Alice's Wonderland
SAMPLER QUILT

100 QUILT BLOCKS
TO IMPROVE YOUR SEWING SKILLS

Alice Caroline

DAVID & CHARLES

www.davidandcharles.com

Contents

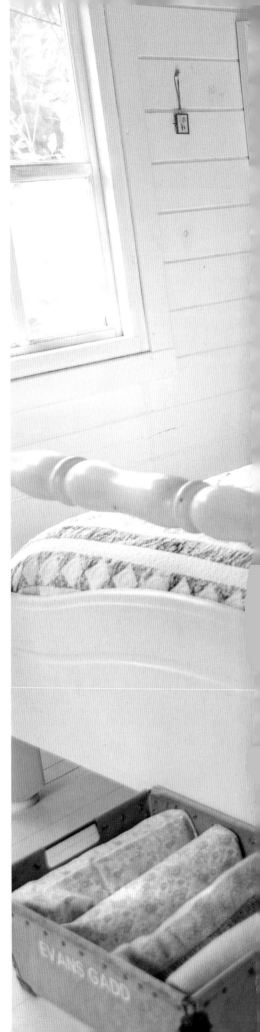

Introduction

I invite you to embark on a delightful journey through the whimsical realm of Alice's Wonderland. Sampler quilts have long held a special place in the hearts of quilters, including mine, partly thanks to the aesthetic of mixing different blocks but also partly because, I'm afraid to admit, I can get bored making the same block over and over for a quilt — I love variety! I also love rainbows, so for this quilt I chose ten rainbows of ten fabrics each, totalling 100 different fabrics for the 100 different blocks. You could choose an entirely different colour scheme if you wish, such as all reds or blues.

Alice's Wonderland began as a Block of the Month Club quilt, which divided the quilt into bite-size chunks of ten blocks a month. The final two months were dedicated to sashing, borders and finishing. You could approach the project this way, too, or go at a different pace, depending on your lifestyle or how you like to work.

The early blocks introduce you gently to the basics, then gradually, you'll encounter more intricate designs. As you journey through my Wonderland, you'll discover which techniques resonate most — perhaps you'll find joy in the rhythmic repetition of patchwork, the artistic freedom of raw-edge appliqué, or the meditative precision of English Paper Piecing.

So, gather your fabrics, sharpen your scissors, and prepare your sewing machine — it's time to embark on a quilting adventure. Savour the handmade process and unleash your creativity as you bring your unique version of Alice's Wonderland to life.

I look forward to seeing what you create!

#ALICESWONDERLANDQUILT

How to Use this Book

The making of the 100 blocks that are included in Alice's Wonderland Sampler Quilt is divided into sections based on their main construction category, as follows: Patchwork, arguably the most recognisable method of quilting, so I have included several sections featuring popular patchwork units, such as Half Square Triangles, Diamond in a Square and Flying Geese; English Paper Piecing (EPP), a simple hand-sewing technique; and Raw Edge Appliqué, which is like collaging with fabric. But before you get started, you should review Standard Piecing, which includes advice on seam allowances.

SKILL LEVELS

The blocks are ordered from simplest to most challenging within each section, and as you work through the 100, you will build on what was previously learnt and master many techniques assisted by the essential how-to information provided at the start of each block chapter. The most novice-friendly patchwork blocks are simple strip-pieced designs such as Block 1: Amish Bar and Block 2: Rail Fence. Beginners to EPP should start with Block 64: Simple Heart, and if new to raw edge appliqué, Block 81: Double Heart is an excellent choice. Make the blocks in order as a skill-building exercise, or flit from patchwork to EPP to appliqué and back again, to your heart's content – the choice is yours!

CUTTING YOUR FABRIC

Cutting lists are provided for each block that should be cross referenced to the Fabric Swatch Chart in The Fabrics section, and handy cutting layout diagrams may be downloaded in digital form through the Alice Caroline or Bookmarked websites. Please refer to these to get the most out of your fabrics. For straight lines, it is best to use a rotary cutter, grid ruler and cutting mat to cut out the required shapes more quickly. Ensure the rotary cutter has a nice sharp blade and the cutting mat is flat and free of deep grooves. For curved lines, a sharp pair of fabric scissors is suitable.

TEMPLATES

All patchwork, EPP and raw edge appliqué templates are provided true to scale; simply trace to use them. For EPP and patchwork templates, I recommend using at least 120gsm paper; for appliqué templates, thinner 80gsm paper is suitable. Some EPP and appliqué templates provided will also need to be reversed to make a mirrored pair and the fabric cutting instructions on each template will specify if this is required, so do make sure to look out for this. In fact, 'Read twice and cut once' is a good adage to keep in mind to avoid mistakes throughout the making of this quilt!

BLOCK NAMES

Quilting has a long history and as a result many of the blocks, if not designed by us specifically for Alice's Wonderland Sampler Quilt, already have a commonly known name. I have made every effort to research and provide the correct name for each block, but where they remain unknown, I have named them myself for this collection – these are block numbers: 8, 36, 37, 38, 40, 49, 56, 60 and 90.

As you build your collection of blocks, keep them stored safely, and once all 100 are made, you'll find everything you need to know in the final two chapters, Layout, Sashing & Borders and Quilting & Binding, to turn them into your very own version of the Alice's Wonderland Sampler Quilt.

Recommended tool lists are included throughout the technique sections but pictured here are the equipment essentials you will need:

Sewing machine (with standard sewing foot)

Grid ruler

Rotary cutter

Cutting mat

Fabric scissors

Pins and/or quilt clips

Hand sewing needle
A longer, sharp needle (size 9–11) makes sewing easier.

Sewing thread for machine and hand sewing
Gütermann 100% polyester Sew-All thread in a neutral off-white, white or cream colour will blend well with all the colours of the quilt, but for decorative stitching on the blocks a contrasting colour is best.

Heat erasable pen
I recommend the Pilot Frixion Heat Erasable Gel Pen, simply iron to remove marks and place in the freezer for 15 minutes to bring them back, if needed. Always test your chosen fabric marker on a scrap piece of fabric before use.

Soluble fabric glue pen
I recommend the Sewline Fabric Glue Pen – it also comes with refills.

Standard craft glue stick

The Fabrics

COTTON LAWN

All coloured fabrics featured in Alice's Wonderland Sampler Quilt are Liberty Tana Lawn® fabrics. Tana Lawn® is an absolute delight to sew with and by far my favourite type of fabric.

The fabric has a long history: Liberty had been experimenting with cotton lawn since the late 1890s, but it was not until the early 1930s that their signature Tana Lawn® was born. The fabric is made from unique, long staple cotton fibres which at the time originated from Lake Tana in Ethiopia, hence the name. While the cotton fibre is now sourced from India, Egypt and the USA, the name has remained, and the very same super high quality, long staple cotton is still used in the fabric today. All the fabric is printed at Liberty's printing mill in northern Italy, coincidentally close to another lake, the beautiful Lake Como. Tana Lawn® behaves well in the sewing machine and is smooth and cool with a subtle lustre, almost silk-like to touch, just as well suited to patchwork quilting, EPP and raw edge appliqué as it is to swishy summer dresses and luxury pyjamas.

FAT SIXTEENTHS

The requirements for the 100 coloured fabrics used in my quilt have been designed to work with Liberty Tana Lawn® fat sixteenths, which measure 9 x 13½in (22.9 x 34.3cm) as Liberty Tana Lawn® fabrics have a bolt width of 54in (137cm). Note that a true fat sixteenth of a more typical 44in (112cm) wide fabric measures only 9 x 11in (22.9 x 27.9cm), so if you choose to use alternative narrower width fabrics, I advise you to cut your fabrics to the required 9 x 13½in (22.9 x 34.3cm) pieces to ensure you will have sufficient fabric. For most of the fabrics, you will need just one piece of 9 x 13½in (22.9 x 34.3cm) fabric; however, for thirty of the fabrics, two pieces are required, as they are used in making both the blocks and pieced borders of the quilt.

LIBERTY PRINTS

The Fabric Swatch Chart has images of the coloured Liberty Tana Lawn® fabrics I have used in my quilt. These come from a variety of Liberty collections, including, but not limited to, the 2022 Classics, 2017/18 Classics, seasonal Spring/Summer and Autumn/Winter collections from 2022 and before, Organics, Alice Caroline Liberty Reprints and Alice Caroline Liberty Exclusives. As such, these exact prints may no longer be available and they may be difficult to acquire. If you cannot find a specific print, I suggest substituting it for one with as similar a colour and print density as possible. Liberty is constantly releasing new prints so it should not be hard to find good substitutes. For a ready-made fabric selection with all 100 different Liberty fabrics chosen for you, visit www.alicecaroline.com for an Alice's Wonderland Quilt kit. But remember, any differences will only add to your quilt's unique charm, so embrace them! You could even incorporate pieces of fabric or clothing that holds sentimental value to make your quilt more personal.

BACKGROUND FABRIC

For the plain white background fabric required for making the blocks and quilt borders (identified as 'W' in the piecing diagrams), I have used a high quality, 100% cotton, quilting weight fabric. I hummed and hawed over whether to go with white or off-white, deciding in the end on an off-white shade, which for me has an instantly timeless appeal, not to mention being more forgiving of the odd mark or stain! A pure white background certainly has its positives, too, such as making the quilt feel fresh and clean, while allowing the colourful fabrics to pop even more. Whatever colour you choose for your background fabric, you'll need a total of 6½ yards (6 metres) of 44in (112cm) wide fabric. For backing and binding requirements, please refer to the Quilting & Binding chapter for further details.

I have always used a combination of Liberty Tana Lawn® fabric and more traditional quilting weight fabrics without issue when making quilts. If you prefer not to mix fabric types, you could, of course, choose a plain Tana Lawn® for the background fabric just the same as you could use quilting cotton fabrics for all the coloured areas on the quilt. All I suggest is that you choose 100% cotton woven fabrics for ease of making and pressing. If you are mixing fabric types, it's a good idea to pre-wash the fabrics as some shrink more than others.

Fabric Swatch Chart

One 9 x 13½in (22.9 x 34.3cm) fabric piece is required for each of the coloured fabrics, and for those marked with an asterisk (*), two pieces are required.

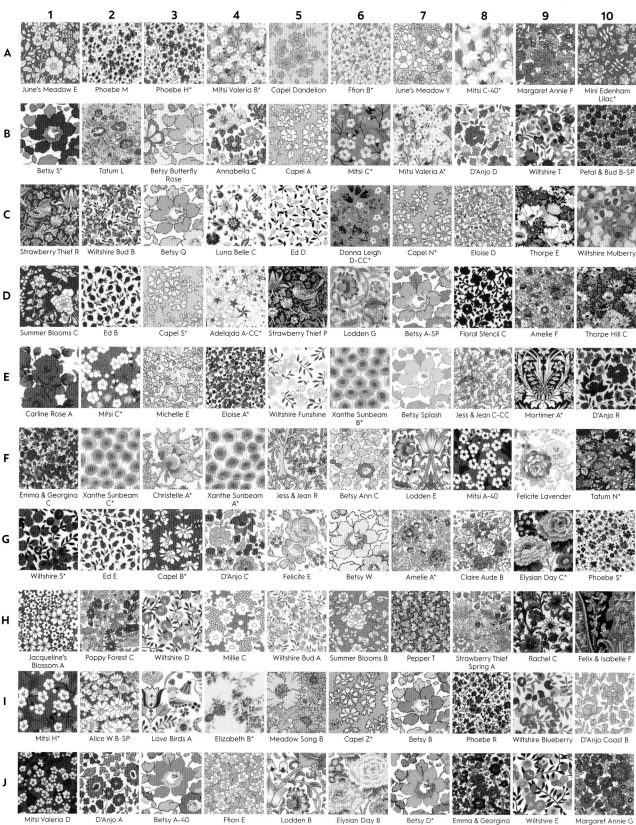

	1	2	3	4	5	6	7	8	9	10
A	June's Meadow E	Phoebe M	Phoebe H*	Mitsi Valeria B*	Capel Dandelion	Ffion B*	June's Meadow Y	Mitsi C-40*	Margaret Annie F	Mini Edenham Lilac*
B	Betsy S*	Tatum L	Betsy Butterfly Rose	Annabella C	Capel A	Mitsi C*	Mitsi Valeria A*	D'Anjo D	Wiltshire T	Petal & Bud B-SP
C	Strawberry Thief R	Wiltshire Bud B	Betsy Q	Luna Belle C	Ed D	Donna Leigh D-CC*	Capel N*	Eloise D	Thorpe E	Wiltshire Mulberry
D	Summer Blooms C	Ed B	Capel S*	Adelajda A-CC*	Strawberry Thief P	Lodden G	Betsy A-SP	Floral Stencil C	Amelie F	Thorpe Hill C
E	Carline Rose A	Mitsi C*	Michelle E	Eloise A*	Wiltshire Funshine	Xanthe Sunbeam B*	Betsy Splash	Jess & Jean C-CC	Mortimer A*	D'Anjo R
F	Emma & Georgina C	Xanthe Sunbeam C*	Christelle A*	Xanthe Sunbeam A*	Jess & Jean R	Betsy Ann C	Lodden E	Mitsi A-40	Felicite Lavender	Tatum N*
G	Wiltshire S*	Ed E	Capel B*	D'Anjo C	Felicite E	Betsy W	Amelie A*	Claire Aude B	Elysian Day C*	Phoebe S*
H	Jacqueline's Blossom A	Poppy Forest C	Wiltshire D	Millie C	Wiltshire Bud A	Summer Blooms B	Pepper T	Strawberry Thief Spring A	Rachel C	Felix & Isabelle F
I	Mitsi H*	Alice W B-SP	Love Birds A	Elizabeth B*	Meadow Song B	Capel Z*	Betsy B	Phoebe R	Wiltshire Blueberry	D'Anjo Coast B
J	Mitsi Valeria D	D'Anjo A	Betsy A-40	Ffion E	Lodden B	Elysian Day B	Betsy D*	Emma & Georgina B*	Wiltshire E	Margaret Annie G

Standard Piecing

SEAM ALLOWANCE

Seams will be sewn using either a standard ¼in (0.635cm, to be exact) seam or a scant ¼in (0.4–0.5cm) seam. The block instructions will indicate which one to use, or even if both are needed, for each block. It is important to stick to the required seam allowance to ensure even units are made, and this may change from step to step.

A standard ¼in (0.6cm) seam is when the seams are sewn together with the needle positioned exactly ¼in (0.6cm) in from the edge of the fabric.

A scant ¼in (0.4–0.5cm) seam is when the needle is positioned approximately 1mm short of the exact ¼in (0.6cm) point, making the seam slightly narrower. In reality, the seam ends up being about ³⁄₁₆in (0.47mm) or ¹³⁄₆₄in (0.51cm) but of course not many rulers show those measurements, hence why it is simply called a scant ¼in (0.4–0.5cm)!

Sewing the seams ever so slightly narrower in this way allows for the little bit of fabric that is lost when it is folded over, and also gives just that bit more width, often enabling the block to be trimmed down to the correct size. Set your seam guide to the same scant ¼in (0.4–0.5cm) position for sewing all parts of a single block together when instructed to do so.

Don't worry if you have to remove the seam guide , then can't remember its position when you need it again. You may set a new scant ¼in (0.4–0.5cm) point for each block as needed. It is not a fixed measurement – if it were there would be a sewing ruler with 16th or 64th inch points marked! All that matters is that a scant seam is sewn slightly narrower than the standard seam.

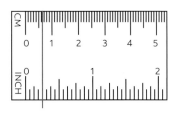

Standard ¼in (0.635cm) seam allowance

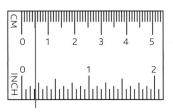

Scant ¼in (0.4–0.5cm) seam allowance

STANDARD PIECING METHOD

When joining two units of fabric together, always use the following method unless the block instructions indicate otherwise.

1. Arrange the units being joined on a flat surface as the instructions indicate, right sides facing up.

2. Flip the right-hand unit over onto the left, with right sides together. Positioning the edges to be sewn together on the right-hand side in this way will make it easier to handle when being fed through the sewing machine.

3. Sew together using the seam allowance indicated by the block instructions. Remove pins as you go just before they pass under the sewing foot to prevent the needle hitting them.

4. Open out and press seams in the direction indicated by the block instructions.

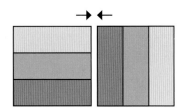

Place two units together

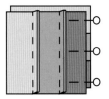

Fold right sides facing, pin and stitch

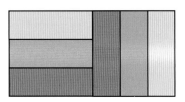

Completed unit

STANDARD PRESSING METHODS

For accurate results, pressing must be done after every sewing step.

FABRIC COLOUR

Use the iron to press seams either open, or to one side/the darkest fabric (or possibly a mix of both!) as indicated by the block instructions. There are no hard rules as to which to do, but there are a couple of factors that may influence which one is used for any given block or section within a block.

They may be pressed towards the darker fabric if the lightest fabric is very translucent so as to not impact the final look of the quilt, or pressed open if all fabrics are suitably opaque.

REDUCING BULK

The direction to press can also depend on the amount of piecing being done using these units. For example, if making a block where lots of seams will be meeting, as for the Checkerboard block, it would be best to press the seams open to help reduce bulk. However, if the block is simpler with fewer seams meeting, as for the Rail Fence block, pressing the seams to just the one side will suit well.

ALTERNATING SIDES

Also, but only if you wish to do so, where seams are pressed to one side, the side to which they are pressed may be alternated along the same seam if the position of the light and dark fabrics change. When doing this, snip no more than ⅛in (0.2–3cm) into the seam at the point the seam direction changes (indicated by the red dot on the diagram) to release the tension in the fabric and help the seam sit neatly. Be very careful not to snip too close to the sewn seam!

I have made recommendations as to how the seams can be pressed on each block; however, if you are a seasoned quilter and wish to press a different way, please do so! There are no rules, only guidelines, so please do as you feel most comfortable.

Seams pressed open

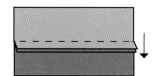

Seams pressed to darkest side

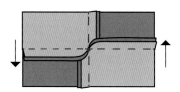

Seams pressed to darkest side along same seam

Strip Piecing

ABOUT STRIP PIECING

Strip piecing is a simple and effective way of speeding up your patchwork quilting. Rather than spending time laboriously cutting out individual rectangles or squares, larger strip shaped sections of fabric are sewn together to make 'strip sets'. Each set is then cut down into smaller units ready for patchworking.

Quilt blocks commonly using this construction method include Rail Fence, Nine Patch, Checkerboard and Roman Square.

Recommended Tools: rotary cutter, cutting mat, grid ruler, seam guide

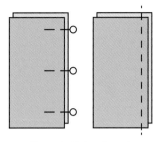

Pin and stitch adjacent strips, right sides facing

STRIP PIECING METHOD

1. Take two adjacent strips as indicated by the block's instructions and place them right sides together, aligning their edges along the edge to be sewn together. Pin together along this edge.

2. Sew strips together, removing pins as you go just before they pass under the sewing foot.

3. Open out fabric. Press seams open or to one side as necessary.

4. Repeat steps 1–3 as many times as necessary to join the strips together into the required strip set, alternating the direction of sewing each time.

5. Use a rotary cutter and grid ruler to cut the strip set into smaller units, following the quantity and dimensions as directed by the block's instructions.

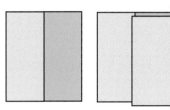

Add additional strips in same way

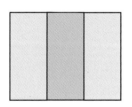

Completed strip set

HANDY TIPS

To prevent fabric rippling or bowing, sew each strip together from alternating directions, i.e. sew first seam from top to bottom, then sew the second seam from bottom to top. This spreads the tension around and will help the fabric keep its shape and sit neatly.

Also to prevent fabric rippling or bowing, avoid sewing more than three strips together in one strip set. Instead, try to break up any larger strip set into smaller sets of ideally two strips each, three if it cannot be avoided. Then, sew the smaller sets together to make a larger set, alternating the direction of sewing as previously described.

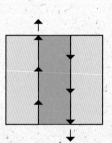

When sewing strip sets, sew seams in alternate directions

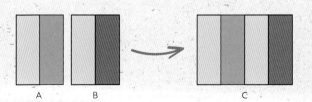

If the block instructions require, for example, a strip set of four strips, start by sewing seam A, then seam B, then join the two smaller sets together, seam C

CHAIN STRIP PIECING METHOD

1. Use the **Strip Piecing Method** to sew the required fabrics together to make strip sets and then cut into smaller units. Follow the dimensions and quantities of the smaller units as described in the block's instructions.

2. Take the required long strip as indicated by the block's instructions and place a smaller unit on top, right sides of fabrics together. Align their edges along the edge to be sewn together. Leave a small gap and then place another smaller unit on the strip, right sides together and edges aligned. Continue placing smaller units on top of the strip in this way, arranging them along the strip so that you have as many as required fitted onto the strip while maintaining a small gap between each small unit. Pin all the smaller units onto the strip along this edge.

3. Sew strips together, removing pins as you go just before they pass under the sewing foot.

4. Open out fabric. Press seams open or to one side as necessary.

5. Use a rotary cutter and grid ruler to roughly cut the chain strip-pieced set into smaller units.

6. Use a rotary cutter and grid ruler to cut the smaller units down to the correct size as directed by the block's instructions.

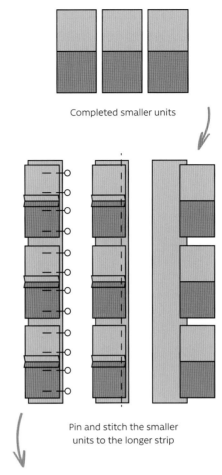

Completed smaller units

Pin and stitch the smaller units to the longer strip

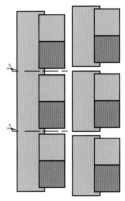

Subcut the longer strip to separate the units

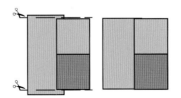

Trim down the unit to the required size

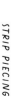

BLOCK 1: Amish Bar

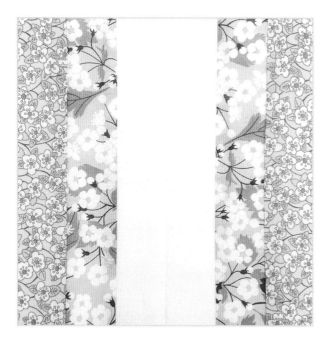

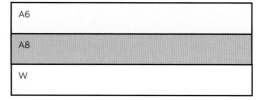

Sew the three strips into a strip set

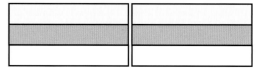

Subcut into two smaller units

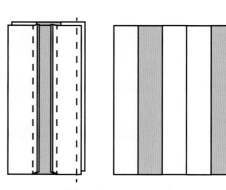

Join units, open out and press

INFO

- Block Size: 6½in (16.5cm) unfinished, 6in (15.2cm) finished
- Seams: ¼in (0.6cm)
- Press Seams: To darkest fabric. Press after each sewing step.

CUTTING

- White Fabric: one 1½ x 13in (3.8 x 33cm)
- Fabric A6: one 1½ x 13in (3.8 x 33cm)
- Fabric A8: one 1½ x 13in (3.8 x 33cm)

CONSTRUCTION

1. Following the **Strip Piecing Method**, sew the three strips together into a strip set as shown. Then, cut the strip set in half to make two smaller units measuring 3½ x 6½in (8.9 x 16.5cm).

2. Following the **Standard Piecing Method**, arrange these units with the white strips at the centre, right sides facing up. Flip the right-hand unit over onto the left, with right sides together. Align their edges along the right-hand side and pin together. Sew together, open out and press.

3. Evenly trim down the whole block to 6½in (16.5cm) square if it is not this size already. Block is complete. Press and store safely.

Fabric Focus

Mitsi is a stylised floral that was first designed in the 1950s by Gillian Farr, a member of the Liberty Fabrics design team. Featuring a Japanese-style blossom, it pays homage to Liberty's historical passion for Asian motifs.

BLOCK 2: *Rail Fence*

INFO

- Block Size: 6½in (16.5cm) unfinished, 6in (15.2cm) finished
- Seams: ¼in (0.6cm)
- Press Seams: To darkest fabric. Press after each sewing step.

CUTTING

- White Fabric: two 1½ x 7in (3.8 x 17.8cm)
- Fabric A1: two 1½ x 7in (3.8 x 17.8cm)
- Fabric A4: two 1½ x 7in (3.8 x 17.8cm)

CONSTRUCTION

1. Following the **Strip Piecing Method**, sew three strips together to make a strip set as shown. Make a second, identical strip set with remaining strips. Then cut both strip sets in half to make four smaller units measuring 3½ x 3½in (8.9 x 8.9cm).

2. Following the **Standard Piecing Method**, arrange two of the smaller units as shown, right sides facing up. Flip the right-hand unit over onto the left, with right sides together. Align their edges along the right-hand side and pin together. Repeat with the two remaining smaller units. Sew a pinned unit together, open out and press. Repeat with other pinned unit.

3. Sew the units together as shown following the **Standard Piecing Method**.

4. Evenly trim down the whole block to 6½in (16.5cm) square if it is not this size already. Block is complete. Press and store safely.

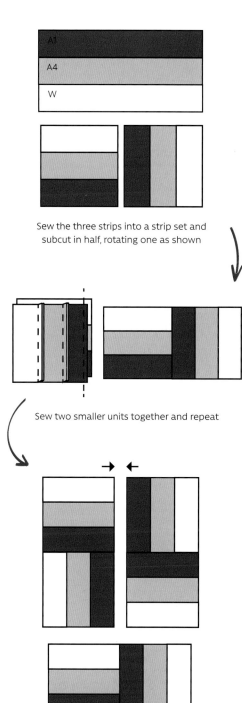

Sew the three strips into a strip set and subcut in half, rotating one as shown

Sew two smaller units together and repeat

Join the two resulting units into final block

BLOCK 3: Nine Patch

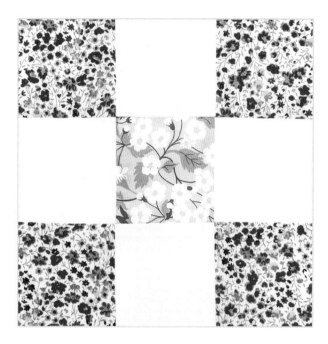

INFO

- Block Size: 6½in (16.5cm) unfinished, 6in (15.2cm) finished
- Seams: ¼in (0.6cm)
- Press Seams: To darkest fabric. Press after each sewing step.

CUTTING

- White Fabric: one 2½ x 5in (6.4 x 12.7cm) and two 2½ x 2½in (6.4 x 6.4cm)
- Fabric A2: two 2½ x 5in (6.4 x 12.7cm)
- Fabric A8: one 2½ x 2½in (6.4 x 6.4cm)

CONSTRUCTION

I. Following the **Strip Piecing Method**, sew three strips together to make two strip sets as shown. Then, cut the wider strip set in half to make two smaller units measuring 2½ x 6½in (6.4 x 16.5cm) as shown.

2. Sew the units together as shown following the **Standard Piecing Method**.

3. Evenly trim down the whole block to 6½in (16.5cm) square if it is not this size already. Block is complete. Press and store safely.

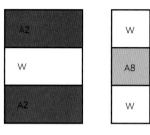

Sew the strips into two units

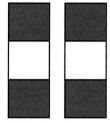

Subcut the wider strip set into two smaller units

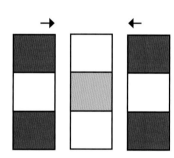

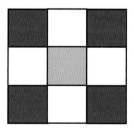

Join the units into final block

BLOCK 4: Checkerboard

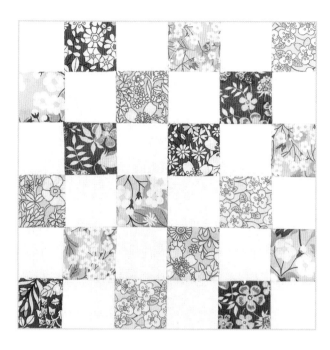

INFO

- Block Size: 6½in (16.5cm) unfinished, 6in (15.2cm) finished
- Seams: ¼in (0.6cm)
- Press Seams: Open. Press after each sewing step.

CUTTING

- White Fabric: six 1½ x 5in (3.8 x 12.7cm)
- Fabric A1: one 1½ x 5in (3.8 x 12.7cm)
- Fabric A4: one 1½ x 5in (3.8 x 12.7cm)
- Fabric A6: one 1½ x 5in (3.8 x 12.7cm)
- Fabric A7: one 1½ x 5in (3.8 x 12.7cm)
- Fabric A8: one 1½ x 5in (3.8 x 12.7cm)
- Fabric A10: one 1½ x 5in (3.8 x 12.7cm)

CONSTRUCTION

1. Following the **Strip Piecing Method**, sew the white fabric strips and coloured strips together to make the strip sets as shown. Then, cut each strip set at 1½in (3.8cm) intervals to make three 1½ x 2½in (3.8 x 6.4cm) units from each. Discard any leftover fabric.

2. Sew the smaller units together following the **Standard Piecing Method**, to make six sections as shown.

Tip: Joining smaller units together in sections in this way first, rather than trying to sew the whole block at once, helps keep piecing consistent and comfortable to handle.

3. Sew the sections together as shown.

4. Evenly trim down the whole block to 6½in (16.5cm) square if it is not this size already. Block is complete. Press and store safely.

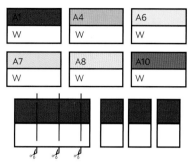

Sew the strips into six units and subcut each of these into three smaller units

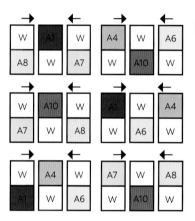

Join smaller units together in threes as shown

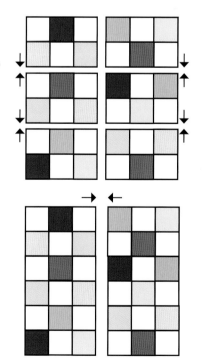

Join the sections together in the sequence shown into final block

BLOCK 5: Log Cabin

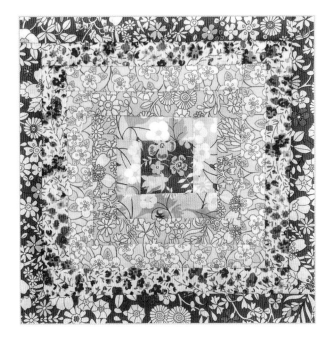

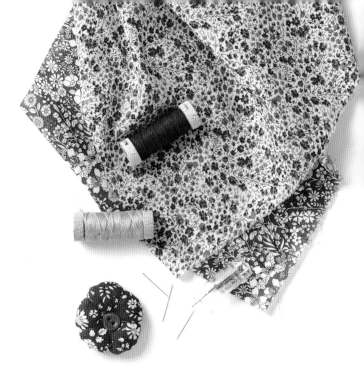

INFO

- Block Size: 6½in (16.5cm) unfinished, 6in (15.2cm) finished
- Seams: ¼in (0.6cm)
- Press Seams: To one side. Press after each sewing step.

CUTTING

- Fabric A1: two 1 x 13in (2.6 x 33cm)
- Fabric A3: two 1 x 13in (2.6 x 33cm)
- Fabric A6: two 1 x 10in (2.6 x 25.4cm)
- Fabric A7: two 1 x 10in (2.6 x 25.4cm)
- Fabric A8: one 1 x 10in (2.6 x 25.4cm)
- Fabric A10: one 1½ x 1½in (3.8 x 3.8cm)

CONSTRUCTION

1. Take the long strip of fabric A8 and the A10 fabric square. *Pin and sew right sides together along one side, matching the square but with a slight overhang of the strip – approx. ⅛–¼in (0.3-0.6cm) – as shown. Use a rotary cutter and ruler to trim away the overhanging strip on the long side to make unit as shown.

2. Take the strip trimmed off and align, pin and sew it onto the unit as shown. Overhang the strip at the top slightly as before. Use rotary cutter and ruler to trim away the overhanging strip on the long side to make unit as shown.

3. Take the strip trimmed off and align, pin and sew it onto the unit as shown. Overhang the strip at the top slightly as before. Use rotary cutter and ruler to trim away the overhanging strip on the long side to make unit as shown.

4. Take the strip trimmed off and align, pin and sew it onto the unit as shown. Overhang the strip at the top slightly as before. Use rotary cutter and ruler to trim away the overhanging strip on the long side to make unit as shown. Discard any trimmed away fabric. Rotate unit so the edge with the shortest strip is facing up.

Tip: Fabrics A7, A6, A3 and A1 have two fabric strips each; simply start one strip when the other runs out.

5. Take the strip of fabric A7 and repeat steps 1*-4 to make the unit as shown.

6. Repeat to add the fabric strips in order: A6, A3 and ending with the A1 fabric strips to make the unit as shown.

7. Evenly trim down the whole block to 6½in (16.5cm) square if it is not this size already. Block is complete. Press and store safely.

Tip: This log cabin block construction method is best suited to small log cabins only. Larger log cabins must have all fabric pieces cut exactly to size and eased together for best results.

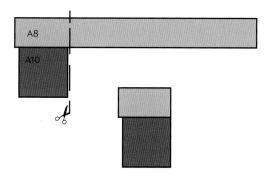

Sew the long strip onto the centre square then trim

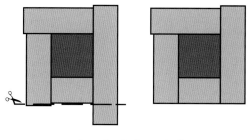

Repeat as before onto the remaining side then trim

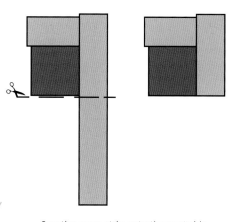

Sew the same strip onto the next side of the centre square then trim

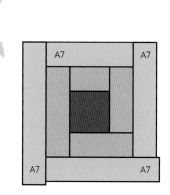

Sew the next coloured fabric strip on in the same way

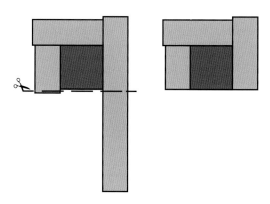

Repeat as before on next side

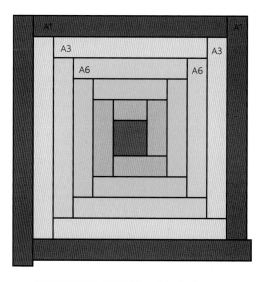

Continue adding remaining strips in the same way until you have the final block as shown

BLOCK 6: Simple Cross

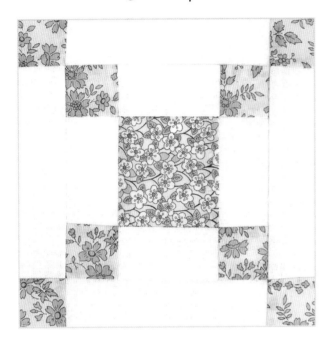

CONSTRUCTION

1. Following the **Strip Piecing Method**, sew one 3 x 4½in (7.6 x 11.4cm) white fabric strip and two 1½ x 3in (3.8 x 7.6cm) A5 fabric strips together to make the strip set as shown. Cut the strip set in half lengthways to make two 1½ x 6½in (3.8 x 16.5cm) smaller units.

2. Following the **Strip Piecing Method**, sew one 2½ x 3in (6.4 x 7.6cm) white fabric strip and two 1½ x 3in (3.8 x 7.6cm) A5 fabric strips together to make the strip set as shown. Cut the strip set in half lengthways to make two 1½ x 4½in (3.8 x 11.4cm) smaller units.

3. Take two 1½ x 2½in (3.8 x 6.4cm) white fabric strips and the 2½ x 2½in (6.4 x 6.4cm) A6 fabric square, and sew the unit shown following the **Standard Piecing Method**. This is the unit at the centre of the block.

4. Take the two 1½ x 4½in (3.8 x 11.4cm) units and align, pin and sew them onto the centre unit as shown.

5. Take the remaining two 1½ x 4½in (3.8 x 11.4cm) strips of white fabric and align, pin and sew them onto the unit as shown.

6. Take the two 1½ x 6½in (3.8 x 16.5cm) units and align, pin and sew them onto the unit as shown.

7. Evenly trim down the whole block to 6½in (16.5cm) square if it is not this size already. Block is complete. Press and store safely.

INFO

- Block Size: 6½in (16.5cm) unfinished, 6in (15.2cm) finished
- Seams: ¼in (0.6cm)
- Press Seams: To darkest fabric. Press after each sewing step.

CUTTING

- White Fabric: one 3 x 4½in (7.6 x 11.4cm), two 1½ x 4½in (3.8 x 11.4cm), one 2½ x 3in (6.4 x 7.6cm) and two 1½ x 2½in (3.8 x 6.4cm)
- Fabric A5: four 1½ x 3in (3.8 x 7.6cm)
- Fabric A6: one 2½ x 2½in (6.4 x 6.4cm)

Fabric Focus

Ffion is a pretty ditsy floral inspired by a woodblock design and created in 1959. This fresh, simple flower pattern on a coloured ground is reminiscent of a much-loved Liberty favourite, Mitsi.

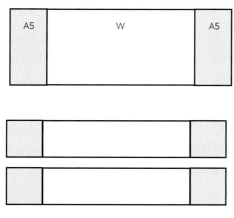

Sew longer strips into a strip set and
subcut into two smaller units

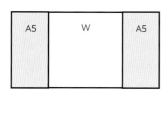

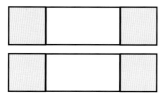

Sew shorter strips into a strip set and
subcut into two smaller units

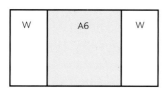

Sew the centre unit

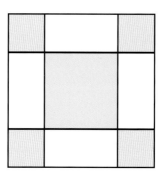

Sew the shorter units onto the top
and bottom of the centre unit

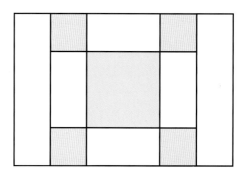

Sew white fabric strips onto either side

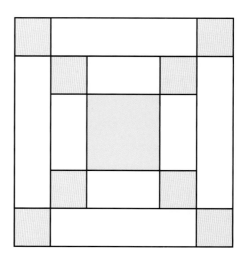

Sew the longer units onto the top and
bottom to complete the block as shown

BLOCK 7: *Simple Cross Variation*

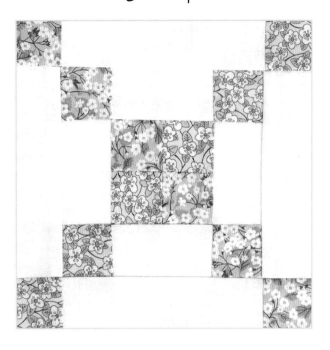

INFO

- Block Size: 6½in (16.5cm) unfinished, 6in (15.2cm) finished
- Seams: ¼in (0.6cm)
- Press Seams: To darkest fabric. Press after each sewing step.

CUTTING

- White Fabric: one 3 x 4½in (7.6 x 11.4cm), two 1½ x 4½in (3.8 x 11.4cm), two 1½ x 2½in (3.8 x 6.4cm) and one 2½ x 3in (6.4 x 7.6cm)
- Fabric A4: three 1½ x 3in (3.8 x 7.6cm)
- Fabric A6: three 1½ x 3in (3.8 x 7.6cm)

CONSTRUCTION

1. Following the **Strip Piecing Method**, sew one 3 x 4½in (7.6 x 11.4cm) white fabric strip and one 1½ x 3in (3.8 x 7.6cm) strip each of A4 and A6 fabric together to make the strip set as shown. Cut the strip set in half lengthways to make two 1½ x 6½in (3.8 x 16.5cm) smaller units.

2. Following the **Strip Piecing Method**, sew one 2½ x 3in (6.4 x 7.6cm) white fabric strip and one 1½ x 3in (3.8 x 7.6cm) strip each of A4 and A6 fabric together to make the strip set as shown. Cut the strip set in half lengthways to make two 1½ x 4½in (3.8 x 11.4cm) smaller units.

3. Following the **Strip Piecing Method**, sew remaining 1½ x 3in (3.8 x 7.6cm) strips of A4 and A6 fabric together to make the strip set as shown. Cut the strip set in half lengthways to make two 1½ x 2½in (3.8 x 6.4cm) smaller units.

4. Follow the **Standard Piecing Method** with the small 1½ x 2½in (3.8 x 6.4cm) units to make a 2½ x 2½in (6.4 x 6.4cm) square unit as shown.

5. Take two 1½ x 2½in (3.8 x 6.4cm) white fabric strips and sew to either side of the 2½ x 2½in (6.4 x 6.4cm) square unit as shown.

6. Take the two 1½ x 4½in (3.8 x 11.4cm) units and sew onto the top and bottom of the unit as shown.

7. Take the two 1½ x 4½in (3.8 x 11.4cm) strips of white fabric and sew to either side of the unit as shown.

8. Take the two 1½ x 6½in (3.8 x 16.5cm) units and sew onto the top and bottom of the unit as shown.

9. Evenly trim down the whole block to 6½in (16.5cm) square if it is not this size already. Block is complete. Press and store safely.

Fabric Focus

Mitsi Valeria is a half-scale version of the well-known Liberty fabric Mitsi, which features the Japanese-style blossom. It first appeared in 2013 and has been part of the Classics collection ever since. Smaller flowers and buds lend the print an increased feeling of delicacy.

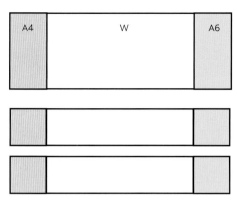

Sew longer strips into a strip set and
subcut into two smaller units

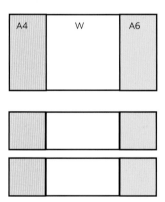

Sew shorter strips into a strip set and
subcut into two smaller units

Sew remaining A4 and A6 strips into a strip
set and subcut into two smaller units

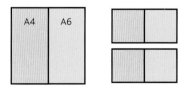

Sew together units just made
to make the centre unit

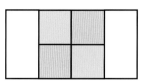

Add white strips onto either
side of the centre unit

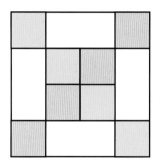

Sew the shorter units onto the top and bottom

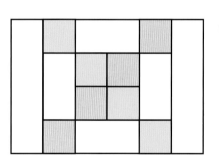

Add white strips onto either side

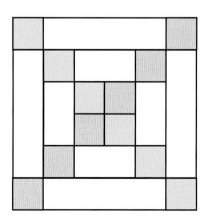

Sew the longer units onto the top and
bottom to complete the block as shown

BLOCK 8: *Corner Tiles*

INFO

- Block Size: 6½in (16.5cm) unfinished, 6in (15.2cm) finished
- Seams: scant ¼in (0.4–0.5cm)
- Press Seams: To darkest fabric. Press after each sewing step.

CUTTING

- White Fabric: one 1½ x 9in (3.8 x 22.9cm) and four 2½ x 2½in (6.4 x 6.4cm)
- Fabric A10: one 1½ x 9in (3.8 x 22.9cm) and one 1½ x 13in (3.8 x 33cm)

CONSTRUCTION

1. Following the **Strip Piecing Method**, use a scant seam to sew the 1½ x 9in (3.8 x 22.9cm) strips of each fabric together to make the strip set as shown. Then cut the strip set at 1½in (3.8cm) intervals to make six 1½ x 2½in (3.8 x 6.4cm) smaller units.

2. Take the long 1½ x 13in (3.8 x 33cm) strip of fabric A10 and following the **Chain Strip Piecing Method**, sew onto this strip just four of the smaller units using a scant seam. Cut them apart and trim down to make four units sized 2½ x 2½in (6.4 x 6.4cm) as shown.

3. Sew the two remaining small units together as shown using a scant seam following the **Standard Piecing Method**.

4. Following the **Standard Piecing Method**, use a scant seam to sew the units together with the 2½ x 2½in (6.4 x 6.4cm) white fabric squares as shown.

5. Evenly trim down the whole block to 6½in (16.5cm) square if it is not this size already. Block is complete. Press and store safely.

Fabric Focus

Mini Edenham, a smaller scale version of Liberty's Edenham print, is an exclusive fabric from Alice Caroline's 2020 Butterfly Garden Collection. The original Edenham was first created for Liberty Fabrics in 1994; its timeless design draws upon their archive florals and features a fresh graphic layout, with bright colours and wider spacing.

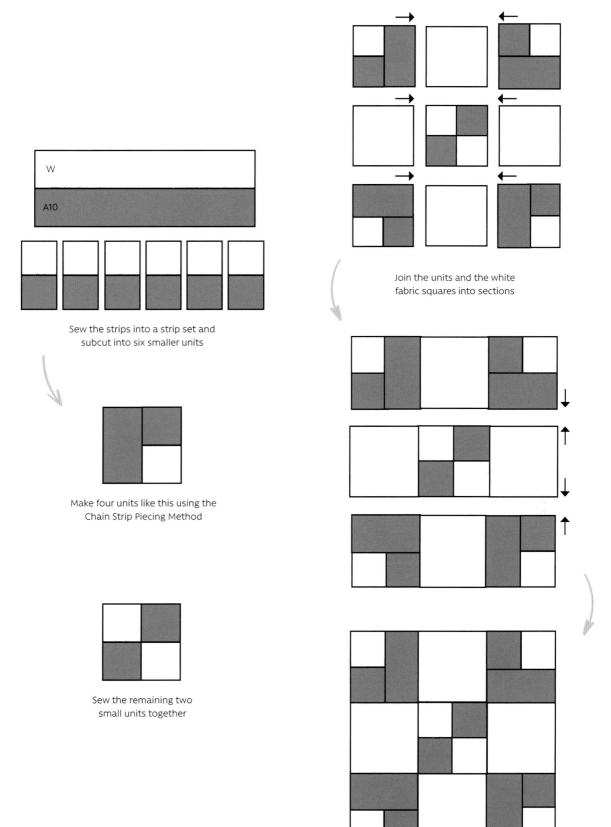

W

A10

Sew the strips into a strip set and
subcut into six smaller units

Make four units like this using the
Chain Strip Piecing Method

Sew the remaining two
small units together

Join the units and the white
fabric squares into sections

Sew the sections together into final block

BLOCK 9: Antique Tile

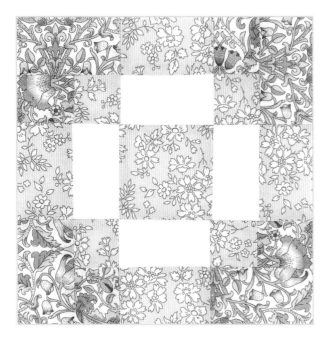

INFO

- Block Size: 6½in (16.5cm) unfinished, 6in (15.2cm) finished
- Seams: scant ¼in (0.4–0.5cm)
- Press Seams: Open. Press after each sewing step.

CUTTING

- White Fabric: one 1½ x 13in (3.8 x 33cm)
- Fabric D3: one 1½ x 7in (3.8 x 17.8cm), one 1½ x 13in (3.8 x 33cm) and one 2½ x 2½in (6.4 x 6.4cm)
- Fabric D6: one 1½ x 7in (3.8 x 17.8cm) and one 1½ x 13in (3.8 x 33cm)

CONSTRUCTION

1. Following the **Strip Piecing Method**, use a scant seam to sew the 1½ x 7in (3.8 x 17.8cm) strips of fabrics D3 and D6 together to make the strip set as shown. Then, cut the strip set at 1½in (3.8cm) intervals to make four 1½ x 2½in (3.8 x 6.4cm) smaller units. Discard any leftover fabric.

2. Take the long 1½ x 13in (3.8 x 33cm) strip of fabric D6 and following the **Chain Strip Piecing Method**, sew onto this strip all four of the smaller units using a scant seam. Cut them apart and trim down to make four units sized 2½ x 2½in (6.4 x 6.4cm) as shown.

3. Following the **Strip Piecing Method**, use a scant seam to sew the 1½ x 13in (3.8 x 33cm) strips of white and D3 fabric together to make the strip set as shown. Then, cut the strip set at 2½in (6.4cm) intervals to make four 2½ x 2½in (6.4 x 6.4cm) smaller units. Discard leftover fabric.

4. Following the **Standard Piecing Method**, sew the units together as shown using a scant seam, first joining the units into sections with the 2½ x 2½in (6.4 x 6.4cm) D3 fabric square, then sewing the sections together.

5. Evenly trim down the whole block to 6½in (16.5cm) square if it is not this size already. Block is complete. Press and store safely.

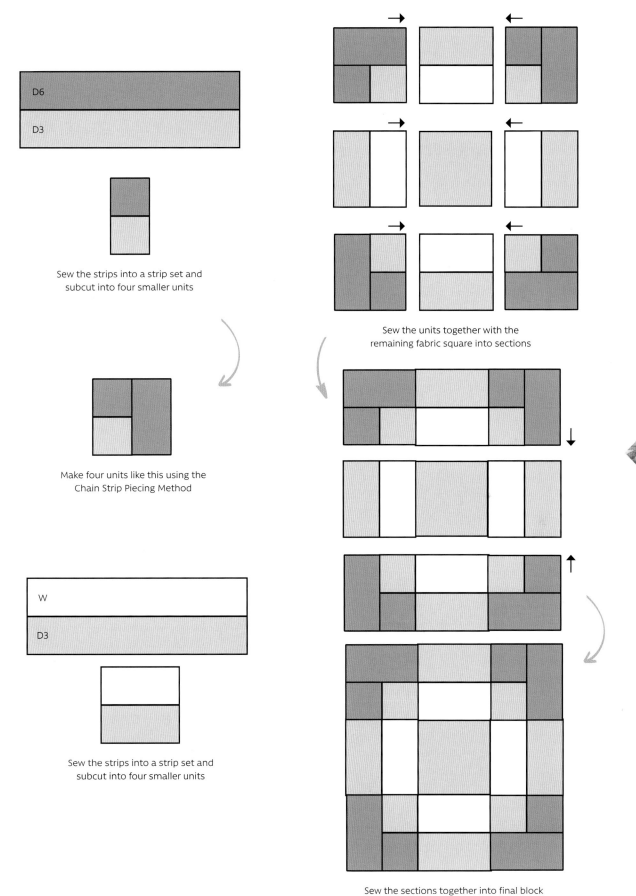

D6

D3

Sew the strips into a strip set and subcut into four smaller units

Make four units like this using the Chain Strip Piecing Method

W

D3

Sew the strips into a strip set and subcut into four smaller units

Sew the units together with the remaining fabric square into sections

Sew the sections together into final block

BLOCK 10: *Checkerboard Variation*

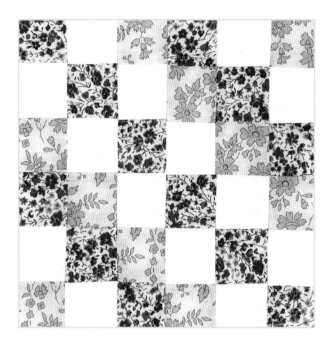

INFO

- Block Size: 6½in (16.5cm) unfinished, 6in (15.2cm) finished
- Seams: ¼in (0.6cm)
- Press Seams: Open. Press after each sewing step.

CUTTING

- White Fabric: one 1½ x 9in (3.8 x 22.9cm) and four 1½ x 3in (3.8 x 7.6cm)
- Fabric A3: one 1½ x 9in (3.8 x 22.9cm) and three 1½ x 3in (3.8 x 7.6cm)
- Fabric A5: one 1½ x 9in (3.8 x 22.9cm) and two 1½ x 3in (3.8 x 7.6cm)

CONSTRUCTION

1. Following the **Strip Piecing Method**, sew the 1½ x 9in (3.8 x 22.9cm) strips of each fabric together to make the strip set as shown. Then, cut the strip set at 1½in (3.8cm) intervals to make six 1½ x 3½in (3.8 x 8.9cm) smaller units.

2. Following the **Strip Piecing Method**, sew the remaining 1½ x 3in (3.8 x 7.6cm) strips of fabric together to make the strip sets as shown. Then, cut each strip set in half to make six 1½ x 3½in (3.8 x 8.9cm) smaller units. You should now have a total of twelve smaller units.

3. Sew the smaller units together into the four nine-patch units as shown following the **Standard Piecing Method**.

4. Sew the nine-patch units together into sections, then join the sections together as shown.

5. Evenly trim down the whole block to 6½in (16.5cm) square if it is not this size already. Block is complete. Press and store safely.

Fabric Focus

Phoebe was first printed as a scarf in 1966 and was inspired by print impressions found at the Liberty Fabrics' printworks at Merton Abbey Mills.

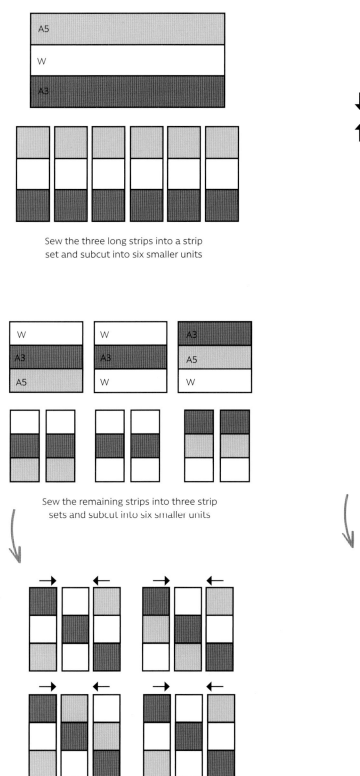

Sew the three long strips into a strip
set and subcut into six smaller units

Sew the remaining strips into three strip
sets and subcut into six smaller units

Sew the units together to make
four nine-patch units

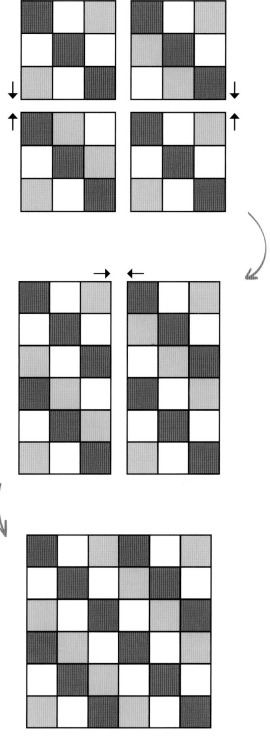

Join the sections together in the
sequence shown into final block

BLOCK 11: Crossroads to Jericho

INFO

- Block Size: 6½in (16.5cm) unfinished, 6in (15.2cm) finished
- Seams: ¼in (0.6cm)
- Press Seams: To darkest fabric. Press after each sewing step.

CUTTING

- White Fabric: two 2 x 4in (5.1 x 10.2cm, one 2 x 2in (5.1 x 5.1cm)
- Fabric A7: two 4 x 4in (10.2 x 10.2cm)
- Fabric A9: one 2 x 4in (5.1 x 10.2cm) and two 2 x 2in (5.1 x 5.1cm)

CONSTRUCTION

1. Cut the two 4 x 4in (10.2 x 10.2cm) squares of fabric A7 into half diagonally to make four triangles. Be very careful with these triangles so as not to change their shape as the diagonal line is on the bias and at risk of stretching. Handle them as little as possible and keep neat and flat until use.

2. Following the **Strip Piecing Method**, sew the two 2 x 4in (5.1 x 10.2cm) strips of white fabric to either side of the 2 x 4in (5.1 x 10.2cm) A9 fabric strip to make the strip set as shown. Then, cut the strip set in half to make two 2 x 5in (5.1 x 12.7cm) smaller units.

3. Following the **Strip Piecing Method**, sew the 2 x 2in (5.1 x 5.1cm) squares of fabric A9 to either side of the 2 x 2in (5.1 x 5.1cm) white fabric square as shown.

4. Sew the strips from steps 2 and 3 into the nine-patch unit as shown. Trim down to 4¾ x 4¾in (12 x 12cm), taking an even amount off each side of the unit. There will not be much to trim.

5. Use a ruler to find the middle point along the long diagonal edge of each of the four A7 fabric triangles and mark with a pin or heat erasable pen. Fold the nine-patch unit in half both ways and also mark the middle points along each edge.

6. Take two triangles and align, pin and sew them onto the nine-patch unit as shown, matching the marked middle points. Be careful not to stretch the triangle pieces. Open out and press.

7. Take the remaining two triangles and align, pin and sew them onto the nine-patch unit as shown, matching the marked middle points. Again, be careful not to stretch the triangle pieces. Open out and press.

8. Evenly trim down the whole block to 6½in (16.5cm) square if it is not this size already. Block is complete. Press and store safely.

Fabric Focus

Margaret Annie was hand-drawn by the Liberty Fabrics' design team and it features detailed layouts of summer perennials.

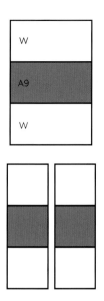

Sew the strips into a strip set and
subcut into two smaller units

Sew the squares together in a strip

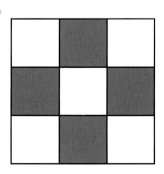

Sew the strips together to
make a nine-patch unit

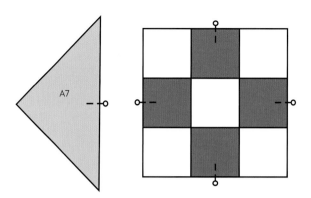

Find the middle points and mark with a pin

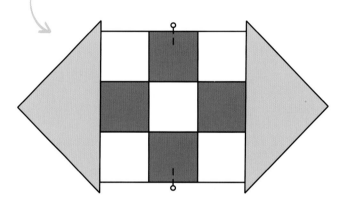

Sew a triangle onto either side of the
nine-patch unit, aligning the middle points

Sew the remaining triangles on, open
out and press to complete as shown

Half Square Triangles

ABOUT HALF SQUARE TRIANGLES (HSTS)

The humble HST is a very important foundational patchworking technique. The units are made from two right-angle triangles which are sewn together along their longest side to form a single square piece. Endlessly useful, the number of designs that can be created using HSTS alone is incredible. In combination with other techniques even more interesting block designs can be made.

Quilt blocks commonly using these units include Broken Dishes, Shoo Fly, Pinwheel and Basket.

Recommended Tool: heat erasable fabric pen

TWO AT A TIME HST METHOD

1. Place two squares of fabric on top of each other, right sides together. Line up the edges exactly. Use a heat erasable pen (or pencil) and ruler to draw a straight line diagonally across the wrong side of the top square. Pin in place.

2. Sew along either side of the drawn line using the seam indicated in the block instructions. Remove the pins.

3. Cut along the drawn line. Open each out and press the seams either open or to one side as needed.

FOUR AT A TIME HST METHOD

1. Place two squares of fabric on top of each other, right sides together. Line up the edges exactly and pin in place.

2. Sew around the outside edges using the seam indicated in the block instruction, removing pins as you go.

3. Cut the unit into quarters diagonally (using a heat erasable pen to draw on the exact cutting lines may help to cut accurately). Open each out and press the seams either open or to one side as needed.

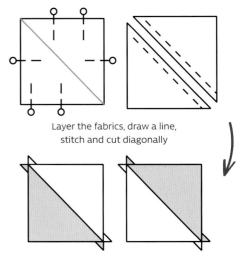

Layer the fabrics, draw a line, stitch and cut diagonally

Makes two untrimmed HSTs

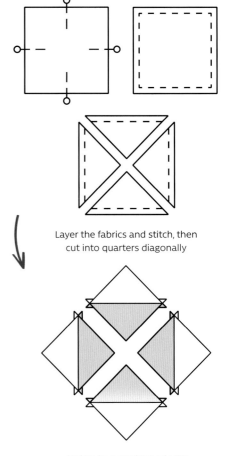

Layer the fabrics and stitch, then cut into quarters diagonally

Makes four untrimmed HSTs

HANDY TIP

When trimming a finished HST to size, trim evenly so that the seam sits exactly in the corners of each unit.

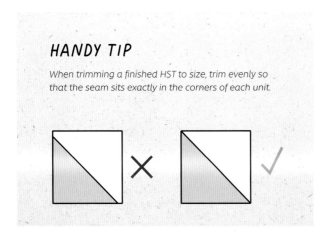

HALF SQUARE TRIANGLES

EIGHT AT A TIME HST METHOD

1. Place two squares of fabric on top of each other, right sides together. Line up the edges exactly. Use a heat erasable pen (or pencil) and ruler to draw two diagonal lines across the wrong side of the top square. Pin in place.

2. Sew along either side of the drawn line using the seam indicated in the block instructions. Remove the pins.

3. Cut the unit in half vertically and horizontally, as well as diagonally along the drawn lines (using a heat erasable pen to draw on the exact cutting lines may help with accuracy). Open each out and press the seams either open or to one side as needed.

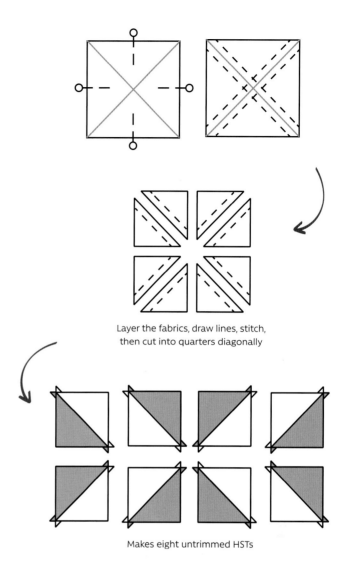

Layer the fabrics, draw lines, stitch, then cut into quarters diagonally

Makes eight untrimmed HSTs

HANDY TIPS

HSTs may be pressed either open or to one side, but there are different methods for handling them.

Pressing seams open means you can easily achieve more accurate seam alignment when joining units together; simply flip back one corner and 'peek' in at how the seams are sitting to check that they are aligned.

If seams are pressed to one side they should face opposite directions to help reduce bulk. Seams can then be 'nested' together, so the bulk of each HST's seam butts up against each other neatly when the seams are aligned. Feel with your fingers and look at the meeting seams from the side to make sure this is happening.

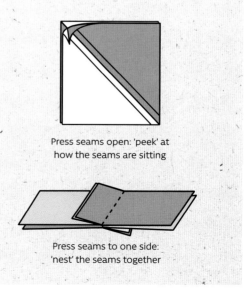

Press seams open: 'peek' at how the seams are sitting

Press seams to one side: 'nest' the seams together

BLOCK 12: Broken Dishes

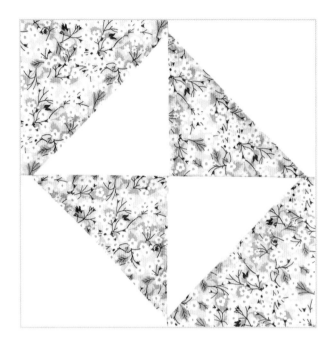

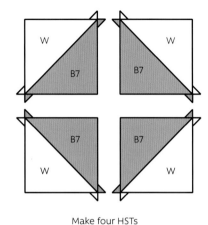

Make four HSTs

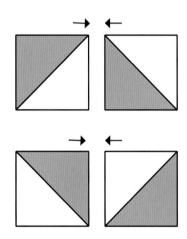

Evenly trim and sew HSTs together in pairs

INFO

- Block Size: 6½in (16.5cm) unfinished, 6in (15.2cm) finished
- Seams: ¼in (0.6cm)
- Press Seams: Open. Press after each sewing step.

CUTTING

- White Fabric: one 6 x 6in (15.2 x 15.2cm)
- Fabric B7: one 6 x 6in (15.2 x 15.2cm)

CONSTRUCTION

1. Following the **Four at a Time HST Method**, sew the two squares together into four HSTs as shown.

2. Evenly trim each HST down to 3½ x 3½in (8.9 x 8.9cm) square.

3. Sew the units as shown following the **Standard Piecing Method**, first sewing two HSTs together, then joining the resulting units.

4. Evenly trim down the whole block to 6½in (16.5cm) square if it is not this size already. Block is complete. Press and store safely.

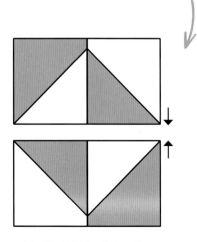

Sew the paired units together to complete the block

BLOCK 13: *Shoo Fly*

INFO

- Block Size: 6½in (16.5cm) unfinished, 6in (15.2cm) finished
- Seams: ¼in (0.6cm)
- Press Seams: Open. Press after each sewing step.

CUTTING

- White Fabric: one 4½ x 4½in (11.4 x 11.4cm) and four 2½ x 2½in (6.4 x 6.4cm)
- Fabric B6: one 4½ x 4½in (11.4 x 11.4cm) and one 2½ x 2½in (6.4 x 6.4cm)

CONSTRUCTION

1. Following the **Four at a Time HST Method**, sew the 4½ x 4½in (11.4 x 11.4cm) squares together into four HSTs as shown.

2. Evenly trim each HST down to 2½ x 2½in (6.4 x 6.4cm) square.

3. Sew the HSTs and the 2½ x 2½in (6.4 x 6.4cm) fabric squares into sections as shown, following the **Standard Piecing Method**, then joining the sections together.

4. Evenly trim down the whole block to 6½in (16.5cm) square if it is not this size already. Block is complete. Press and store safely.

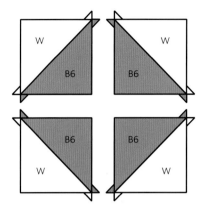

Make four HSTs

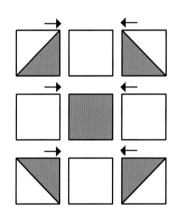

Evenly trim HSTs and sew together with the remaining fabric squares into sections

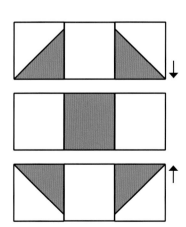

Sew the sections together to complete the block

BLOCK 14: The Spool

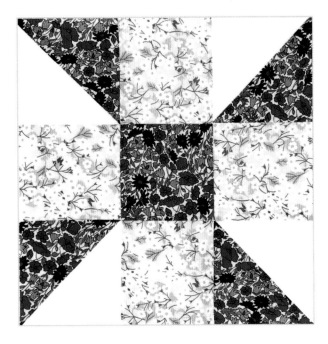

INFO

- Block Size: 6½in (16.5cm) unfinished, 6in (15.2cm) finished
- Seams: ¼in (0.6cm) and scant ¼in (0.4–0.5cm)
- Press Seams: Open. Press after each sewing step.

CUTTING

- White Fabric: one 4½ x 4½in (11.4 x 11.4cm)
- Fabric B7: four 2½ x 2½in (6.4 x 6.4cm)
- Fabric B10: one 4½ x 4½in (11.4 x 11.4cm) and one 2½ x 2½in (6.4 x 6.4cm)

CONSTRUCTION

1. Using a standard ¼in (0.6cm) seam, follow the **Four at a Time HST Method** to sew the 4½ x 4½in (11.4 x 11.4cm) squares together into four HSTs as shown.

2. Evenly trim each HST down to 2½ x 2½in (6.4 x 6.4cm) square.

3. Using a scant ¼in (0.4–0.5cm) seam, sew the HSTs and 2½ x 2½in (6.4 x 6.4cm) B7 and B10 fabric squares into sections as shown following the **Standard Piecing Method**, then join the sections together, again using a scant seam.

4. Evenly trim down the whole block to 6½in (16.5cm) square if it is not this size already. Block is complete. Press and store safely.

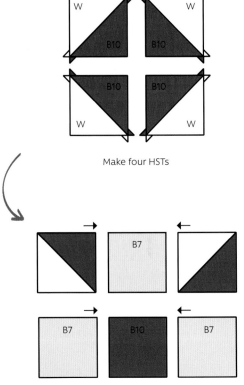

Make four HSTs

Evenly trim HSTs and sew together with the remaining fabric squares into sections

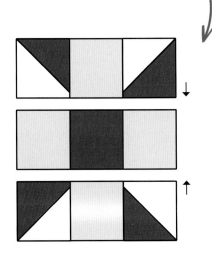

Sew the sections together to complete the block

BLOCK 15: Old Maid's Puzzle

INFO

- Block Size: 6½in (16.5cm) unfinished, 6in (15.2cm) finished
- Seams: ¼in (0.6cm)
- Press Seams: Open. Press after each sewing step.

CUTTING

- White Fabric: one 4½ x 4½in (11.4 x 11.4cm), three 2½ x 2½in (6.4 x 6.4cm) and one 3¼ x 3¼in (8.3 x 8.3cm)
- Fabric B5: one 3¼ x 3¼in (8.3 x 8.3cm)
- Fabric B9: one 4½ x 4½in (11.4 x 11.4cm)

CONSTRUCTION

1. Following the **Four at a Time HST Method**, sew the 4½ x 4½in (11.4 x 11.4cm) squares together into four HSTs as shown.

2. Following the **Two at a Time HST Method**, sew the 3¼ x 3¼in (8.3 x 8.3cm) squares together into two HSTs as shown.

3. Evenly trim each HST down to 2½ x 2½in (6.4 x 6.4cm) square.

4. Sew the units together as shown following the **Standard Piecing Method**, first sewing the HSTs with the 2½ x 2½in (6.4 x 6.4cm) white fabric squares into sections, then joining the sections together.

5. Evenly trim down the whole block to 6½in (16.5cm) square if it is not this size already. Block is complete. Press and store safely.

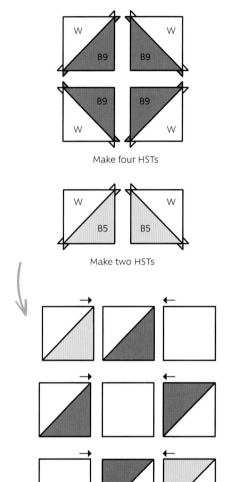

Make four HSTs

Make two HSTs

Evenly trim HSTs and sew together with the remaining white fabric squares into sections

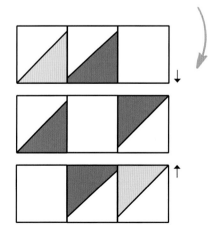

Sew the sections together to complete the block

BLOCK 16: *Spider*

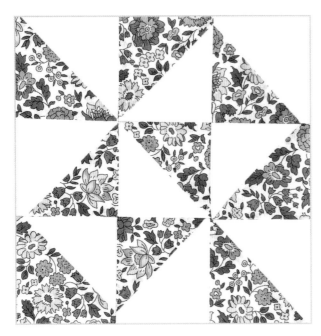

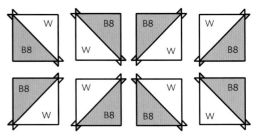

Make eight HSTs from larger fabric squares

Make two HSTs from smaller fabric squares and discard one

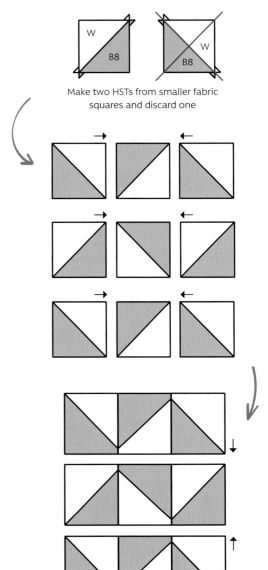

Evenly trim HSTs, sew together into sections, then sew sections together to complete the block

INFO

- Block Size: 6½in (16.5cm) unfinished, 6in (15.2cm) finished
- Seams: ¼in (0.6cm)
- Press Seams: Open. Press after each sewing step.

CUTTING

- White Fabric: one 6¼ x 6¼in (15.9 x 15.9cm) and one 3¼ x 3¼in (8.3 x 8.3cm)
- Fabric B8: one 6¼ x 6¼in (15.9 x 15.9cm) and one 3¼ x 3¼in (8.3 x 8.3cm)

CONSTRUCTION

1. Following the **Eight at a Time HST Method**, sew the 6¼ x 6¼in (15.9 x 15.9cm) squares of white fabric and B8 fabric together into eight HSTs as shown.

2. Following the **Two at a Time HST Method**, sew the 3¼ x 3¼in (8.3 x 8.3cm) squares of white fabric and B8 fabric together into two HSTs as shown. Discard one.

3. Evenly trim each HST down to 2½ x 2½in (6.4 x 6.4cm) square.

4. Sew the units together as shown following the **Standard Piecing Method**, first sewing three HSTs into sections, then joining the sections together.

5. Evenly trim down the whole block to 6½in (16.5cm) square if it is not this size already. Block is complete. Press and store safely.

BLOCK 17: Wild Geese

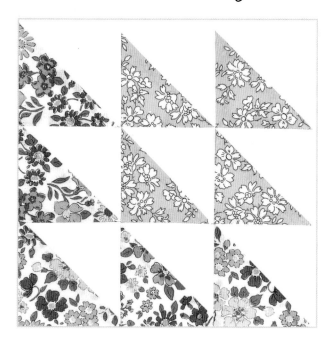

INFO

- Block Size: 6½in (16.5cm) unfinished, 6in (15.2cm) finished
- Seams: ¼in (0.6cm)
- Press Seams: Open. Press after each sewing step.

CUTTING

- White Fabric: two 4½ x 4½in (11.4 x 11.4cm) and one 3¼ x 3¼in (8.3 x 8.3cm)
- Fabric B4: one 4½ x 4½in (11.4 x 11.4cm) and one 3¼ x 3¼in (8.3 x 8.3cm)
- Fabric B5: one 3¼ x 3¼in (8.3 x 8.3cm)

CONSTRUCTION

1. Following the **Four at a Time HST Method**, sew one 4½ x 4½in (11.4 x 11.4cm) square of white fabric and B4 fabric together into four HSTs as shown. Sew one 4½ x 4½in (11.4 x 11.4cm) square of white fabric and B5 fabric together into four HSTs as shown.

2. Following the **Two at a Time HST Method**, sew the 3¼ x 3¼in (8.3 x 8.3cm) squares of white fabric and B4 fabric together into two HSTs. Discard one.

3. Evenly trim each HST down to 2½ x 2½in (6.4 x 6.4cm) square.

4. Sew the units together as shown following the **Standard Piecing Method**, first sewing three HSTs, then joining the resulting units.

5. Evenly trim down the whole block to 6½in (16.5cm) square if it is not this size already. Block is complete. Press and store safely.

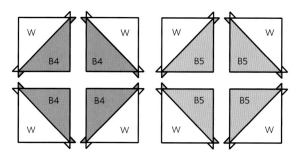

Make four HSTs from each pair of the larger fabric squares

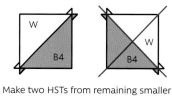

Make two HSTs from remaining smaller fabric squares and discard one

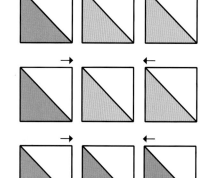

Evenly trim HSTs and sew together into sections

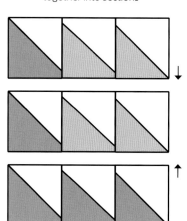

Sew the sections together to complete the block

BLOCK 18: Baby Bud

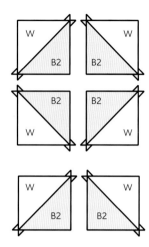

Make four HSTs and two HSTs

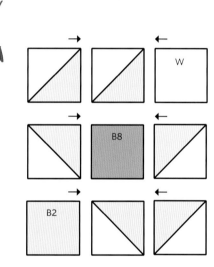

Evenly trim HSTs and sew together with the remaining fabric squares into sections

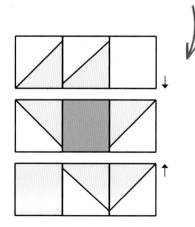

Sew the sections together to complete the block

INFO

- Block Size: 6½in (16.5cm) unfinished, 6in (15.2cm) finished
- Seams: ¼in (0.6cm) and scant ¼in (0.4–0.5cm)
- Press Seams: Open. Press after each sewing step.

CUTTING

- White Fabric: one 4½ x 4½in (11.4 x 11.4cm), one 3¼ x 3¼in (8.3 x 8.3cm) and one 2½ x 2½in (6.4 x 6.4cm)
- Fabric B2: one 4½ x 4½in (11.4 x 11.4cm), one 3¼ x 3¼in (8.3 x 8.3cm) and one 2½ x 2½in (6.4 x 6.4cm)
- Fabric B8: one 2½ x 2½in (6.4 x 6.4cm)

CONSTRUCTION

1. Using a standard ¼in (0.6cm) seam, follow the **Four at a Time HST Method** to sew the 4½ x 4½in (11.4 x 11.4cm) squares together into four HSTs as shown.

2. Using a standard ¼in (0.6cm) seam, follow the **Two at a Time HST Method** to sew the 3¼ x 3¼in (8.3 x 8.3cm) squares together into two HSTs as shown.

3. Evenly trim each HST down to 2½ x 2½in (6.4 x 6.4cm) square.

4. Using a scant ¼in (0.4–0.5cm) seam, sew the HSTs and 2½ x 2½in (6.4 x 6.4cm) fabric squares into sections as shown following the **Standard Piecing Method**, then join the sections together, again using a scant seam.

5. Evenly trim down the whole block to 6½in (16.5cm) square if it is not this size already. Block is complete. Press and store safely.

BLOCK 19: Maple Leaf

INFO

- Block Size: 6½in (16.5cm) unfinished, 6in (15.2cm) finished
- Seams: ¼in (0.6cm) and scant ¼in (0.4–0.5cm)
- Press Seams: Open. Press after each sewing step.

CUTTING

- White Fabric: one 4½ x 4½in (11.4 x 11.4cm), one 2½ x 2½in (6.4 x 6.4cm) and two 2 x 2in (5.1 x 5.1cm)
- Fabric B1: one 4½ x 4½in (11.4 x 11.4cm) and four 2½ x 2½in (6.4 x 6.4cm)

CONSTRUCTION

1. Using a ¼in (0.6cm) seam, follow the **Four at a Time HST Method** to sew the 4½ x 4½in (11.4 x 11.4cm) squares together into four HSTs as shown. Evenly trim each HST down to 2½ x 2½in (6.4 x 6.4cm) square.

2. Use a heat erasable pen and ruler to draw a straight line diagonally across both 2 x 2in (5.1 x 5.1cm) white fabric squares.

3. Pin one of the marked squares in the corner of a 2½ x 2½in (6.4 x 6.4cm) B1 fabric square, right sides together. Sew slightly to the outside of the drawn line. Remove pins. Cut ¼in (0.6cm) from the seam line as shown. Open out and press. Then sew remaining marked square to the opposite corner. This unit is the 'stalk' of the leaf. Evenly trim down to 2½ x 2½in (6.4 x 6.4cm) square.

4. Using a scant ¼in (0.4–0.5cm) seam, sew the HSTs, the stalk unit and the 2½ x 2½in (6.4 x 6.4cm) fabric squares into sections as shown following the **Standard Piecing Method**, then join the sections together.

5. Evenly trim down the whole block to 6½in (16.5cm) square. Press and store safely.

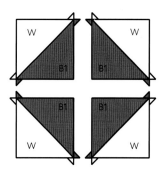

Make four HSTs, then evenly trim

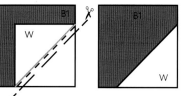

Sew small square in corner of large square, trim and press out. Repeat at opposite corner

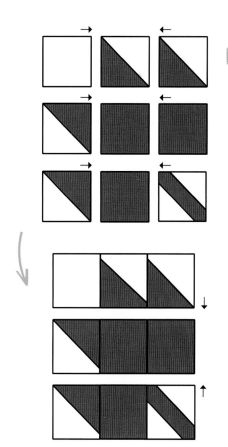

Sew the units together with the remaining fabric squares into sections, then sew sections together to complete the block

BLOCK 20: Split Nine Patch

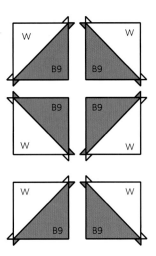

Make four HSTs and two HSTs

INFO

- Block Size: 6½in (16.5cm) unfinished, 6in (15.2cm) finished
- Seams: ¼in (0.6cm) and scant ¼in (0.4–0.5cm)
- Press Seams: Open. Press after each sewing step.

CUTTING

- White Fabric: one 4½ x 4½in (11.4 x 11.4cm), one 3¼ x 3¼in (8.3 x 8.3cm) and two 2½ x 2½in (6.4 x 6.4cm)
- Fabric B6: one 2½ x 2½in (6.4 x 6.4cm
- Fabric B9: one 4½ x 4½in (11.4 x 11.4cm) and one 3¼ x 3¼in (8.3 x 8.3cm)

CONSTRUCTION

1. Using a standard ¼in (0.6cm) seam, follow the **Four at a Time HST Method** to sew the 4½ x 4½in (11.4 x 11.4cm) squares together into four HSTs as shown.

2. Using a standard ¼in (0.6cm) seam, follow the **Two at a Time HST Method** to sew the 3¼ x 3¼in (8.3 x 8.3cm) squares together into two HSTs as shown.

3. Evenly trim each HST down to 2½ x 2½in (6.4 x 6.4cm) square.

4. Using a scant ¼in (0.4–0.5cm) seam, sew the HSTs and 2½ x 2½in (6.4 x 6.4cm) fabric squares into sections as shown following the **Standard Piecing Method**, then join the sections as shown, again using a scant seam.

5. Evenly trim down the whole block to 6½in (16.5cm) square if it is not this size already. Block is complete. Press and store safely.

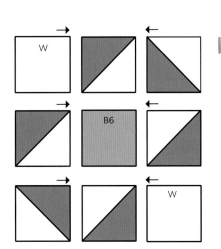

Evenly trim HSTs and sew together with the remaining fabric squares into sections

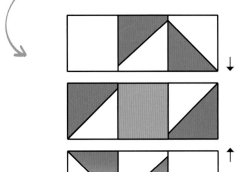

Sew the sections together to complete the block

BLOCK 21: Eccentric Star

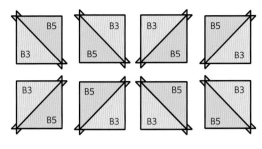

Make eight HSTs

INFO

- Block Size: 6½in (16.5cm) unfinished, 6in (15.2cm) finished
- Seams: ¼in (0.6cm) and scant ¼in (0.4–0.5cm)
- Press Seams: Open. Press after each sewing step.

CUTTING

- White Fabric: one 2½ x 2½in (6.4 x 6.4cm)
- Fabric B3: one 6¼ x 6¼in (15.9 x 15.9cm)
- Fabric B5: one 6¼ x 6¼in (15.9 x 15.9cm)

CONSTRUCTION

1. Using a standard ¼in (0.6cm) seam, follow the **Eight at a Time HST Method** to sew the 6¼ x 6¼in (15.9 x 15.9cm) squares together into eight HSTs as shown.

2. Evenly trim each HST down to 2½ x 2½in (6.4 x 6.4cm) square.

3. Using a scant ¼in (0.4–0.5cm) seam, sew the HSTs and 2½ x 2½in (6.4 x 6.4cm) white fabric square into sections as shown following the **Standard Piecing Method**, then join the sections as shown, again using a scant seam.

4. Evenly trim down the whole block to 6½in (16.5cm) square if it is not this size already. Block is complete. Press and store safely.

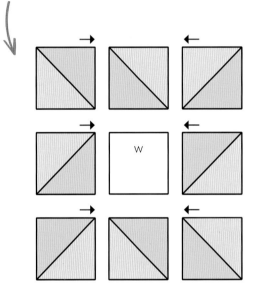

Evenly trim HSTs and sew together with the remaining white fabric square into sections

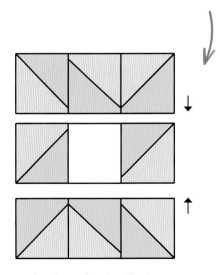

Sew the sections together to complete the block

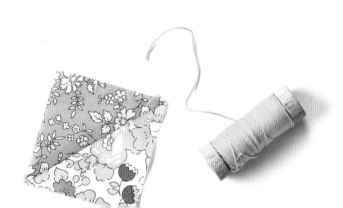

BLOCK 22: Monkey Wrench

INFO

- Block Size: 6½in (16.5cm) unfinished, 6in (15.2cm) finished
- Seams: scant ¼in (0.4–0.5cm) and ¼in (0.6cm)
- Press Seams: Open. Press after each sewing step.

CUTTING

- White Fabric: one 1½ x 13in (3.8 x 33cm), one 4½ x 4½in (11.4 x 11.4cm) and one 2½ x 2½in (6.4 x 6.4cm)
- Fabric C1: one 1½ x 13in (3.8 x 33cm) and one 4½ x 4½in (11.4 x 11.4cm)

CONSTRUCTION

1. Following the **Strip Piecing Method**, sew the 1½ x 13in (3.8 x 33cm) strips of fabric together to make the strip set as shown. Then, cut the strip set at 2½in (6.4cm) intervals to make four 2½ x 2½in (6.4 x 6.4cm) smaller units. Discard any leftover fabric.

2. Following the **Four at a Time HST Method**, use a scant ¼in (0.4–0.5cm) seam to sew the 4½ x 4½in (11.4 x 11.4cm) squares together into four HSTs as shown. Evenly trim each HST down to 2½ x 2½in (6.4 x 6.4cm) square.

3. Sew the units together as shown following the **Standard Piecing Method**, using a standard ¼in (0.6cm) seam, first joining them into sections with the 2½ x 2½in (6.4 x 6.4cm) white fabric square, then sewing the sections together.

4. Evenly trim down the whole block to 6½in (16.5cm) square if it is not this size already. Block is complete. Press and store safely.

Fabric Focus

Strawberry Thief was designed by William Morris in 1883. Liberty Fabrics first produced it as a furnishing fabric in 1979 and it has since been redrawn for Tana Lawn® in a smaller scale. It has become one of the most popular classic Liberty prints.

Sew the strips into a strip set and
subcut into four smaller units

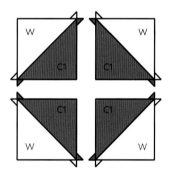

Make four HSTs, then evenly trim

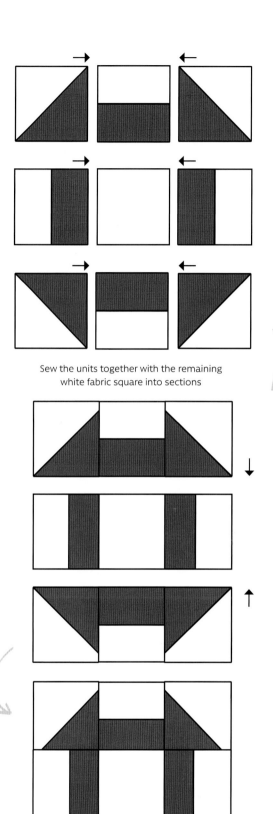

Sew the units together with the remaining
white fabric square into sections

Sew the sections together into the final block

BLOCK 23: Forest Paths

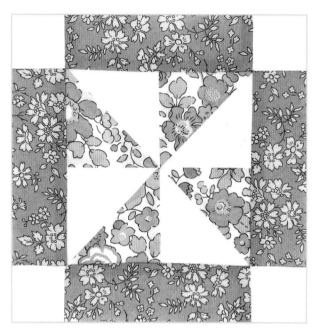

INFO

- Block Size: 6½in (16.5cm) unfinished, 6in (15.2cm) finished
- Seams: scant ¼in (0.4–0.5cm)
- Press Seams: Open. Press after each sewing step.

CUTTING

- White Fabric: one 4½ x 4½in (11.4 x 11.4cm) and four 1½ x 1½in (3.8 x 3.8cm)
- Fabric C3: one 4½ x 4½in (11.4 x 11.4cm)
- Fabric C7: four 1½ x 4½in (3.8 x 11.4cm)

CONSTRUCTION

1. Following the **Four at a Time HST Method**, use a scant seam to sew the 4½ x 4½in (11.4 x 11.4cm) squares together into four HSTs as shown. Evenly trim each HST down to 2½ x 2½in (6.4 x 6.4cm) square.

2. Sew the units shown following the **Standard Piecing Method** using a scant seam, first sewing two HSTs together, then joining the resulting units.

3. Sew 1½ x 4½in (3.8 x 11.4cm) C7 fabric strips to the top and bottom of the unit using a scant seam.

4. Sew the 1½ x 1½in (3.8 x 3.8cm) white fabric squares to each end of the remaining C7 fabric strips using a scant seam, then sew these strips to the sides of the unit as shown, again using a scant seam.

5. Evenly trim down the whole block to 6½in (16.5cm) square if it is not this size already. Block is complete. Press and store safely.

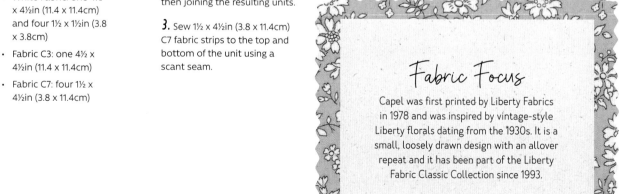

Fabric Focus

Capel was first printed by Liberty Fabrics in 1978 and was inspired by vintage-style Liberty florals dating from the 1930s. It is a small, loosely drawn design with an allover repeat and it has been part of the Liberty Fabric Classic Collection since 1993.

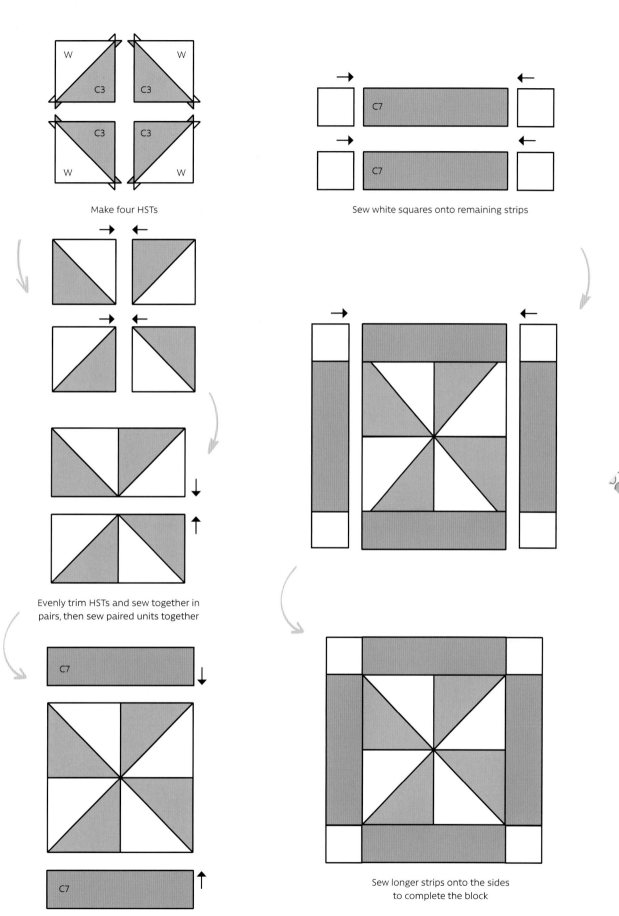

Make four HSTs

Sew white squares onto remaining strips

Evenly trim HSTs and sew together in
pairs, then sew paired units together

Sew strips onto the top and bottom

Sew longer strips onto the sides
to complete the block

BLOCK 24: Friendship Star Variation

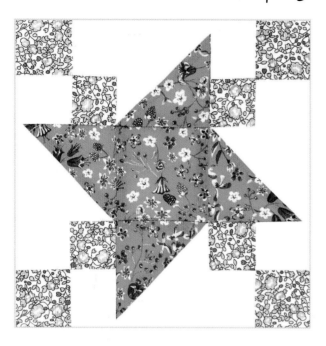

CONSTRUCTION

1. Following the **Strip Piecing Method**, use a scant seam to sew the 1½ x 13in (3.8 x 33cm) strips of white fabric and C8 fabric together to make the strip set as shown. Then, cut the strip set at 1½in (3.8cm) intervals to make eight 1½ x 2½in (3.8 x 6.4cm) smaller units. Discard any leftover fabric.

2. Sew four of the units shown following the **Standard Piecing Method**. Evenly trim down to 2½ x 2½in (6.4 x 6.4cm) square if not already this size.

3. Following the **Four at a Time HST Method**, use a scant seam to sew the 4½ x 4½in (11.4 x 11.4cm) squares together into four HSTs as shown. Evenly trim each HST down to 2½ x 2½in (6.4 x 6.4cm) square.

4. Following the **Standard Piecing Method**, sew the units together as shown using a scant seam, first joining the units into sections with the 2½ x 2½in (6.4 x 6.4cm) C6 fabric square, then sewing the sections together.

5. Evenly trim down the whole block to 6½in (16.5cm) square if it is not this size already. Block is complete. Press and store safely.

INFO

- Block Size: 6½in (16.5cm) unfinished, 6in (15.2cm) finished
- Seams: scant ¼in (0.4–0.5cm)
- Press Seams: Open. Press after each sewing step.

CUTTING

- White Fabric: one 1½ x 13in (3.8 x 33cm) and one 4½ x 4½in (11.4 x 11.4cm)
- Fabric C6: one 2½ x 2½in (6.4 x 6.4cm) and one 4½ x 4½in (11.4 x 11.4cm)
- Fabric C8: one 1½ x 13in (3.8 x 33cm)

Fabric Focus

Eloise is derived from an archival 1966 Liberty design and it is one of a group of prints that was inspired by Victorian florals. It was first revived for Autumn/Winter 2005 and quickly joined the Classics collection.

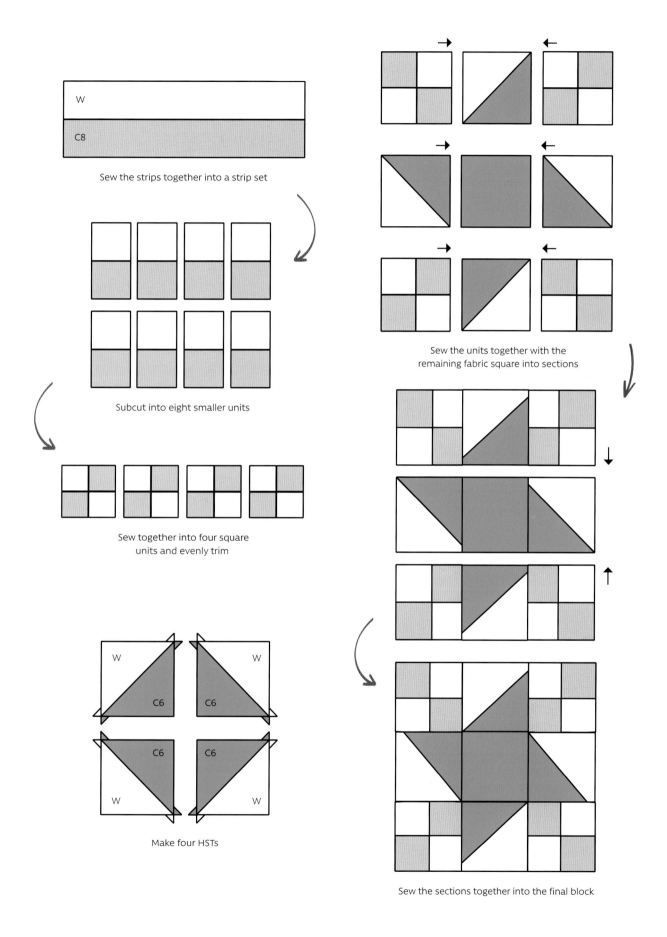

Sew the strips together into a strip set

Subcut into eight smaller units

Sew together into four square units and evenly trim

Make four HSTs

W

C8

W

W

C6

C6

C6

C6

W

W

Sew the units together with the remaining fabric square into sections

Sew the sections together into the final block

BLOCK 25: Home Queen

INFO

- Block Size: 6½in (16.5cm) unfinished, 6in (15.2cm) finished
- Seams: scant ¼in (0.4–0.5cm)
- Press Seams: Open. Press after each sewing step.

CUTTING

- White Fabric: one 4½ x 4½in (11.4 x 11.4cm) and one 1½ x 10in (3.8 x 25.4cm)
- Fabric C2: one 4½ x 4½in (11.4 x 11.4cm), one 1½ x 10in (3.8 x 25.4cm) and two 2½ x 2½in (6.4 x 6.4cm)

CONSTRUCTION

1. Following the **Strip Piecing Method**, use a scant seam to sew the 1½ x 10in (3.8 x 25.4cm) strips of fabric together to make the strip set as shown. Then, cut the strip set at 1½in (3.8cm) intervals to make six 1½ x 2½in (3.8 x 6.4cm) smaller units. Discard any leftover fabric.

2. Sew the smaller units together to make three of the units shown following the **Standard Piecing Method** using a scant seam. Evenly trim down to 2½ x 2½in (6.4 x 6.4cm) square if not already this size.

3. Following the **Four at a Time HST Method**, use a scant seam to sew the 4½ x 4½in (11.4 x 11.4cm) squares together into four HSTs as shown. Evenly trim each HST down to 2½ x 2½in (6.4 x 6.4cm) square.

4. Following the **Standard Piecing Method**, sew the units together as shown using a scant seam, first joining the units into sections with the 2½ x 2½in (6.4 x 6.4cm) C2 fabric squares, then sewing the sections together.

5. Evenly trim down the whole block to 6½in (16.5cm) square if it is not this size already. Block is complete. Press and store safely.

Fabric Focus

Wiltshire Bud is a small-scale version of that much-loved classic, the Wiltshire print. Its lovely allover leaf and berry pattern was redrawn in a light colour palette to give a modern, polished effect.

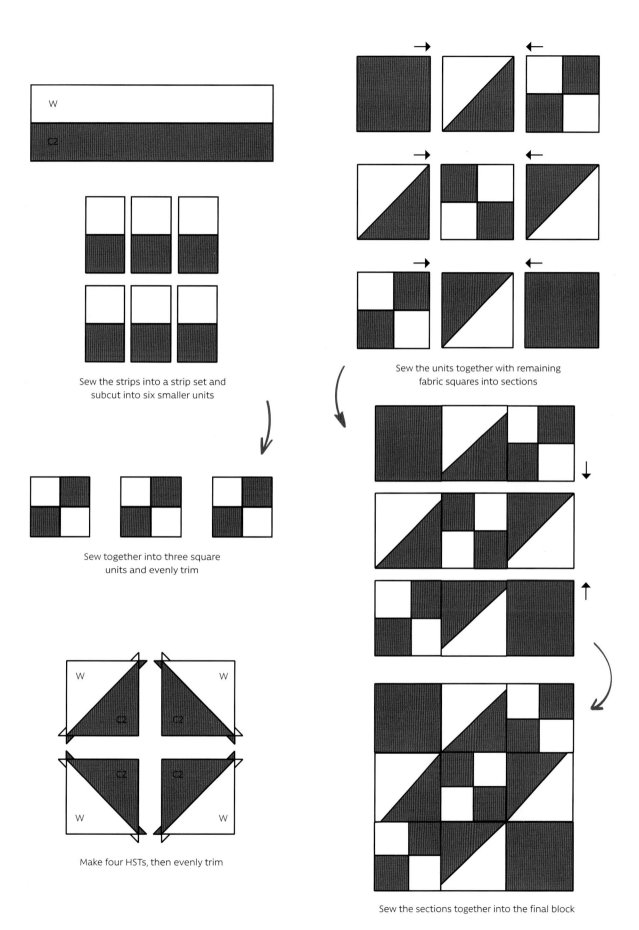

Sew the strips into a strip set and subcut into six smaller units

Sew together into three square units and evenly trim

Make four HSTs, then evenly trim

Sew the units together with remaining fabric squares into sections

Sew the sections together into the final block

BLOCK 26: Jacob's Ladder

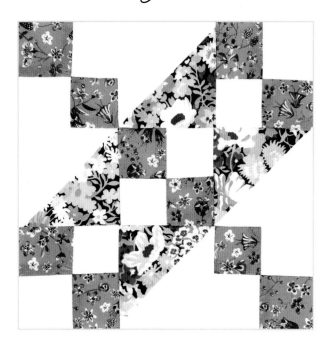

INFO

- Block Size: 6½in (16.5cm) unfinished, 6in (15.2cm) finished
- Seams: scant ¼in (0.4–0.5cm)
- Press Seams: Open. Press after each sewing step.

CUTTING

- White Fabric: one 4½ x 4½in (11.4 x 11.4cm) and two 1½ x 9in (3.8 x 22.9cm)
- Fabric C6: two 1½ x 9in (3.8 x 22.9cm)
- Fabric C9: one 4½ x 4½in (11.4 x 11.4cm)

CONSTRUCTION

1. Following the **Strip Piecing Method**, use a scant seam to sew the 1½ x 9in (3.8 x 22.9cm) strips of white and C6 fabric together to make the strip set as shown. Make a second, identical strip set with the remaining 1½ x 9in (3.8 x 22.9cm) strips.

2. Cut the strip sets at 1½in (3.8cm) intervals to make ten 1½ x 2½in (3.8 x 6.4cm) smaller units. Discard any leftover fabric.

3. Sew the smaller units together to make five of the units shown following the **Standard Piecing Method** using a scant seam. Evenly trim down to 2½ x 2½in (6.4 x 6.4cm) square if not already this size.

4. Following the **Four at a Time HST Method**, use a scant seam to sew the 4½ x 4½in (11.4 x 11.4cm) squares together into four HSTs as shown. Evenly trim each HST down to 2½ x 2½in (6.4 x 6.4cm) square.

5. Following the **Standard Piecing Method**, sew the units together as shown using a scant seam, first joining the units into sections, then sewing the sections together.

6. Evenly trim down the whole block to 6½in (16.5cm) square if it is not this size already. Block is complete. Press and store safely.

Fabric Focus

Donna Leigh was inspired by a design from botanical artist and engraver William Kilburn, who was also one of the 18th century's most well-regarded calico-printers. During the late 1700s he produced many patterns, often with rich, dark backgrounds and contrasting flowers.

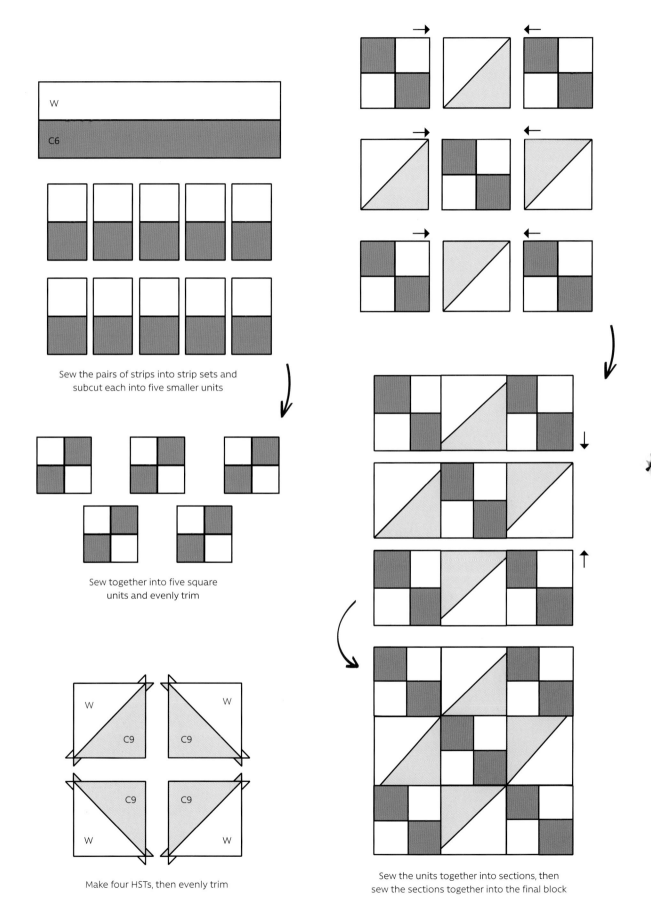

W

C6

Sew the pairs of strips into strip sets and
subcut each into five smaller units

Sew together into five square
units and evenly trim

W | W
C9 | C9

C9 | C9
W | W

Make four HSTs, then evenly trim

Sew the units together into sections, then
sew the sections together into the final block

BLOCK 27: Water Wheel

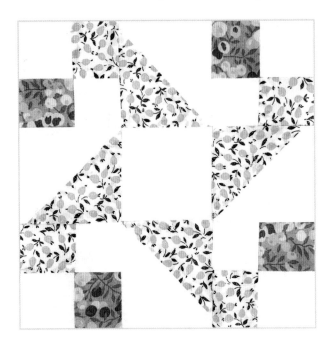

INFO

- Block Size: 6½in (16.5cm) unfinished, 6in (15.2cm) finished
- Seams: scant ¼in (0.4–0.5cm)
- Press Seams: Open. Press after each sewing step.

CUTTING

- White Fabric: two 1½ x 7in (3.8 x 17.8cm), one 4½ x 4½in (11.4 x 11.4cm) and one 2½ x 2½in (6.4 x 6.4cm)
- Fabric C5: one 1½ x 7in (3.8 x 17.8cm) and one 4½ x 4½in (11.4 x 11.4cm)
- Fabric C10: one 1½ x 7in (3.8 x 17.8cm)

CONSTRUCTION

1. Following the **Strip Piecing Method**, use a scant seam to sew a 1½ x 7in (3.8 x 17.8cm) strip of white fabric and C5 fabric together to make the strip set as shown. Then, cut the strip set at 1½in (3.8cm) intervals to make four 1½ x 2½in (3.8 x 6.4cm) smaller units. Discard any leftover fabric.

2. Following the **Strip Piecing Method**, use a scant seam to sew a 1½ x 7in (3.8 x 17.8cm) strip of white fabric and C10 fabric together to make the strip set as shown. Then, cut the strip set at 1½in (3.8cm) intervals to make four 1½ x 2½in (3.8 x 6.4cm) smaller units. Discard any leftover fabric.

3. Sew four of the units shown following the **Standard Piecing Method** using a scant seam. Evenly trim down to 2½ x 2½in (6.4 x 6.4cm) square if not already this size.

4. Following the **Four at a Time HST Method**, use a scant seam to sew the 4½ x 4½in (11.4 x 11.4cm) squares together into four HSTs as shown. Evenly trim each HST down to 2½ x 2½in (6.4 x 6.4cm) square.

5. Following the **Standard Piecing Method**, sew the units together as shown using a scant seam, first joining the units and 2½ x 2½in (6.4 x 6.4cm) white fabric square into sections, then sewing the sections together.

6. Evenly trim down the whole block to 6½in (16.5cm) square if it is not this size already. Block is complete. Press and store safely.

Fabric Focus

Wiltshire is a yew tree leaf and berry pattern designed for Liberty Fabrics in 1933. It has been part of the Classics collection since 1979 and is one of the most popular and well-known Liberty prints today.

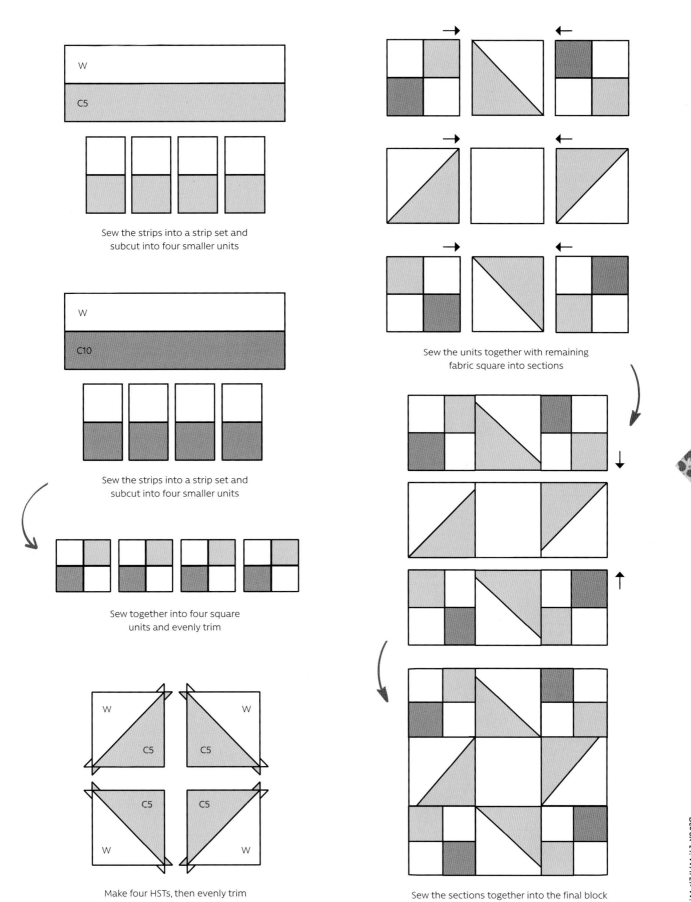

Sew the strips into a strip set and subcut into four smaller units

Sew the strips into a strip set and subcut into four smaller units

Sew together into four square units and evenly trim

Make four HSTs, then evenly trim

Sew the units together with remaining fabric square into sections

Sew the sections together into the final block

Quarter Square Triangles

ABOUT QUARTER SQUARE TRIANGLES (QSTS)

A true QST involves four different fabrics, whereas one that uses only two different fabrics may instead be called an Hourglass or Bow Tie. However, the method for constructing QSTs using two or four different fabrics is exactly the same and, luckily, very simple.

Quilt blocks commonly using these units include Swamp Angel and Ohio Star.

Recommended Tool: heat erasable pen

Match two HSTs together

ONE AT A TIME QST METHOD

1. Take two pre-made HSTs of the same size. Their seams may be pressed either open or to one side. Place them right sides together, paying attention to how the colours meet. If seams are pressed to one side they should face opposite directions to help reduce bulk. This is called 'nesting seams' (see **Half Square Triangles: Handy Tips**).

2. Use a heat erasable pen (or pencil) and ruler to draw a straight line diagonally across the wrong side of the top HST as shown. Pin in place.

3. Sew along the drawn line if a standard ¼in (0.6cm) seam, or slightly to the outside of the drawn line if a scant seam, as indicated by the specific block instructions. Remove pins. Trim down the outside to ¼in (0.6cm) seam as shown.

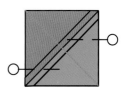

Draw a diagonal line on the top HST then pin HSTs together

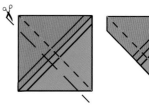

After stitching along or just outside of the marked line, trim down to the seam allowance

Makes one untrimmed QST

Split QSTs

ABOUT SPLIT QUARTER SQUARE TRIANGLES

The split QST unit has two small triangles on one half of the square and one larger triangle on the other half.

Quilt blocks commonly using these units include Air Castle, Card Trick and Twin Star.

Recommended Tool: heat erasable pen

ONE AT A TIME SPLIT QST METHOD

1. Take a single pre-made HST and one fabric square of the same size. Place them right sides together as shown, paying attention to where the colours meet.

2. Use a heat erasable pen (or pencil) and ruler to draw a straight line diagonally across the wrong side of the top square. Pin in place.

3. Sew along the drawn line if a standard ¼in (0.6cm) seam, or slightly to the outside of the drawn line if a scant seam, as indicated by the specific block instructions. Remove pins. Trim down the outside to ¼in (0.6cm) seam as shown. Open out and press.

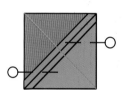

Match one fabric square and one HST together

Draw a diagonal line on the top HST then pin fabrics together

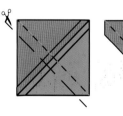

After stitching along or just outside of the marked line, trim down to the seam allowance

HANDY TIPS

When making QSTs and split QSTs, pay attention to where the different fabrics meet and how that may affect the end result. Fold back the seams and double check before sewing to be sure everything is sitting as you want it to be.

Evenly trim each QST unit and split QST unit so the joined point in the middle is exactly in the centre. Note: using a scant ¼in (0.4-5cm) seam rather than a standard ¼in (0.6cm) seam will result in slightly more fabric to trim off at the end, thereby allowing more room for error.

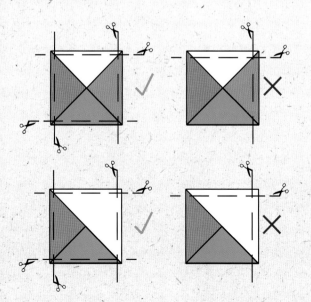

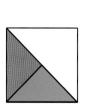

Makes one untrimmed split QST

BLOCK 28: Ohio Star

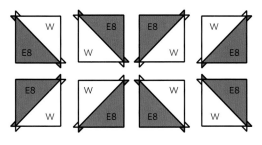

Make eight HSTs

Make four QSTs and evenly trim

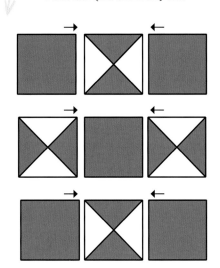

Sew QST units together with the remaining fabric squares into sections

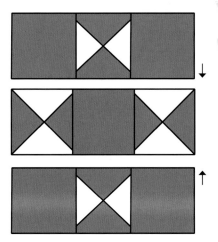

Sew the sections together to complete the block

INFO

- Block Size: 6½in (16.5cm) unfinished, 6in (15.2cm) finished
- Seams: ¼in (0.6cm)
- Press Seams: Open. Press after each sewing step.

CUTTING

- White Fabric: one 6¼ x 6¼in (15.9 x 15.9cm)
- Fabric E8: one 6¼ x 6¼in (15.9 x 15.9cm) and five 2½ x 2½in (6.4 x 6.4cm)

CONSTRUCTION

1. Following the **Eight at a Time HST Method**, sew the 6¼ x 6¼in (15.9 x 15.9cm) squares together into eight HSTs as shown.

2. Following the **One at a Time QST Method**, sew pairs of the HSTs together to make four QSTs as shown.

3. Evenly trim each QST down to 2½ x 2½in (6.4 x 6.4cm) square.

4. Sew the units together as shown following the **Standard Piecing Method**, first sewing the QSTs with the 2½ x 2½in (6.4 x 6.4cm) E8 fabric squares into sections, then joining the sections together.

5. Evenly trim down the whole block to 6½in (16.5cm) square if it is not this size already. Block is complete. Press and store safely.

BLOCK 29: Star X

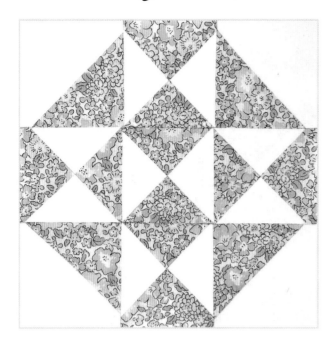

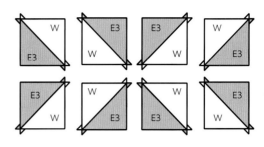

Make sixteen HSTs using the Eight at a Time HST Method

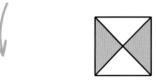

Make five QSTs and evenly trim

INFO

- Block Size: 6½in (16.5cm) unfinished, 6in (15.2cm) finished
- Seams: ¼in (0.6cm)
- Press Seams: Open. Press after each sewing step.

CUTTING

- White Fabric: two 6¼ x 6¼in (15.9 x 15.9cm)
- Fabric E3: two 6¼ x 6¼in (15.9 x 15.9cm)

CONSTRUCTION

1. Following the **Eight at a Time HST Method**, sew one E3 fabric square and one white fabric square together into eight HSTs as shown. Then repeat with the remaining squares to make a total of sixteen HSTs.

2. Evenly trim just four of the HST units down to 2½ x 2½in (6.4 x 6.4cm) square. Set these trimmed four aside until step 5.

3. Following the **One at a Time QST Method**, sew two of the HSTs together into one QST as shown. Repeat with eight of the remaining HSTs to make a total of five QSTs. Discard the two remaining HSTs.

4. Evenly trim each QST down to 2½ x 2½in (6.4 x 6.4cm) square.

5. Sew the units together as shown following the **Standard Piecing Method**, first sewing them into sections, then joining the sections together.

6. Evenly trim down the whole block to 6½in (16.5cm) square if it is not this size already. Block is complete. Press and store safely.

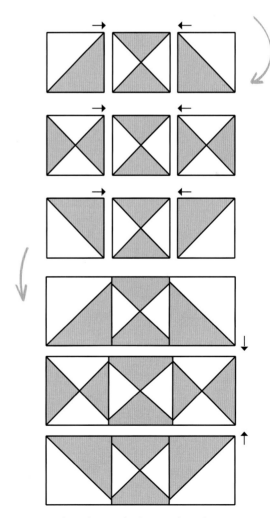

Sew the units together into sections, then sew the sections together to complete the block

BLOCK 30: Four X

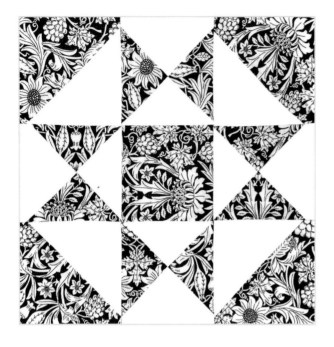

INFO

- Block Size: 6½in (16.5cm) unfinished, 6in (15.2cm) finished
- Seams: ¼in (0.6cm)
- Press Seams: Open. Press after each sewing step.

CUTTING

- White Fabric: one 6¼ x 6¼in (15.9 x 15.9cm) and one 4½ x 4½in (11.4 x 11.4cm)
- Fabric E9: one 6¼ x 6¼in (15.9 x 15.9cm), one 4½ x 4½in (11.4 x 11.4cm) and one 2½ x 2½in (6.4 x 6.4cm)

CONSTRUCTION

1. Following the **Eight at a Time HST Method**, sew the 6¼ x 6¼in (15.9 x 15.9cm) squares together into eight HSTs as shown.

2. Following the **Four at a Time HST Method**, sew the 4½ x 4½in (11.4 x 11.4cm) squares together into four HSTs as shown.

3. Evenly trim just four of the HST units down to 2½ x 2½in (6.4 x 6.4cm) square. Set these trimmed four aside until step 6.

4. Following the **One at a Time QST Method**, sew two of the HSTs together into one QST as shown. Repeat with six of the remaining HSTs to make a total of four QSTs.

5. Evenly trim each QST down to 2½ x 2½in (6.4 x 6.4cm) square.

6. Sew the units together as shown following the **Standard Piecing Method**, first sewing them into sections with the 2½ x 2½in (6.4 x 6.4cm) E9 fabric square, then joining the sections together.

7. Evenly trim down the whole block to 6½in (16.5cm) square if it is not this size already. Block is complete. Press and store safely.

Fabric Focus

Mortimer has a timelessly charming appeal, featuring an Arts and Crafts style design brimming with luscious foliage and fruit. It is, in fact, a simplified version of William Morris's 'Sunflower' design.

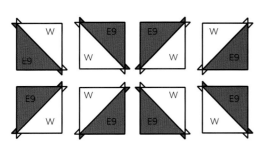

Make eight HSTs

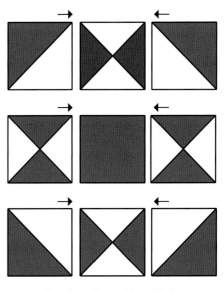

Sew the units together with the remaining fabric square into sections

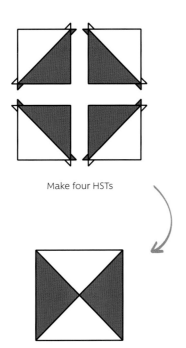

Make four HSTs

Make four QSTs and evenly trim

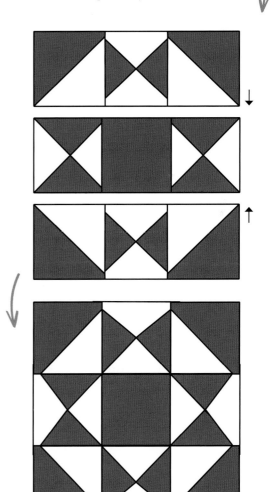

Sew the sections together into the final block

BLOCK 31: Whirlwind

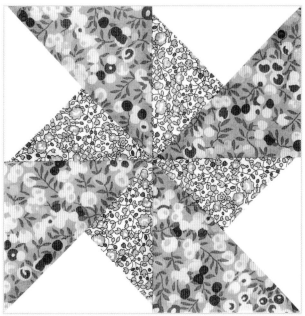

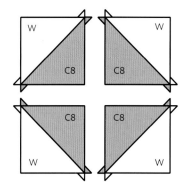

Make four HSTs, then evenly trim

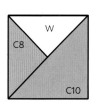

Make four split QSTs and evenly trim

INFO

- Block Size: 6½in (16.5cm) unfinished, 6in (15.2cm) finished
- Seams: scant ¼in (0.4–0.5cm)
- Press Seams: Open. Press after each sewing step.

CUTTING

- White Fabric: one 6 x 6in (15.2 x 15.2cm)
- Fabric C8: one 6 x 6in (15.2 x 15.2cm)
- Fabric C10: four 3½ x 3½in (8.9 x 8.9cm)

CONSTRUCTION

1. Following the **Four at a Time HST Method**, use a scant seam to sew the 6 x 6in (15.2 x 15.2cm) squares together into four HSTs as shown. Evenly trim each HST down to 3½ x 3½in (8.9 x 8.9cm) square.

2. Following the **One at a Time Split QST Method**, use a scant seam to sew the four HSTs and the four 3½ x 3½in (8.9 x 8.9cm) C10 fabric squares into four identical units as shown. Evenly trim each split QST down to 3½ x 3½in (8.9 x 8.9cm) square.

3. Sew the units together as shown using a scant seam and following the **Standard Piecing Method**, first sewing two units together, then joining the resulting units.

4. Evenly trim down the whole block to 6½in (16.5cm) square if it is not this size already. Block is complete. Press and store safely.

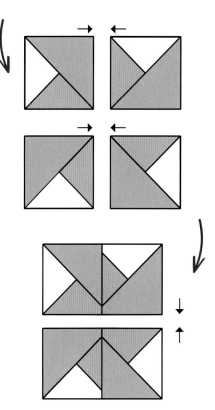

Sew the split QSTs together in pairs, then sew the paired units together to complete the block

BLOCK 32: Card Trick

INFO

- Block Size: 6½in (16.5cm) unfinished, 6in (15.2cm) finished
- Seams: ¼in (0.6cm)
- Press Seams: Open. Press after each sewing step.

CUTTING

- White Fabric: two 4½ x 4½in (11.4 x 11.4cm)
- Fabric C4: one 4½ x 4½in (11.4 x 11.4cm), two 2½ x 2½in (6.4 x 6.4cm) and one 3¼ x 3¼in (8.3 x 8.3cm)
- Fabric C9: one 4½ x 4½in (11.4 x 11.4cm), two 2½ x 2½in (6.4 x 6.4cm) and one 3¼ x 3¼in (8.3 x 8.3cm)

CONSTRUCTION

1. Following the **Four at a Time HST Method**, sew one 4½ x 4½in (11.4 x 11.4cm) square of white fabric and C4 fabric together into four HSTs as shown. Sew one 4½ x 4½in (11.4 x 11.4cm) square of white fabric and C9 fabric together into four HSTs as shown.

2. Evenly trim each of these eight HSTs down to 2½ x 2½in (6.4 x 6.4cm) square.

3. Following the **Two at a Time HST Method**, sew the 3¼ x 3¼in (8.3 x 8.3cm) squares of C4 and C9 fabrics together into two HSTs. Following the **One at a Time QST Method**, sew these HSTs together into one QST as shown and evenly trim down to 2½ x 2½in (6.4 x 6.4cm) square.

4. Following the **One at a Time Split QST Method**, sew two white fabric and C9 fabric HSTs and the two 2½ x 2½in (6.4 x 6.4cm) C4 fabric squares into two identical units. Repeat to sew two white fabric and C4 fabric HSTs and the two 2½ x 2½in (6.4 x 6.4cm) C9 fabric squares into two identical units, to give you four split QSTs in total.

5. Evenly trim each split QST down to 2½ x 2½in (6.4 x 6.4cm) square.

6. Sew the units together as shown following the **Standard Piecing Method**, first sewing the units into sections, then joining the sections together.

7. Evenly trim down the whole block to 6½in (16.5cm) square if it is not this size already. Block is complete. Press and store safely.

Fabric Focus

Thorpe is named after the artist John Hall Thorpe, whose paintings from the early 1900s inspired its dense floral layout. Its flourishing design, drawn and coloured in 1968, evokes the classic style of 1930s Liberty florals.

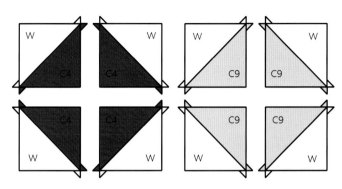

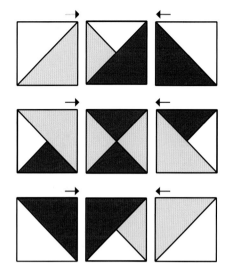

Make four HSTs from each pair of
the largest fabric squares

Sew trimmed units together into sections

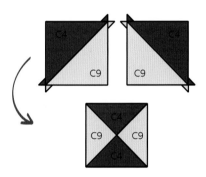

Make two HSTs, evenly trim then
use these to make one QST

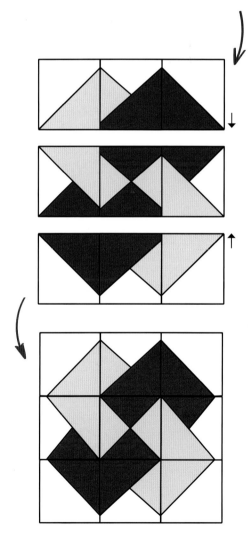

Make four split QSTs, making
two identical units each

Sew the sections together
into the final block

Diamond in a Square

ABOUT DIAMOND IN A SQUARE

Also known as Square in a Square, or simply Diamond Square, this block has been around since at least the 1870s. At its most simple it involves a single diamond set on-point within a square. More visually complicated versions can involve multiple diamonds and squares growing ever larger, giving the illusion of shapes within shapes within shapes. The good news is that the technique for making the more complicated looking versions and the simple looking versions is the same and very easy to achieve.

Quilt blocks commonly using these units include Evening Star, Nonsense and Union.

Recommended Tool: heat erasable pen

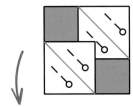

Pin marked small squares in opposite corners of large square

DIAMOND IN A SQUARE METHOD

I. You will need one large fabric square (which becomes the 'diamond') and four smaller fabric squares (which become the corner pieces of the 'square') and the exact dimensions will be indicated by the block instructions. Draw a straight line diagonally across the wrong side of each of the smaller squares using a heat erasable pen (or pencil) and ruler.

2. Place two of the small fabric squares in the opposite corners of the large fabric square, right sides together, as shown. The small squares should overlap in the middle of the large square. Pin in place.

3. Sew either directly on the drawn line for a standard seam, or slightly beside the drawn line for a scant seam (see diagrams), as indicated by the specific block instructions. Remove the pins. Trim off fabric from the sewn corners to ¼in (0.6cm) seam. Open out and press.

4. Repeat steps 2 and 3 to sew the remaining two small squares in the other two corners of the large square.

5. Evenly trim the block down to the required size as directed by the block's instructions, being sure to leave ¼in (0.6cm) space between each of the inner diamond points and the outer block edge.

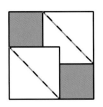 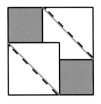

Sewing with a standard seam   Sewing with a scant seam

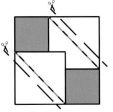

Trim the corners down

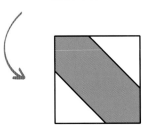

Open out and press

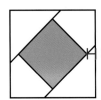

¼in (0.6 cm) space

Makes one Diamond in a Square unit

HANDY TIPS

Sewing a Diamond in a Square with a scant ¼in (0.4–0.5cm) instead of a standard ¼in (0.6cm) seam will result in slightly more fabric to trim off at the end, allowing more room for error.

If using a directional fabric for the corner pieces of the 'square' you may want them to be facing a certain way. When placing the small fabric squares on the large square in step 2, flip each corner fabric piece back to check it will be facing the right way once opened out. Do take the time to check this before pinning and sewing to avoid unpicking later.

BLOCK 33: Broken Sash

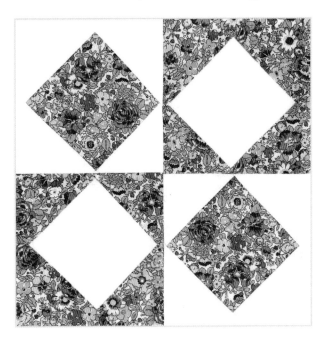

INFO

- Block Size: 6½in (16.5cm) unfinished, 6in (15.2cm) finished
- Seams: scant ¼in (0.4–0.5cm) and ¼in (0.6cm)
- Press Seams: Open. Press after each sewing step.

CUTTING

- White Fabric: two 3½ x 3½in (8.9 x 8.9cm) and eight 2⅛ x 2⅛in (5.4 x 5.4cm)
- Fabric D9: two 3½ x 3½in (8.9 x 8.9cm) and eight 2⅛ x 2⅛in (5.4 x 5.4cm)

CONSTRUCTION

1. Following the **Diamond in a Square Method**, use a scant ¼in (0.4–0.5cm) seam to sew four of the 2⅛ x 2⅛in (5.4 x 5.4cm) white fabric squares onto one 3½ x 3½in (8.9 x 8.9cm) D9 fabric square to make the unit shown. Evenly trim down to 2½ x 2½in (6.4 x 6.4cm) square. Repeat to make one more identical unit.

2. Repeat step 1 to make two Diamond in a Square units from the eight 2⅛ x 2⅛in (5.4 x 5.4cm) D9 fabric squares and the two 3½ x 3½in (8.9 x 8.9cm) white fabric squares.

3. Evenly trim each Diamond in a Square unit down to 3½ x 3½in (8.9 x 8.9cm) square.

4. Following the **Standard Piecing Method** and using a standard ¼in (0.6cm) seam, sew the units together in pairs (your points may not touch perfectly, but that's okay), then joining the paired units into sections and finally sewing the sections together.

5. Evenly trim down the whole block to 6½in (16.5cm) square if it is not this size already. Block is complete. Press and store safely.

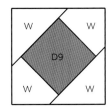

Make two Diamond in a Square units as shown and evenly trim

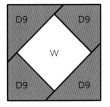

Make two Diamond in a Square units as shown and evenly trim

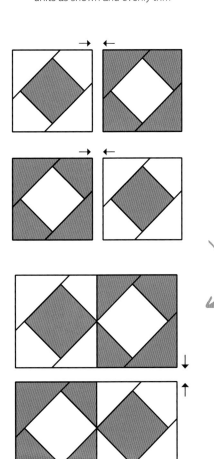

Sew units together into sections, then sew the sections together into the final block

BLOCK 34: Sawtooth Star Variation

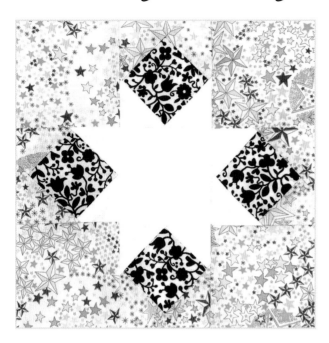

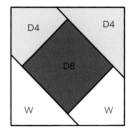

Make four Diamond in a Square units as shown and evenly trim

INFO

- Block Size: 6½in (16.5cm) unfinished, 6in (15.2cm) finished
- Seams: scant ¼in (0.4–0.5cm) and ¼in (0.6cm)
- Press Seams: Open. Press after each sewing step

CUTTING

- White Fabric: one 2½ x 2½in (6.4 x 6.4cm), eight 1½ x 1½in (3.8 x 3.8cm)
- Fabric D4: eight 1½ x 1½in (3.8 x 3.8cm), four 2½ x 2½in (6.4 x 6.4cm)
- Fabric D8: four 2½ x 2½in (6.4 x 6.4cm)

CONSTRUCTION

I. Following the **Diamond in a Square Method**, use a scant ¼in (0.4–0.5cm) seam to sew two of the 1½ x 1½in (3.8 x 3.8cm) D4 fabric squares and two of the 1½ x 1½in (3.8 x 3.8cm) white fabric squares onto the 2½ x 2½in (6.4 x 6.4cm) D8 fabric square to make the unit shown. Evenly trim down to 2½ x 2½in (6.4 x 6.4cm) square.

2. Repeat step 1 to make three more identical units.

3. Following the **Standard Piecing Method**, sew the units together as shown using a standard ¼in (0.6cm) seam, first joining the Diamond in a Square units with the 2½ x 2½in (6.4 x 6.4cm) white and D4 fabric squares into sections, then sewing the sections together.

4. Evenly trim down the whole block to 6½in (16.5cm) square if it is not this size already. Block is complete. Press and store safely.

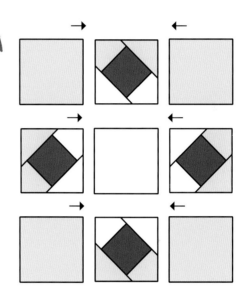

Sew the units together with remaining fabric squares into sections

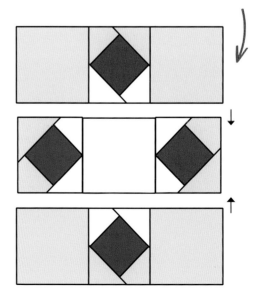

Sew the sections together into the final block

BLOCK 35: *Hourglass*

INFO

- Block Size: 6½in (16.5cm) unfinished, 6in (15.2cm) finished
- Seams: scant ¼in (0.4–0.5cm) and ¼in (0.6cm)
- Press Seams: Open. Press after each sewing step.

CUTTING

- White Fabric: one 3⅜ x 3⅜in (8.6 x 8.6cm) and two 3½ x 3½in (8.9 x 8.9cm)
- Fabric D8: four 2 x 2in (5.1 x 5.1cm)
- Fabric D10: two 1½ x 4½in (3.8 x 11.4cm) and two 1½ x 6½in (3.8 x 16.5cm)

CONSTRUCTION

1. Following the **Diamond in a Square Method**, use a scant ¼in (0.4–0.5cm) seam to sew the four 2 x 2in (5.1 x 5.1cm) squares of fabric D8 onto the 3⅜ x 3⅜in (8.6 x 8.6cm) white fabric square to make the unit shown. Evenly trim down to 3⅜ x 3⅜in (8.6 x 8.6cm) square.

2. Cut the two 3½ x 3½in (8.9 x 8.9cm) white fabric squares in half diagonally to make four triangles. Be very careful with these triangles so as not to change their shape as the diagonal line is on the bias and at risk of stretching. Handle them as little as possible and keep neat and flat until use.

3. Use a ruler to find the middle point along the long diagonal edge of each triangle and mark with a pin or heat erasable pen. Fold the Diamond in a Square unit in half both ways and mark the middle points.

4. Take two triangles and align, pin and sew them onto the Diamond in a Square unit as shown using a standard ¼in (0.6cm) seam, matching the marked middle points. Be careful not to stretch the triangle pieces. Open out and press.

5. Take the remaining two triangles and align, pin and sew them onto the unit as shown using a standard ¼in (0.6cm) seam, matching the marked middle points as before. Open out and press. Evenly trim down to 4½ x 4½in (11.4 x 11.4cm) square.

6. Following the **Standard Piecing Method**, use a standard ¼in (0.6cm) seam to sew the two 1½ x 4½in (3.8 x 11.4cm) D10 fabric strips onto the top and bottom of the unit as shown.

7. Sew the two 1½ x 6½in (3.8 x 16.5cm) D10 fabric strips onto the sides of the unit as shown

8. Evenly trim down the whole block to 6½in (16.5cm) square if it is not this size already. Block is complete. Press and store safely.

Fabric Focus

Thorpe Hill is a small-scale version of the much-loved Liberty classic, Thorpe. Originally created in 1968, this dense and detailed floral was one of the designs included in Liberty's first ever Classics collection of 1979.

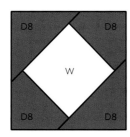

Make one Diamond in a Square
unit and evenly trim

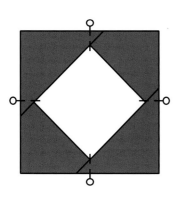

Find the middle points of each edge and mark

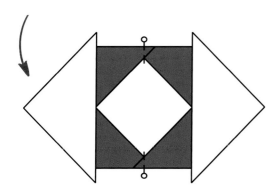

Sew two white fabric triangles onto
either side, aligning the middle points

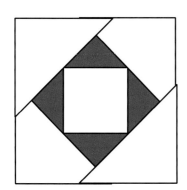

Sew on the remaining triangles,
open out and press

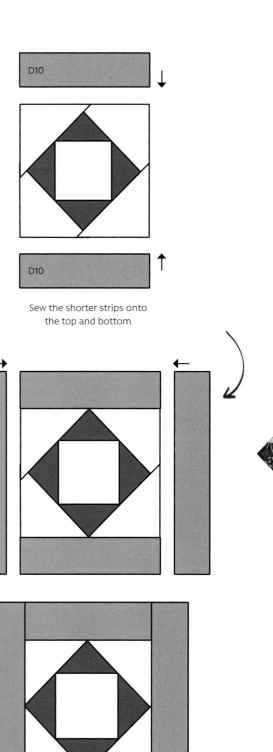

Sew the shorter strips onto
the top and bottom

Sew the longer strips onto the
sides to complete the block

BLOCK 36: Corner Tiles Variation

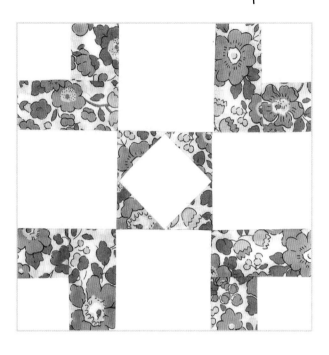

CONSTRUCTION

1. Following the **Diamond in a Square Method**, use a scant ¼in (0.4–0.5cm) seam to sew the four 1½ x 1½in (3.8 x 3.8cm) squares of D7 fabric onto one 2½ x 2½in (6.4 x 6.4cm) white fabric square to make the unit shown. Evenly trim down to 2½ x 2½in (6.4 x 6.4cm) square.

2. Following the **Strip Piecing Method**, use a standard ¼in (0.6cm) seam to sew the 1½ x 7in (3.8 x 17.8cm) strips of white fabric and fabric D7 together to make the strip set as shown. Then, cut the strip set at 1½in (3.8cm) intervals to make four 1½ x 2½in (3.8 x 6.4cm) smaller units. Discard leftover fabric.

3. Take the long 1½ x 13in (3.8 x 33cm) strip of fabric D7 and following the **Chain Strip Piecing Method**, use a standard ¼in (0.6cm) seam to sew onto this strip all four of the smaller units. Cut them apart and trim down to make four units sized 2½ x 2½in (6.4 x 6.4cm) as shown.

4. Using a scant seam, sew the units together with the remaining 2½ x 2½in (6.4 x 6.4cm) white fabric squares into sections as shown following the **Standard Piecing Method**, then join the sections together.

5. Evenly trim down the whole block to 6½in (16.5cm) square if it is not this size already. Block is complete. Press and store safely.

INFO

- Block Size: 6½in (16.5cm) unfinished, 6in (15.2cm) finished
- Seams: scant ¼in (0.4–0.5cm) and ¼in (0.6cm)
- Press Seams: Open. Press after each sewing step.

CUTTING

- White Fabric: one 1½ x 7in (3.8 x 17.8cm) and five 2½ x 2½in (6.4 x 6.4cm)
- Fabric D7: four 1½ x 1½in (3.8 x 3.8cm), one 1½ x 7in (3.8 x 17.8cm) and one 1½ x 13in (3.8 x 33cm)

Fabric Focus

Betsy is a stylised floral that was created for Liberty Fabrics in 1933 by the enigmatic D.S. whose work makes up many of the favourite Tana Lawn® patterns. Betsy in particular is one of the most popular Liberty fabrics of all time.

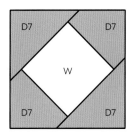

Make one Diamond in a Square
unit and evenly trim

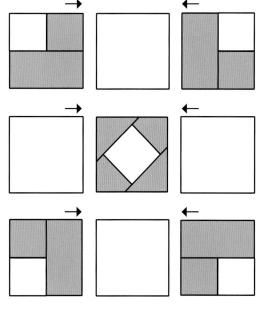

Sew the units together with remaining
fabric squares into sections

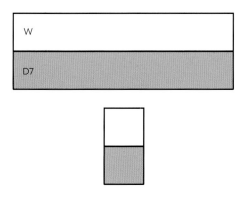

Sew the strips into a strip set and
subcut into four smaller units

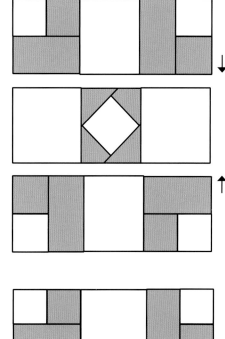

Make four units like this using Chain
Strip Piecing Method and evenly trim

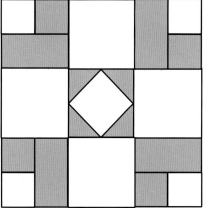

Sew the sections together into the final block

BLOCK 37: *Bits and Pieces*

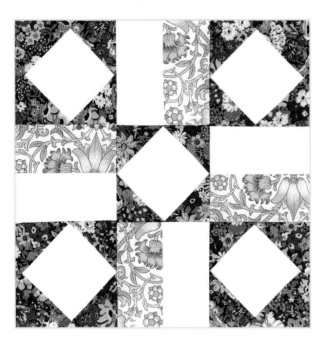

INFO

- Block Size: 6½in (16.5cm) unfinished, 6in (15.2cm) finished
- Seams: scant ¼in (0.4–0.5cm) and ¼in (0.6cm)
- Press Seams: Open. Press after each sewing step.

CUTTING

- White Fabric: one 1½ x 11in (3.8 x 27.9cm) and five 2½ x 2½in (6.4 x 6.4cm)
- Fabric D6: one 1½ x 11in (3.8 x 27.9cm)
- Fabric D10: twenty 1½ x 1½in (3.8 x 3.8cm)

CONSTRUCTION

1. Following the **Diamond in a Square Method**, use a scant ¼in (0.4–0.5cm) seam to sew four of the 1½ x 1½in (3.8 x 3.8cm) D10 fabric squares onto one 2½ x 2½in (6.4 x 6.4cm) white fabric square to make the unit shown. Evenly trim down to 2½ x 2½in (6.4 x 6.4cm) square.

2. Repeat step 1 to make four more identical units.

3. Following the **Strip Piecing Method**, use a standard ¼in (0.6cm) seam to sew the 1½ x 11in (3.8 x 27.9cm) strips of D6 fabric and white fabric together to make the strip set as shown. Then, cut the strip set at 2½in (6.4cm) intervals to make four 2½ x 2½in (6.4 x 6.4cm) smaller units. Discard leftover fabric.

4. Following the **Standard Piecing Method**, sew the units together as shown using a scant seam, first joining the units into sections, then sewing the sections together.

5. Evenly trim down the whole block to 6½in (16.5cm) square if it is not this size already. Block is complete. Press and store safely.

Fabric Focus

Lodden is one of the great Arts and Crafts textile designs of the past. It was originally designed by William Morris in 1884, but was transformed into Liberty's own design by rescaling and recolouring.

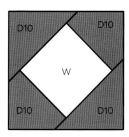

Make five Diamond in a Square units
as shown and evenly trim

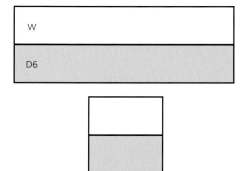

Sew the strips into a strip set and
subcut into four smaller units

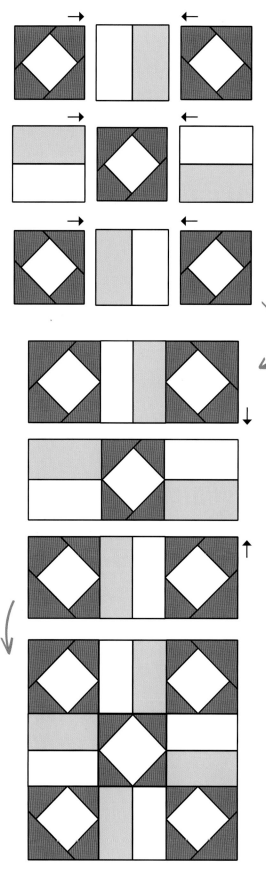

Sew the units together into sections, then sew
the sections together into the final block

BLOCK 38: *Wheel Spokes*

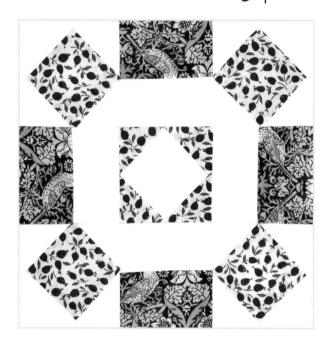

INFO

- Block Size: 6½in (16.5cm) unfinished, 6in (15.2cm) finished
- Seams: scant ¼in (0.4–0.5cm) and ¼in (0.6cm)
- Press Seams: Open. Press after each sewing step.

CUTTING

- White Fabric: one 1½ x 11in (3.8 x 27.9cm), one 2½ x 2½in (6.4 x 6.4cm) and sixteen 1½ x 1½in (3.8 x 3.8cm)
- Fabric D2: four 1½ x 1½in (3.8 x 3.8cm) and four 2½ x 2½in (6.4 x 6.4cm)
- Fabric D5: one 1½ x 11in (3.8 x 27.9cm)

CONSTRUCTION

1. Following the **Diamond in a Square Method**, use a scant ¼in (0.4–0.5cm) seam to sew the four 1½ x 1½in (3.8 x 3.8cm) D2 fabric squares onto the 2½ x 2½in (6.4 x 6.4cm) white fabric square to make the unit shown. Evenly trim down to 2½ x 2½in (6.4 x 6.4cm) square.

2. Repeat step 1 to make four Diamond in a Square units from the sixteen 1½ x 1½in (3.8 x 3.8cm) white fabric squares and the four 2½ x 2½in (6.4 x 6.4cm) D2 fabric squares.

3. Following the **Strip Piecing Method**, use a standard ¼in (0.6cm) seam to sew the 1½ x 11in (3.8 x 27.9cm) strips of D5 fabric and white fabric together to make the strip set as shown. Then, cut the strip set at 2½in (6.4cm) intervals to make four 2½ x 2½in (6.4 x 6.4cm) smaller units. Discard leftover fabric.

4. Following the **Standard Piecing Method**, sew the units together as shown using a scant seam, first joining the units into sections, then sewing the sections together.

5. Evenly trim down the whole block to 6½in (16.5cm) square if it is not this size already. Block is complete. Press and store safely.

Fabric Focus

Ed is an allover two-colour print of small scattered rosehips. It is based on a design created for Liberty in the 1940s by Rex Silver of the Silver Studio, one of the most influential textile design studios in Britain from 1880 until the middle of the 20th century.

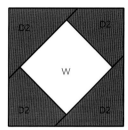

Make one Diamond in a Square
unit and evenly trim

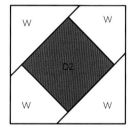

Make four Diamond in a Square
units as shown and evenly trim

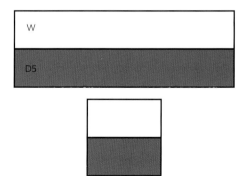

Sew the strips into a strip set and
subcut into four smaller units

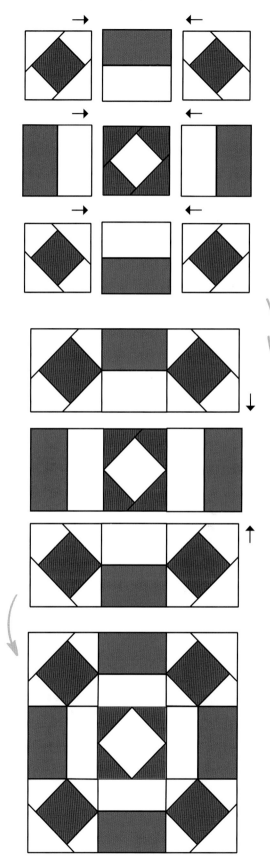

Sew the units together into sections, then sew
the sections together into the final block

BLOCK 39: *Broken Wheel*

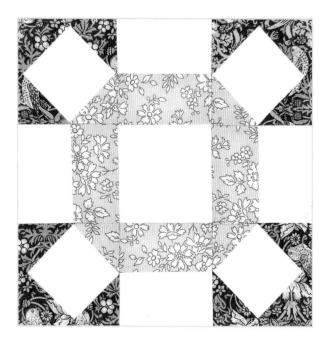

INFO

- Block Size: 6½in (16.5cm) unfinished, 6in (15.2cm) finished
- Seams: scant ¼in (0.4–0.5cm) and ¼in (0.6cm)
- Press Seams: Open. Press after each sewing step.

CUTTING

- White Fabric: one 1½ x 11in (3.8 x 27.9cm) and five 2½ x 2½in (6.4 x 6.4cm)
- Fabric D3: four 1½ x 1½in (3.8 x 3.8cm) and one 1½ x 11in (3.8 x 27.9cm)
- Fabric D5: twelve 1½ x 1½in (3.8 x 3.8cm)

CONSTRUCTION

1. Following the **Diamond in a Square Method**, use a scant ¼in (0.4–0.5cm) seam to sew three of the 1½ x 1½in (3.8 x 3.8cm) D5 fabric squares and one of the 1½ x 1½in (3.8 x 3.8cm) D3 fabric squares onto one of the 2½ x 2½in (6.4 x 6.4cm) white fabric squares to make the unit shown. Evenly trim down to 2½ x 2½in (6.4 x 6.4cm) square.

2. Repeat step 1 to make three more identical units.

3. Following the **Strip Piecing Method**, use a standard ¼in (0.6cm) seam to sew the 1½ x 11in (3.8 x 27.9cm) strips of D3 fabric and white fabric together to make the strip set as shown. Then, cut the strip set at 2½in (6.4cm) intervals to make four 2½ x 2½in (6.4 x 6.4cm) smaller units. Discard leftover fabric.

4. Following the **Standard Piecing Method**, sew the units together as shown using a scant seam, first joining the units into sections with the remaining 2½ x 2½in (6.4 x 6.4cm) white fabric square, then sewing the sections together.

5. Evenly trim down the whole block to 6½in (16.5cm) square if it is not this size already. Block is complete. Press and store safely.

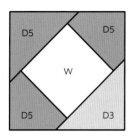

Make four Diamond in a Square
units as shown and evenly trim

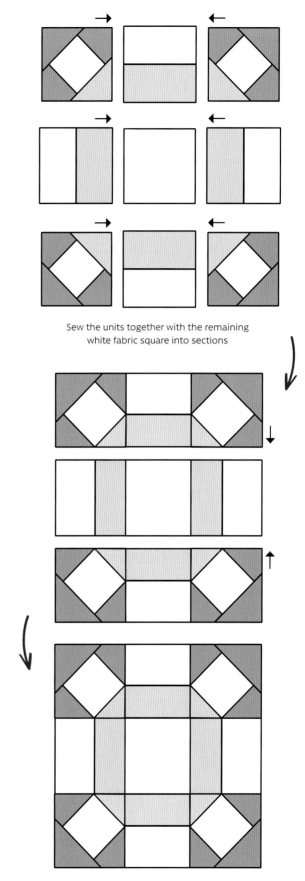

Sew the strips into a strip set and
subcut into four smaller units

Sew the units together with the remaining
white fabric square into sections

Sew the sections together into the final block

BLOCK 40: *Antique Tile Variation*

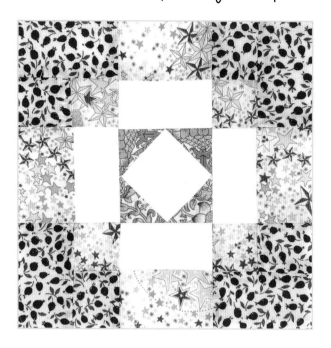

INFO

- Block Size: 6½in (16.5cm) unfinished, 6in (15.2cm) finished

- Seams: scant ¼in (0.4–0.5cm) and ¼in (0.6cm)

- Press Seams: To darkest fabric. Press after each sewing step.

CUTTING

- White Fabric: one 1½ x 11in (3.8 x 27.9cm) and one 2½ x 2½in (6.4 x 6.4cm)

- Fabric D2: one 1½ x 7in (3.8 x 17.8cm), and one 1½ x 13in (3.8 x 33cm)

- Fabric D4: one 1½ x 7in (3.8 x 17.8cm) and one 1½ x 11in (3.8 x 27.9cm)

- Fabric D6: four 1½ x 1½in (3.8 x 3.8cm)

CONSTRUCTION

1. Following the **Diamond in a Square Method**, use a scant ¼in (0.4–0.5cm) seam to sew the four 1½ x 1½in (3.8 x 3.8cm) D6 fabric squares onto the 2½ x 2½in (6.4 x 6.4cm) white fabric square to make the unit shown. Evenly trim down to 2½ x 2½in (6.4 x 6.4cm) square.

2. Following the **Strip Piecing Method**, use a standard ¼in (0.6cm) seam to sew the 1½ x 7in (3.8 x 17.8cm) strips of D2 and D4 fabric together to make the strip set as shown. Then, cut the strip set at 1½in (3.8cm) intervals to make four 1½ x 2½in (3.8 x 6.4cm) smaller units. Discard leftover fabric.

3. Take the long 1½ x 13in (3.8 x 33cm) strip of D2 fabric and following the **Chain Strip Piecing Method**, use a standard ¼in (0.6cm) seam to sew onto this strip all four of the smaller units. Cut them apart and trim down to make four units sized 2½ x 2½in (6.4 x 6.4cm) as shown.

4. Following the **Strip Piecing Method**, use a standard ¼in (0.6cm) seam to sew the 1½ x 11in (3.8 x 27.9cm) strips of D4 and white fabric together to make the strip set as shown. Then, cut the strip set at 2½in (6.4cm) intervals to make four 2½ x 2½in (6.4 x 6.4cm) smaller units. Discard leftover fabric.

5. Following the **Standard Piecing Method**, sew the units together as shown using a scant seam, first joining the units into sections, then sewing the sections together.

6. Evenly trim down the whole block to 6½in (16.5cm) square if it is not this size already. Block is complete. Press and store safely.

Fabric Focus

Adelajda (pronounced ah-de-LIE-dah) features a galaxy of swirling stars in a whirl of vivid shades. A Liberty Fabrics design studio original, it was created for the Autumn/Winter 2011 collection.

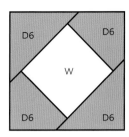

Make one Diamond in a Square
unit and evenly trim

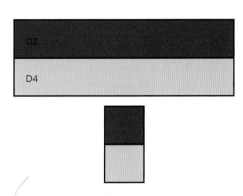

Sew the strips into a strip set and
subcut into four smaller units

Make four units like this using the
Chain Strip Piecing Method

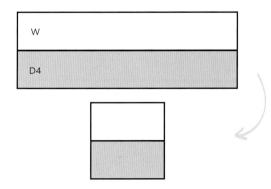

Sew the strips into a strip set and
subcut into four smaller units

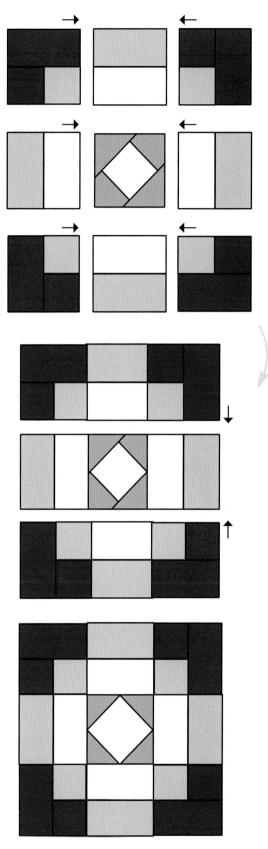

Sew the units together into sections, then sew
the sections together into the final block

BLOCK 41: Mrs Brown's Choice

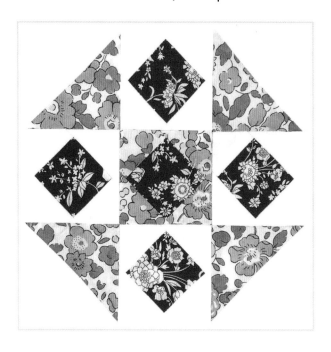

INFO

- Block Size: 6½in (16.5cm) unfinished, 6in (15.2cm) finished
- Seams: scant ¼in (0.4–0.5cm) and ¼in (0.6cm)
- Press Seams: Open. Press after each sewing step.

CUTTING

- White Fabric: one 4½ x 4½in (11.4 x 11.4cm) and sixteen 1½ x 1½in (3.8 x 3.8cm)
- Fabric D1: five 2½ x 2½in (6.4 x 6.4cm)
- Fabric D7: one 4½ x 4½in (11.4 x 11.4cm) and four 1½ x 1½in (3.8 x 3.8cm)

CONSTRUCTION

1. Following the **Diamond in a Square Method**, use a scant ¼in (0.4–0.5cm) seam to sew the four 1½ x 1½in (3.8 x 3.8cm) D7 fabric squares onto one of the 2½ x 2½in (6.4 x 6.4cm) D1 fabric squares to make the unit shown. Evenly trim down to 2½ x 2½in (6.4 x 6.4cm) square.

2. Repeat step 1 to make four Diamond in a Square units from the sixteen 1½ x 1½in (3.8 x 3.8cm) white fabric squares and the four remaining 2½ x 2½in (6.4 x 6.4cm) D1 fabric squares.

3. Following the **Four at a Time HST Method**, use a standard ¼in (0.6cm) seam to sew the 4½ x 4½in (11.4 x 11.4cm) white and D7 fabric squares together into four HSTs as shown. Evenly trim each HST down to 2½ x 2½in (6.4 x 6.4cm) square.

4. Following the **Standard Piecing Method**, sew the units together as shown using a scant seam, first joining the units into sections, then sewing the sections together.

5. Evenly trim down the whole block to 6½in (16.5cm) square if it is not this size already. Block is complete. Press and store safely.

Fabric Focus

Summer Blooms is a two-colour floral first created for Liberty Fabrics in 1965. It has now been reinterpreted and recoloured in bold shades.

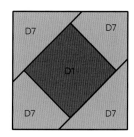

Make one Diamond in a Square
unit and evenly trim

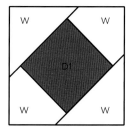

Make four Diamond in a Square
units as shown and evenly trim

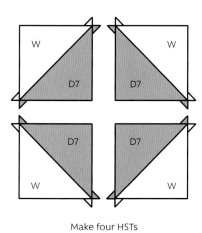

Make four HSTs

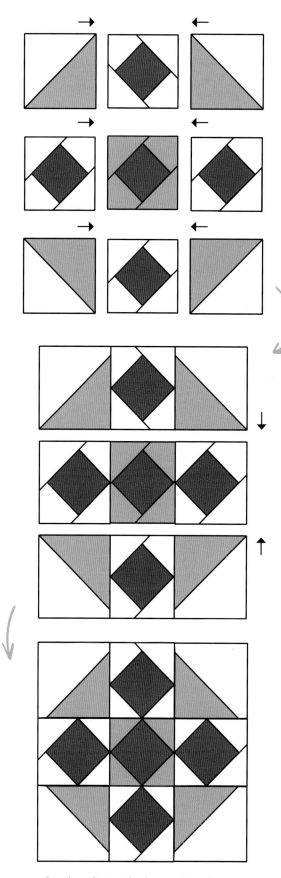

Sew the units together into sections, then sew
the sections together into the final block

BLOCK 42: Braced Star

INFO

- Block Size: 6½in (16.5cm) unfinished, 6in (15.2cm) finished
- Seams: ¼in (0.4–0.5cm) and ¼in (0.6cm)
- Press Seams: Open. Press after each sewing step.

CUTTING

- White Fabric: one 4½ x 4½in (11.4 x 11.4cm), four 2½ x 2½in (6.4 x 6.4cm)
- Fabric E1: two 4½ x 4½in (11.4 x 11.4cm)
- Fabric E4: one 4½ x 4½in (11.4 x 11.4cm), four 1½ x 1½in (3.8 x 3.8cm)
- Fabric E8: one 2½ x 2½in (6.4 x 6.4cm)

CONSTRUCTION

1. Following the **Diamond in a Square Method**, sew the four 1½ x 1½in (3.8 x 3.8cm) E4 fabric squares onto the 2½ x 2½in (6.4 x 6.4cm) E8 fabric square using a scant ¼in (0.4-0.5cm) seam to make the unit as shown. Evenly trim down to 2½ x 2½in (6.4 x 6.4cm).

2. Following the **Four at a Time HST Method**, use a standard ¼in (0.6cm) seam to sew a 4½ x 4½in (11.4 x 11.4cm) E1 fabric square and white fabric square together into four HSTs as shown. Repeat with remaining 4½ x 4½in (11.4 x 11.4cm) E1 and E4 fabric squares to make four HSTs as shown.

3. Following the **One at a Time QST Method**, sew two of the HSTs together into one QST as shown. Repeat with the remaining HSTs to make a total of four QSTs.

4. Evenly trim each QST down to 2½ x 2½in (6.4 x 6.4cm) square.

5. Sew the units together with the 2½ x 2½in (6.4 x 6.4cm) white fabric squares into sections as shown following the **Standard Piecing Method**, then join the sections together.

6. Evenly trim down the whole block to 6½in (16.5cm) square if it is not this size already. Block is complete. Press and store safely.

Fabric Focus

Carline Rose is an archival classic originally painted in the 1990s. It emulates the round, bold forms of vintage 1950s florals.

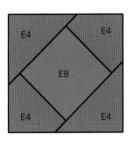

Make one Diamond in a Square
unit and evenly trim

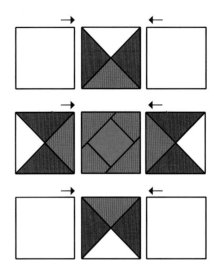

Sew the units together with remaining
fabric squares into sections

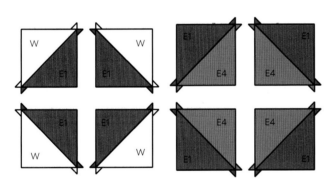

Make four HSTs from each pair of
the larger fabric squares

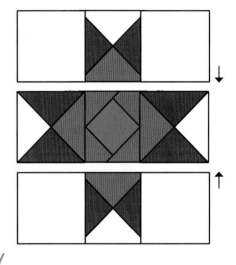

Make four QSTs and evenly trim

Sew the sections together into the final block

BLOCK 43: Air Castle

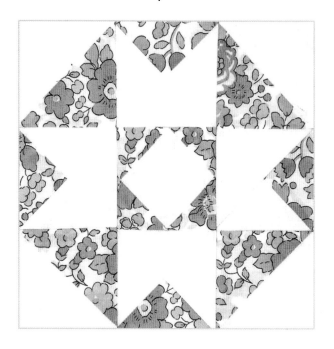

INFO

- Block Size: 6½in (16.5cm) unfinished, 6in (15.2cm) finished
- Seams: scant ¼in (0.4–0.5cm) and ¼in (0.6cm)
- Press Seams: Open. Press after each sewing step.

CUTTING

- White Fabric: one 6¼ x 6¼in (15.9 x 15.9cm) and five 2½ x 2½in (6.4 x 6.4cm)
- Fabric C3: one 6¼ x 6¼in (15.9 x 15.9cm) and four 1½ x 1½in (3.8 x 3.8cm)

CONSTRUCTION

1. Following the **Diamond in a Square Method**, use a scant ¼in (0.4–0.5cm) seam to sew the four 1½ x 1½in (3.8 x 3.8cm) squares of fabric C3 onto one 2½ x 2½in (6.4 x 6.4cm) white fabric square to make the unit shown. Evenly trim down to 2½ x 2½in (6.4 x 6.4cm) square.

2. Following the **Eight at a Time HST Method**, use a scant seam to sew the 6¼ x 6¼in (15.9 x 15.9cm) squares together into eight HSTs as shown. Evenly trim all HSTs down to 2½ x 2½in (6.4 x 6.4cm) square. Set four of the HSTs aside until step 4.

3. Following the **One at a Time Split QST Method**, use a scant seam to sew the four remaining HSTs and the four 2½ x 2½in (6.4 x 6.4cm) white fabric squares into four identical split QSTs as shown. Evenly trim each down to 2½ x 2½in (6.4 x 6.4cm) square.

4. Sew the units together as shown following the **Standard Piecing Method**, using a standard ¼in (0.6cm) seam, first joining the units into sections, then sewing the sections together.

5. Evenly trim down the whole block to 6½in (16.5cm) square if it is not this size already. Block is complete. Press and store safely.

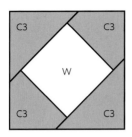

Make one Diamond in a Square
unit and evenly trim

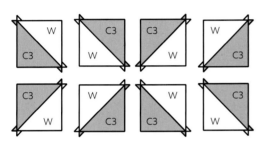

Make eight HSTs, then evenly trim

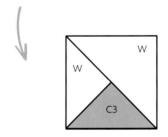

Make four split QSTs and evenly trim

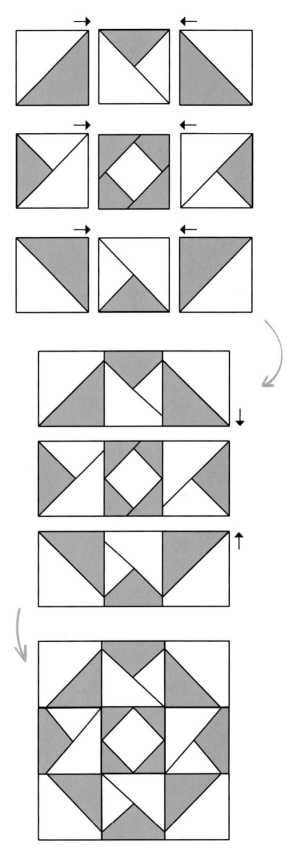

Sew the units together into sections, then
sew the sections together into the final block

BLOCK 44: *Air Castle Variation*

INFO

- Block Size: 6½in (16.5cm) unfinished, 6in (15.2cm) finished
- Seams: scant ¼in (0.4–0.5cm) and ¼in (0.6cm)
- Press Seams: Open. Press after each sewing step.

CUTTING

- White Fabric: one 6¼ x 6¼in (15.9 x 15.9cm) and four 1½ x 1½in (3.8 x 3.8cm)
- Fabric C1: one 6¼ x 6¼in (15.9 x 15.9cm)
- Fabric C7: five 2½ x 2½in (6.4 x 6.4cm)

CONSTRUCTION

1. Following the **Diamond in a Square Method**, use a scant ¼in (0.4–0.5cm) seam to sew the four 1½ x 1½in (3.8 x 3.8cm) white fabric squares onto one 2½ x 2½in (6.4 x 6.4cm) square of C7 fabric to make the unit shown. Evenly trim down to 2½ x 2½in (6.4 x 6.4cm) square.

2. Following the **Eight at a Time HST Method**, use a scant seam to sew the 6¼ x 6¼in (15.9 x 15.9cm) squares together into eight HSTs as shown. Evenly trim all HSTs down to 2½ x 2½in (6.4 x 6.4cm) square. Set four of the HSTs aside until step 4.

3. Following the **One at a Time Split QST Method**, use a scant seam to sew the four remaining HSTs and the four remaining 2½ x 2½in (6.4 x 6.4cm) C7 fabric squares into four identical split QSTs as shown. Evenly trim each down to 2½ x 2½in (6.4 x 6.4cm) square.

4. Sew the units together as shown following the **Standard Piecing Method**, using a standard ¼in (0.6cm) seam, first sewing the units into sections, then joining the sections together.

5. Evenly trim down the whole block to 6½in (16.5cm) square if it is not this size already. Block is complete. Press and store safely.

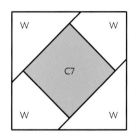

Make one Diamond in a Square
unit and evenly trim

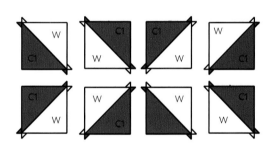

Make eight HSTs, then evenly trim

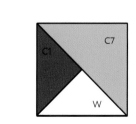

Make four split QSTs and evenly trim

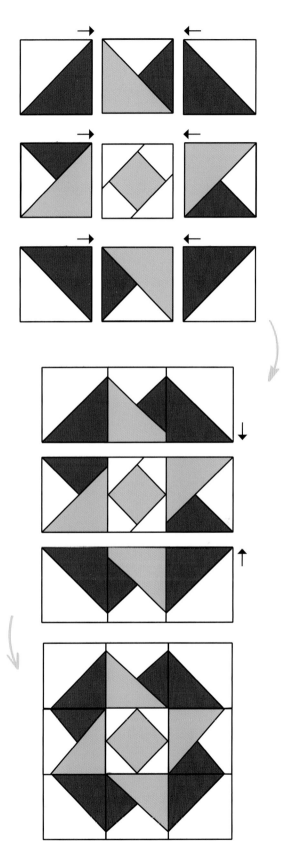

Sew the units together into
sections, then sew the sections
together into the final block

Flying Geese

ABOUT FLYING GEESE

Flying Geese are made up of a central right-angle triangle and two smaller triangles on either side. A quilting basic, these useful units can be spotted in all sorts of blocks, on their own or in combination with other shapes. They are simple and fast to make, especially when constructing multiple at a time.

Quilt blocks commonly using these units include Evening Star, Sawtooth Star and Dutchman's Puzzle.

Recommended Tool: heat erasable pen

FOUR AT A TIME FLYING GEESE METHOD

1. Draw a straight line diagonally across the wrong side of all of the smaller squares with a heat erasable pen (or pencil) and ruler.

2. Place two smaller squares of fabric in opposite corners on top of a larger fabric square, right sides together and drawn diagonal lines angled into the corners. The smaller squares should overlap in the middle of the larger square and the drawn diagonal line should run perfectly straight across the fabrics. Pin in place.

3. Sew a scant ¼in (0.4–0.5cm) seam on either side of this drawn line. Remove pins. Cut directly along the drawn line to make two units. Flip corners open and press.

4. Right sides together, place another of the small squares in the corner of each of the units, drawn line angled into the corner. Pin in place.

5. Sew a scant ¼in (0.4–0.5cm) seam on either side of the drawn line. Remove pins. Cut directly along the drawn line to make two Flying Geese units. Flip corners open and press.

6. Repeat steps 2–5 with the remaining unit and another small square to make a total of four Flying Geese units.

7. Evenly trim each Flying Geese unit down to the required size. Ensure the edges are all right angles and that the bottom points of the triangle end directly in the bottom corners. Leave a ¼in (0.6cm) space between the top inner triangle point and the outer edge.

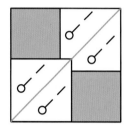
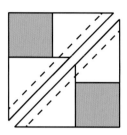

Mark up small squares and place two in corners of a larger square; sew and cut diagonally

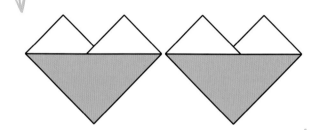

Flip corners open for units as shown

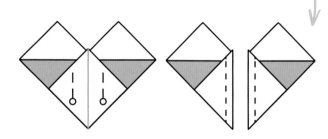

Place small marked up square in corner of each unit; sew then cut along the drawn line

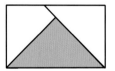
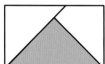

This results in two of the units shown, and a total of four untrimmed flying geese in all

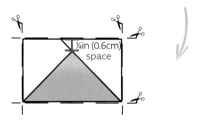

Evenly trim the units to the required size

BLOCK 45: Wild Goose Chase

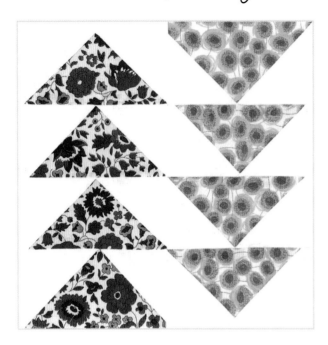

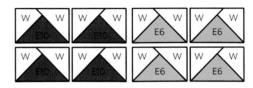

Make eight Flying Geese units and evenly trim

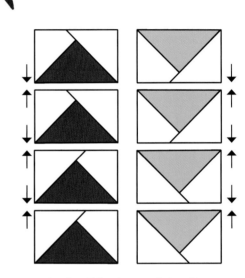

Sew four Flying Geese units together

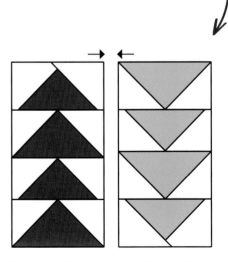

Sew the sections together into the final block

INFO

- Block Size: 6½in (16.5cm) unfinished, 6in (15.2cm) finished
- Seams: ¼in (0.4–0.5cm) and ¼in (0.6cm)
- Press Seams: To one side. Press after each sewing step.

CUTTING

- White Fabric: eight 2⅝ x 2⅝in (6.7 x 6.7cm)
- Fabric E6: one 4½ x 4½in (11.4 x 11.4cm)
- Fabric E10: one 4½ x 4½in (11.4 x 11.4cm)

CONSTRUCTION

1. Following the **Four at a Time Flying Geese Method**, use a scant ¼in (0.4–0.5cm) seam to sew four of the white fabric squares onto each of the coloured fabric squares to make eight Flying Geese units. Evenly trim all units down to 3½ x 2in (8.9 x 5.1cm).

2. Sew the units together as shown following the **Standard Piecing Method** using a standard ¼in (0.6cm) seam, first sewing each set of four Flying Geese units together as shown, then joining the sections together.

3. Evenly trim down the whole block to 6½in (16.5cm) square if it is not this size already. Block is complete. Press and store safely.

BLOCK 46: *Return of the Swallows*

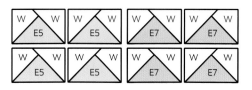

Make eight Flying Geese units and evenly trim

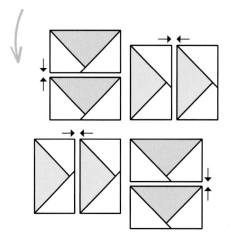

Sew the Flying Geese units together in pairs

INFO

- Block Size: 6½in (16.5cm) unfinished, 6in (15.2cm) finished
- Seams: ¼in (0.4–0.5cm) and ¼in (0.6cm)
- Press Seams: To one side. Press after each sewing step.

CUTTING

- White Fabric: eight 2⅝ x 2⅝in (6.7 x 6.7cm)
- Fabric E5: one 4½ x 4½in (11.4 x 11.4cm)
- Fabric E7: one 4½ x 4½in (11.4 x 11.4cm)

CONSTRUCTION

1. Following the **Four at a Time Flying Geese Method**, use a scant ¼in (0.4–0.5cm) seam to sew four of the white fabric squares onto each of the coloured fabric squares to make eight Flying Geese units. Evenly trim all units down to 3½ x 2in (8.9 x 5.1cm).

2. Sew the units together as shown following the **Standard Piecing Method** using a standard ¼in (0.6cm) seam, first sewing the Flying Geese units together in pairs, then joining the paired units into sections and finally sewing the sections together.

3. Evenly trim down the whole block to 6½in (16.5cm) square if it is not this size already. Block is complete. Press and store safely.

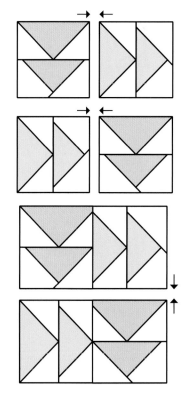

Sew paired units together into sections, then sew the sections together into the final block

BLOCK 47: Dutchman's Puzzle

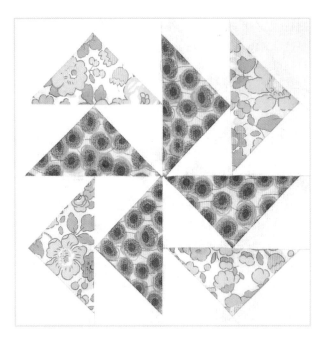

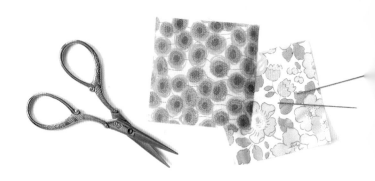

INFO

- Block Size: 6½in (16.5cm) unfinished, 6in (15.2cm) finished
- Seams: ¼in (0.4–0.5cm) and ¼in (0.6cm)
- Press Seams: To one side. Press after each sewing step.

CUTTING

- White Fabric: eight 2⅝ x 2⅝in (6.7 x 6.7cm)
- Fabric E6: one 4½ x 4½in (11.4 x 11.4cm)
- Fabric E7: one 4½ x 4½in (11.4 x 11.4cm)

CONSTRUCTION

1. Following the **Four at a Time Flying Geese Method**, use a scant ¼in (0.4–0.5cm) seam to sew four of the white fabric squares onto each of the coloured fabric squares to make eight Flying Geese units. Evenly trim all units down to 3½ x 2in (8.9 x 5.1cm).

2. Sew the units together as shown following the **Standard Piecing Method** using a standard ¼in (0.6cm) seam, first sewing the Flying Geese units together in pairs, then joining the paired units into sections and finally sewing the sections together.

3. Evenly trim down the whole block to 6½in (16.5cm) square if it is not this size already. Block is complete. Press and store safely.

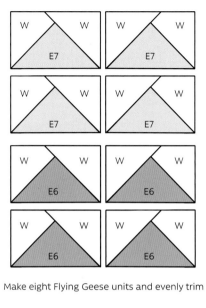

Make eight Flying Geese units and evenly trim

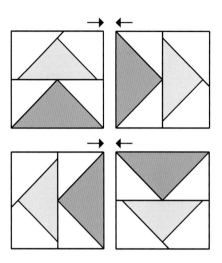

Sew the paired units together into sections

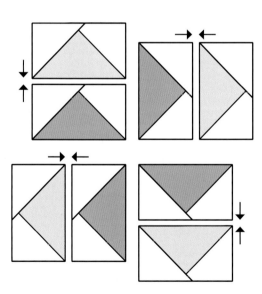

Sew the Flying Geese units together in pairs

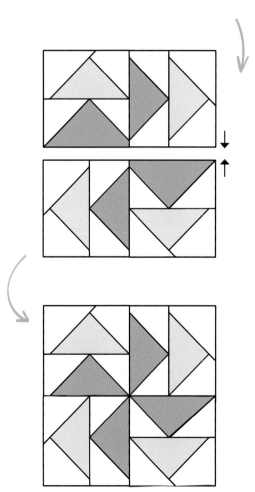

Sew the sections together into the final block

BLOCK 48: *Capital T*

INFO

- Block Size: 6½in (16.5cm) unfinished, 6in (15.2cm) finished
- Seams: scant ¼in (0.4–0.5cm) and ¼in (0.6cm)
- Press Seams: To one side and open. Press after each sewing step.

CUTTING

- White Fabric: one 2½ x 2½in (6.4 x 6.4cm), one 4½ x 4½in (11.4 x 11.4cm), two 4 x 4in (10.2 x 10.2cm)
- Fabric E4: eight 2⅜ x 2⅜in (6 x 6cm)
- Fabric E5: one 4½ x 4½in (11.4 x 11.4cm)

CONSTRUCTION

1. Following the **Four at a Time HST Method**, use a standard ¼in (0.6cm) seam to sew a 4½ x 4½in (11.4 x 11.4cm) E5 fabric square and white fabric square together into four HSTs as shown. Press seams open.

2. Evenly trim the HST units down to 2½ x 2½in (6.4 x 6.4cm) square.

3. Following the **Four at a Time Flying Geese Method**, use a scant ¼in (0.4–0.5cm) seam to sew four 2⅜ x 2⅜in (6 x 6cm) E4 fabric squares onto a 4 x 4in (10.2 x 10.2cm) white fabric square to make four Flying Geese units, and repeat to give you a total of eight Flying Geese units. Evenly trim all units down to 1½ x 2½in (3.8 x 6.4cm).

4. Sew the Flying Geese units together in pairs as shown following the **Standard Piecing Method** and using a standard ¼in (0.6cm) seam.

5. Sew the units together as shown following the **Standard Piecing Method** using a standard ¼in (0.6cm) seam, first sewing them into sections with the 2½ x 2½in (6.4 x 6.4cm) white fabric square, then joining the sections together.

6. Evenly trim down the whole block to 6½in (16.5cm) square if it is not this size already. Block is complete. Press and store safely.

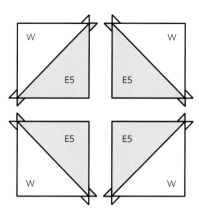

Make four HSTs and evenly trim

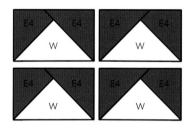

Make a total of eight Flying Geese units and evenly trim

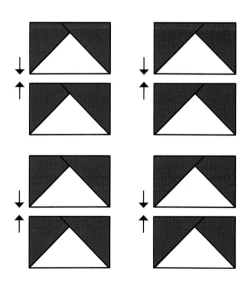

Sew the Flying Geese units together in pairs

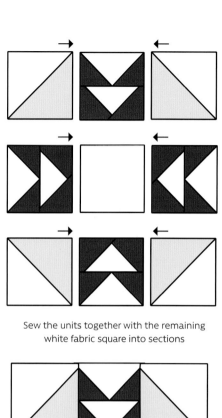

Sew the units together with the remaining white fabric square into sections

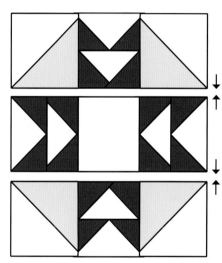

Sew the sections together into the final block

BLOCK 49: *Lady's Fancy*

CONSTRUCTION

1. Following the **Diamond in a Square Method**, sew the four 2½ x 2½in (6.4 x 6.4cm) E7 fabric squares onto the 4½ x 4½in (11.4 x 11.4cm) E5 fabric square using a scant ¼in (0.4–0.5cm) seam to make the unit shown. Evenly trim down to 4½ x 4½in (11.4 x 11.4cm) square.

2. Following the **Four at a Time Flying Geese Method**, use a scant ¼in (0.4–0.5cm) seam to sew four of the 2⅜ x 2⅜in (6 x 6cm) E10 fabric squares onto a 4 x 4in (10.2 x 10.2cm) white fabric square to make four Flying Geese units.

3. Repeat with the remaining 2⅜ x 2⅜in (6 x 6cm) E10 fabric squares and 4 x 4in (10.2 x 10.2cm) white fabric square. You will now have a total of eight Flying Geese units. Evenly trim all units down to 3½ x 2in (8.9 x 5.1cm).

4. Sew the units together as shown following the **Standard Piecing Method** using a standard ¼in (0.6cm) seam, first sewing the Flying Geese units together in pairs. Then on two of the joined pairs, sew a 1½ x 1½in (3.8 x 3.8cm) white fabric square to either end as shown.

5. Sew the shorter strips shown to the top and bottom of the Diamond in a Square, then sew the remaining two longer strips to either side as shown.

6. Evenly trim down the whole block to 6½in (16.5cm) square if not this size already. Block is complete. Press and store safely.

INFO

- Block Size: 6½in (16.5cm) unfinished, 6in (15.2cm) finished
- Seams: ¼in (0.4–0.5cm) and ¼in (0.6cm)
- Press Seams: To one side. Press after each sewing step.

CUTTING

- White Fabric: two 4 x 4in (10.2 x 10.2cm), four 1½ x 1½in (3.8 x 3.8cm)
- Fabric E5: one 4½ x 4½in (11.4 x 11.4cm)
- Fabric E7: four 2½ x 2½in (6.4 x 6.4cm)
- Fabric E10: eight 2⅜ x 2⅜in (6 x 6cm)

Fabric Focus

D'Anjo is a classic Liberty floral based on a design from the 1930s, updated in a fresh, modern style. It was originally designed by the Silver Studio, a London-based design house that created prints for Liberty from the art nouveau period to the 1940s.

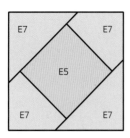

Make one Diamond in a Square
unit and evenly trim

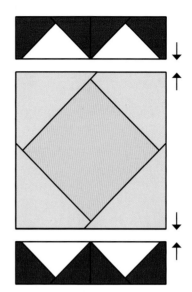

Sew the shorter strips onto the top and
bottom of the Diamond in a Square

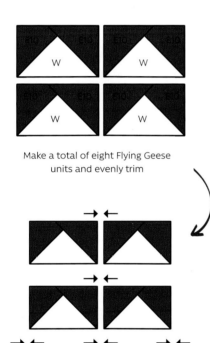

Make a total of eight Flying Geese
units and evenly trim

Sew the units into strips adding the remaining
fabric squares to two of the strips as shown

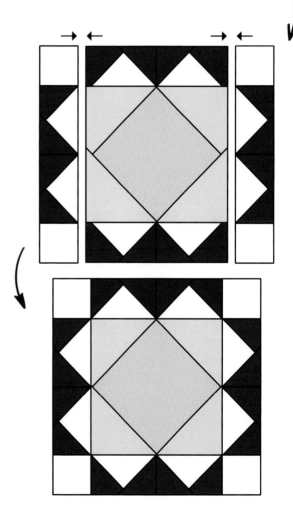

Sew the longer strips onto the
sides to complete the block

BLOCK 50: Gentleman's Fancy Variation

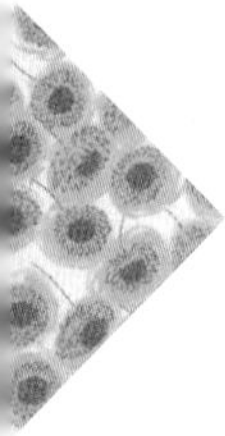

INFO

- Block Size: 6½in (16.5cm) unfinished, 6in (15.2cm) finished
- Seams: ¼in (0.4–0.5cm) and ¼in (0.6cm)
- Press Seams: To one side. Press after each sewing step.

CUTTING

- White Fabric: two 4 x 4in (10.2 x 10.2cm), four 2 x 2in (5.1 x 5.1cm)
- Fabric E2: eight 2⅜ x 2⅜in (6 x 6cm), four 1½ x 1½in (3.8 x 3.8cm)
- Fabric E6: two 3½ x 3½in (8.9 x 8.9cm)
- Fabric E7: one 3⅜ x 3⅜in (8.6 x 8.6cm)

CONSTRUCTION

1. Following the **Diamond in a Square Method**, sew the four 2 x 2in (5.1 x 5.1cm) white fabric squares onto the 3⅜ x 3⅜in (8.6 x 8.6cm) E7 fabric square using a scant ¼in (0.4–0.5cm) seam to make the unit shown. Evenly trim down to 3⅜ x 3⅜in (8.6 x 8.6cm) square.

2. Cut the two 3½ x 3½in (8.9 x 8.9cm) E6 fabric squares into half diagonally to make four triangles. Be very careful with these triangles so as not to change their shape as the diagonal line is on the bias and at risk of stretching. Handle them as little as possible and keep neat and flat until use.

3. Use a ruler to find the middle point along the long diagonal edge of each triangle and mark with a pin or heat erasable pen. Fold the Diamond in a Square unit in half both ways and mark the middle points.

4. Take two triangles and align, pin and sew them onto the Diamond in a Square unit as shown using a standard ¼in (0.6cm) seam, matching the marked middle points. Be careful not to stretch the triangle pieces. Open out and press.

5. Take the remaining two triangles and align, pin and sew them onto the unit as shown using a standard ¼in (0.6cm) seam, matching the marked middle points as before. Open out and press. Evenly trim down to 4½ x 4½in (11.4 x 11.4cm) square.

6. Following the **Four at a Time Flying Geese Method**, use a scant ¼in (0.4–0.5cm) seam to sew four 2⅜ x 2⅜in (6 x 6cm) E2 fabric squares onto each of the 4 x 4in (10.2 x 10.2cm) white fabric squares to make eight Flying Geese units. Evenly trim all units down to 3½ x 2in (8.9 x 5.1cm).

7. Sew the units together as shown following the **Standard Piecing Method** using a standard ¼in (0.6cm) seam, first sewing the Flying Geese units together in pairs. Then on two of the joined pairs, sew a 1½ x 1½in (3.8 x 3.8cm) E2 fabric square to either end as shown.

8. Sew the shorter strips shown to the top and the bottom of the centre unit, then sew the remaining two longer strips to either side as shown.

9. Evenly trim down the whole block to 6½in (16.5cm) square if it is not this size already. Block is complete. Press and store safely.

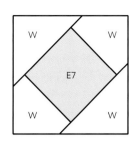

Make one Diamond in a Square
unit and evenly trim

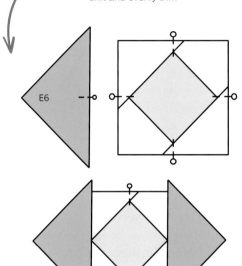

Mark the middle points of each
edge. Sew triangles on either side,
aligning the middle points

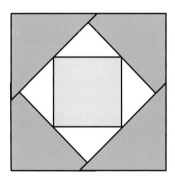

Sew the remaining triangles
on, open out and press

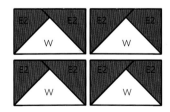

Make a total of eight Flying Geese
units and evenly trim

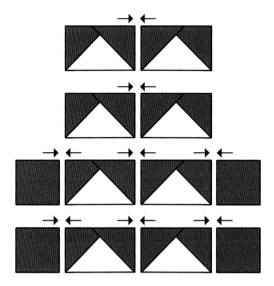

Sew the units into strips, adding the remaining
fabric squares to two of the strips as shown

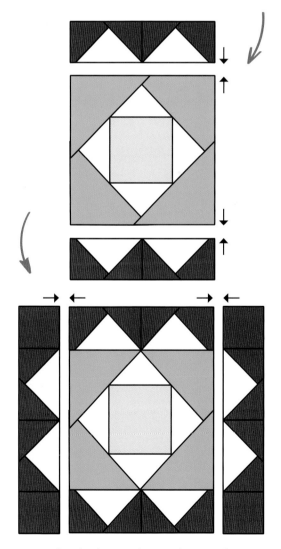

Sew the shorter strips onto the top and
bottom and the longer strips onto the sides

Piecing with Templates

ABOUT PIECING WITH TEMPLATES

Using ready-made templates is a handy way to achieve the more irregular patchwork fabric shapes that would be difficult to sew any other way, including curved and odd angle shapes. Traditionally joined by hand, some curved designs can be pieced using the sewing machine. Templates can be fiddly, so be sure to follow the template's required grainline (marked with an arrow) when cutting fabric pieces, use lots of pins when joining them, and sew them using the correct seam allowance, stopping exactly where required at corners to get the best results.

Quilt blocks commonly using this construction method include Melon Patch and Sunrays.

Recommended Tools: heat erasable pen, fabric scissors, paper scissors, starch

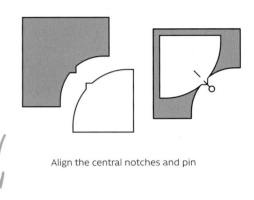

Align the central notches and pin

TEMPLATE PREPARATION METHOD

1. Trace the template onto card or at least 120gsm paper, transferring all text and grainline arrows too. Cut out the template using paper scissors directly on its outline.

2. Place the template onto the fabric, both right side facing up and oriented for the correct grainline. Trace around the template using a heat erasable pen (or lightly with a pencil). Remove template.

3. Cut out traced shape using fabric scissors directly on its outline.

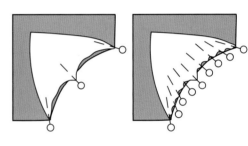

Pin at even intervals to ease the curves together

SEWING CURVES METHOD

Start by cutting out the fabric shapes required using the templates provided, following the **Template Preparaton Method**.

SEWING CONVEX CURVE TO CONCAVE CURVE

1. Placing the smaller piece on top of the larger one, right sides together, align the central notches and pin at a right angle to the curved edge. Next, pin at each end of the curve, gently easing the edges of each piece together, almost as if you are slightly straightening their curves, in order to make them meet.

2. Continue to pin in between at even intervals along the curve, easing the pieces together and gradually closing the remaining gaps one section at a time. For example, start pinning at the halfway points, then the quarter points, and so on, until the whole curved length is pinned together evenly. The fabric will form small gathers at the curved edge outside the pins – this is normal.

3. Sew along the edge, removing pins as you go. Open out. Press the seam towards the concave edge so that it lies flat.

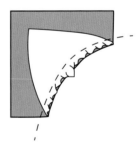

Sew along the curve

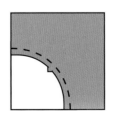

Wrong side   Right side

Open out and press seam towards the concave edge

SEWING SHAPES WITH A SECOND CURVED EDGE

1. For units that have a second curved edge (such as on a Melon Patch unit, pictured), pin the second shaped piece on in the same way as described for **Sewing Convex Curve to Concave Curve** but at the corners of the curve (points A and B) start and end as if the seam allowance on the inner shape has not been pressed inwards. Treat the curve like it is the full length of the shape.

2. Sew along the edge, removing pins before they pass under the needle. Open out. Press the seam towards the concave edge so that it lies flat.

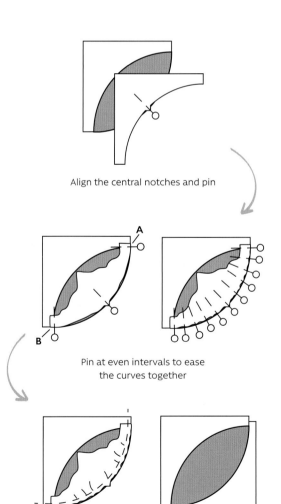

Align the central notches and pin

Pin at even intervals to ease the curves together

Sew along the curve, open out and press

HANDY TIPS

Use a heat erasable pen to draw the stitching line onto the wrong side of the fabric before pinning. This will give you a clear guide to follow while stitching the curve, so you can concentrate on ensuring the fabric is not puckering under the needle!

Due to the curve being on the bias, the more you handle each curve the more risk there is of it stretching out of shape. Practise pinning curves together using scrap pieces of fabric first to build up confidence. The longer the curve, the more pins will be needed to pin it down, at the sixteenth points, thirty-second points, and so on. Alternatively, you may prefer to hand tack (baste) the curve in place.

Stay stitching along each curved edge of the cut pieces will help them to keep their shape. Simply use the machine to sew a line of stitches close to the edge of all individual curved pieces, sewing through one layer of fabric only. Alternatively, when working with smaller curved pieces, you may wish to starch them before sewing.

Sew slowly: patience is key when sewing curves!

When trimming Melon Patch units down to size, always do so evenly. Once trimmed, you should be able to draw an imaginary straight line from each corner of the trimmed unit, through the points of the inner curved shape.

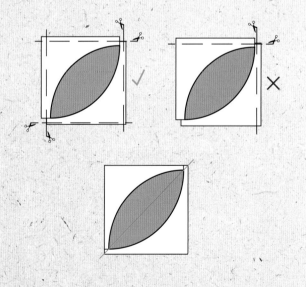

TEMPLATES

You will need these templates to make the ten blocks featured in this section. Place onto fabric so that the grainline arrows on each template align with the fabric selvedge, i.e. running lengthwise down the fabric. They are shown at full size and printable versions can be downloaded from www.bookmarkedhub.com.

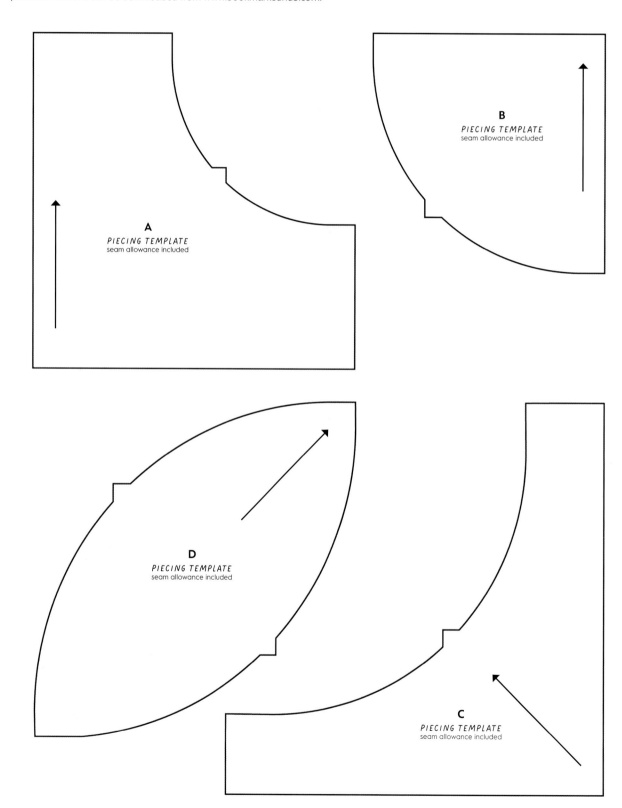

A
PIECING TEMPLATE
seam allowance included

B
PIECING TEMPLATE
seam allowance included

D
PIECING TEMPLATE
seam allowance included

C
PIECING TEMPLATE
seam allowance included

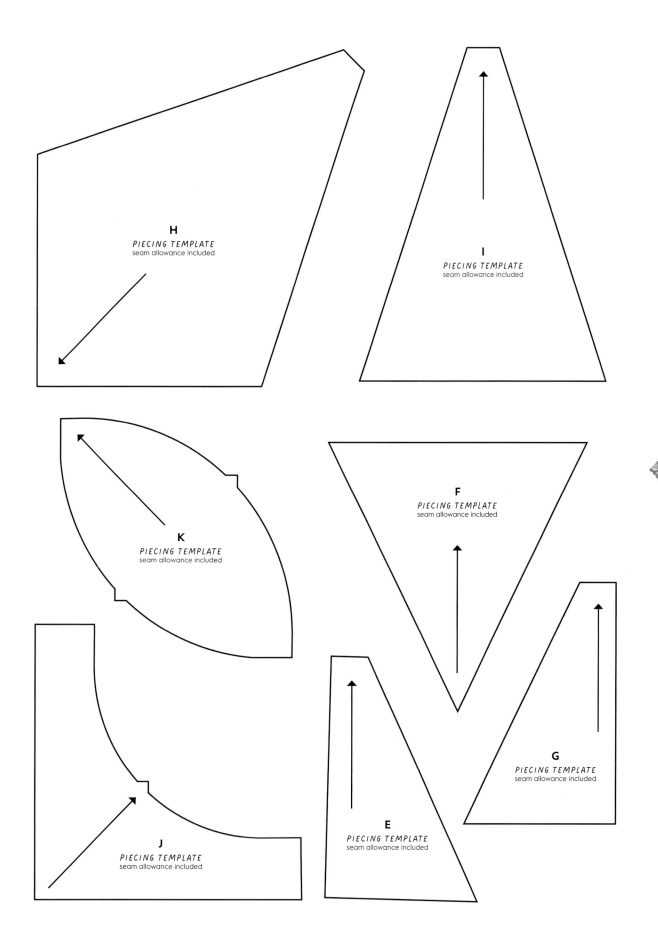

H
PIECING TEMPLATE
seam allowance included

I
PIECING TEMPLATE
seam allowance included

K
PIECING TEMPLATE
seam allowance included

F
PIECING TEMPLATE
seam allowance included

G
PIECING TEMPLATE
seam allowance included

J
PIECING TEMPLATE
seam allowance included

E
PIECING TEMPLATE
seam allowance included

BLOCK 51: Square Dance

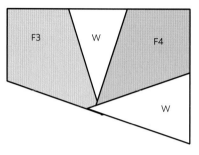

Use the patchwork templates to make two of the units shown

INFO

- Block Size: 6½in (16.5cm) unfinished, 6in (15.2cm) finished
- Seams: scant ¼in (0.4–0.5cm)
- Press Seams: Open. Press after each sewing step.

CUTTING

- White Fabric: four of template I
- Fabric F3: two of template H
- Fabric F4: two of template H

Refer to the start of the Piecing with Templates chapter for the templates.

CONSTRUCTION

1. Following the **Standard Piecing Method**, sew together two of the template H fabric pieces (one fabric F3 and one fabric F4) and two of the template I fabric pieces (white fabric) as shown.

2. Repeat to make an identical unit.

3. Sew the units together as shown.

4. Evenly trim down the whole block to 6½in (16.5cm) square if it is not this size already. Block is complete. Press and store safely.

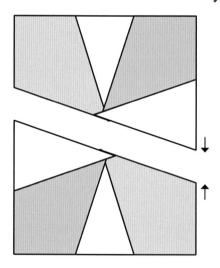

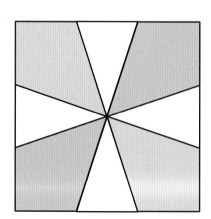

Sew the units together into the final block

BLOCK 52: Sunrays

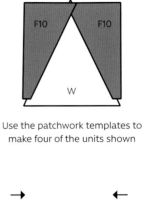

Use the patchwork templates to make four of the units shown

INFO

- Block Size: 6½in (16.5cm) unfinished, 6in (15.2cm) finished
- Seams: scant ¼in (0.4–0.5cm)
- Press Seams: To one side. Press after each sewing step.

CUTTING

- White Fabric: four of template F and four 2½ x 2½in (6.4 x 6.4cm)
- Fabric F6: one 2½ x 2½in (6.4 x 6.4cm)
- Fabric F10: four of template E and four of template G

Refer to the start of the Piecing with Templates chapter for the templates.

CONSTRUCTION

1. Following the **Standard Piecing Method**, sew one of templates E and G fabric pieces (fabric F10) to one of template F fabric pieces (white fabric) to make the unit shown.

2. Repeat three more times to make a total of four identical units. Evenly trim down all units to 2½ x 2½in (6.4 x 6.4cm) square.

3. Sew the units together as shown following the **Standard Piecing Method**, first sewing them in sections with the 2½ x 2½in (6.4 x 6.4cm) fabric squares, then joining the sections together.

4. Evenly trim down the whole block to 6½in (16.5cm) square if it is not this size already. Block is complete. Press and store safely.

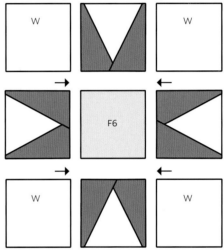

Sew the units together with the remaining fabric squares into sections

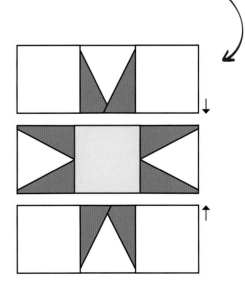

Sew the sections together into the final block

BLOCK 53: *Star of Alamo Variation*

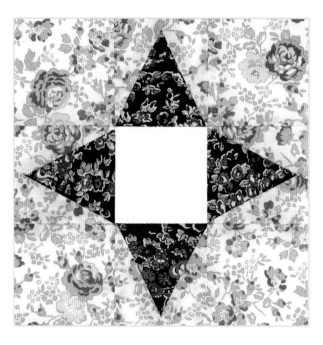

INFO

- Block Size: 6½in (16.5cm) unfinished, 6in (15.2cm) finished
- Seams: scant ¼in (0.4–0.5cm)
- Press Seams: To one side. Press after each sewing step.

CUTTING

- White Fabric: one 2½ x 2½in (6.4 x 6.4cm)
- Fabric F9: four of template E, four of template G and four 2½ x 2½in (6.4 x 6.4cm)
- Fabric F10: four of template F

Refer to the start of the Piecing with Templates chapter for the templates.

CONSTRUCTION

1. Following the **Standard Piecing Method**, sew one of templates E and G fabric pieces (fabric F9) to one of template F fabric pieces (fabric F10) to make the unit shown.

2. Repeat three more times to make a total of four identical units. Evenly trim down all units to 2½ x 2½in (6.4 x 6.4cm) square.

3. Sew the units together as shown following the **Standard Piecing Method**, first sewing them in sections together with the 2½ x 2½in (6.4 x 6.4cm) white and E9 fabric squares, then joining the sections together.

4. Evenly trim down the whole block to 6½in (16.5cm) square if it is not this size already. Block is complete. Press and store safely.

Fabric Focus

Felicite is a rose trail pattern that was created for Liberty Fabrics in 1933, along with the popular Betsy and Wiltshire prints, by a designer we know very little about who had the initials D.S. It joined the Liberty Classics collection in 2001.

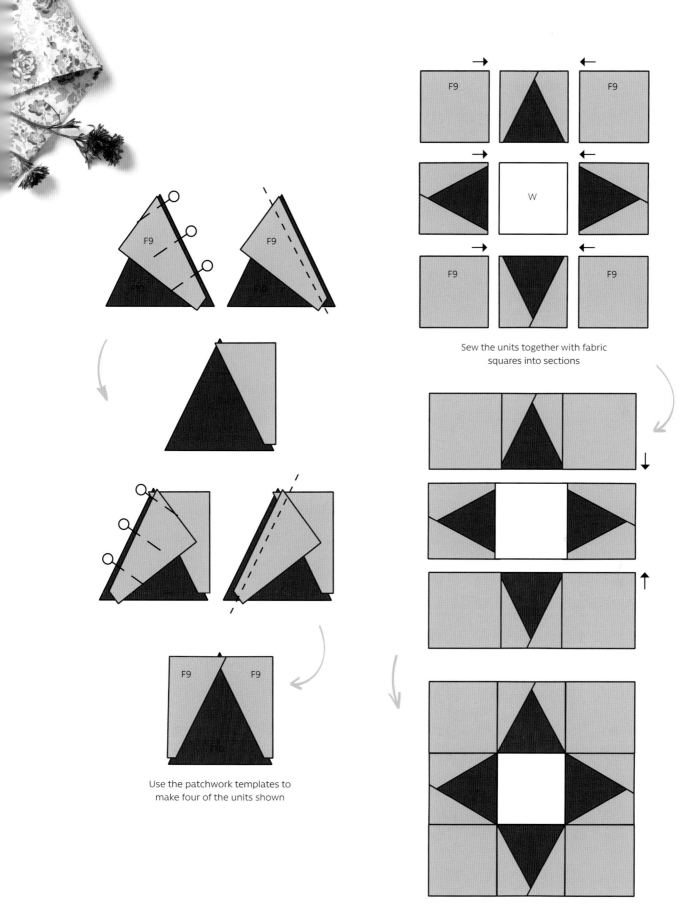

Use the patchwork templates to
make four of the units shown

Sew the units together with fabric
squares into sections

Sew the sections together into the final block

BLOCK 54: *Judy in Arabia*

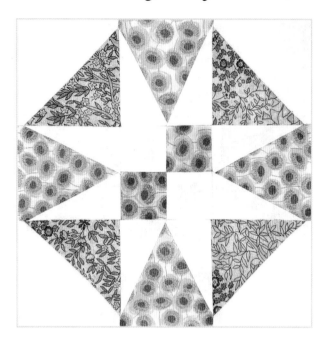

INFO

- Block Size: 6½in (16.5cm) unfinished, 6in (15.2cm) finished
- Seams: scant ¼in (0.4–0.5cm)
- Press Seams: To one side and open. Press after each sewing step.

CUTTING

- White Fabric: four of template E, four of template G, one 4½ x 4½in (11.4 x 11.4cm) and one 1½ x 3in (3.8 x 7.6cm)
- Fabric F2: four of template F
- Fabric F4: one 1½ x 3in (3.8 x 7.6cm)
- Fabric F5: one 4½ x 4½in (11.4 x 11.4cm)

Refer to the start of the Piecing with Templates chapter for the templates.

CONSTRUCTION

1. Following the **Strip Piecing Method**, sew the 1½ x 3in (3.8 x 7.6cm) strips of white fabric and fabric F4 together to make a strip set as shown.

2. Press open. Then, cut the strip set at 1½in (3.8cm) intervals to make two 1½ x 2½in (3.8 x 6.4cm) smaller units. Discard leftover fabric.

3. Sew these units together as shown following the **Standard Piecing Method**. Evenly trim down to 2½ x 2½in (6.4 x 6.4cm) square. Press open.

4. Following the **Four at a Time HST Method**, sew the 4½ x 4½in (11.4 x 11.4cm) white fabric and F5 fabric squares together into four HSTs as shown.

5. Following the **Standard Piecing Method**, sew one of templates E and G fabric pieces (white fabric) to one of template F fabric pieces (fabric F2) to make the unit shown. Press seams to one side.

6. Repeat step 5 to make a total of four identical units. Evenly trim down all units to 2½ x 2½in (6.4 x 6.4cm) square.

7. Sew the units together as shown following the **Standard Piecing Method** and pressing seams open, first sewing them in sections, then joining the sections together.

8. Evenly trim down the whole block to 6½in (16.5cm) square if it is not this size already. Block is complete. Press and store safely.

Fabric Focus

Jess & Jean was drawn in the Liberty Fabrics design studio using make-up items from cosmetic brands NARS, Shu Uemura and Laura Mercier. It is based on an archival furnishing print and inspired by the Arts and Crafts movement.

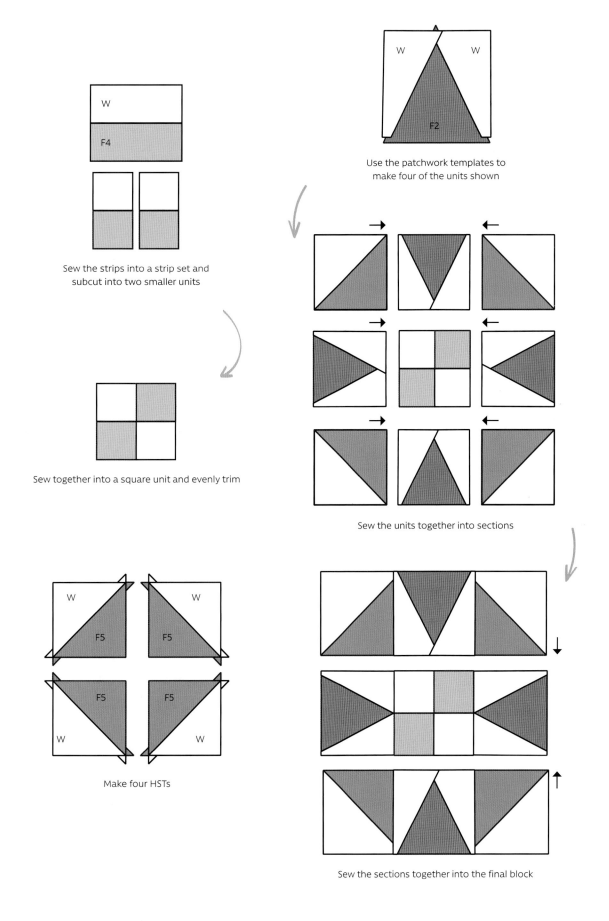

W

F4

Sew the strips into a strip set and
subcut into two smaller units

Sew together into a square unit and evenly trim

W   W

F2

Use the patchwork templates to
make four of the units shown

Sew the units together into sections

W   W

F5   F5

F5   F5

W   W

Make four HSTs

Sew the sections together into the final block

BLOCK 55: Snowball

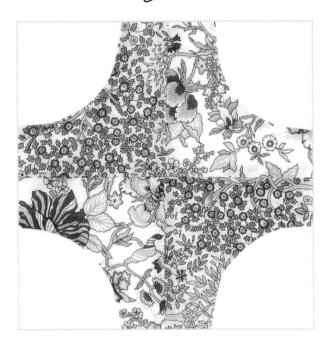

INFO

- Block Size: 6½in (16.5cm) unfinished, 6in (15.2cm) finished
- Seams: scant ¼in (0.4–0.5cm) and ¼in (0.6cm)
- Press Seams: To one side and open. Press after each sewing step.

CUTTING

- White Fabric: four of template B
- Fabric F3: two of template A
- Fabric F5: two of template A

Refer to the start of the Piecing with Templates chapter for the templates.

CONSTRUCTION

I. Following the **Sewing Curves Method**, use a scant ¼in (0.4–0.5cm) seam to sew one of template A fabric pieces (fabric F3) to a template B fabric piece (white fabric) to make the unit shown. Then repeat to make an identical unit.

2. Following step 1, sew two more units using the remaining template A (fabric F5) and template B (white fabric) pieces.

3. Sew the units together as shown following the **Standard Piecing Method**. Use a ¼in (0.6cm) seam and press seams open, first sewing them together in pairs, then joining the paired units together.

4. Evenly trim down the whole block to 6½in (16.5cm) square if it is not this size already. Block is complete. Press and store safely.

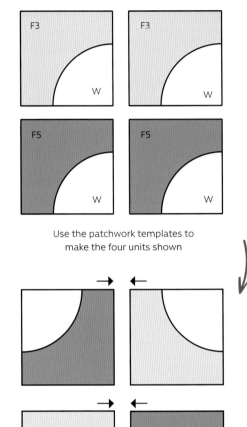

Use the patchwork templates to make the four units shown

Sew the units together in pairs

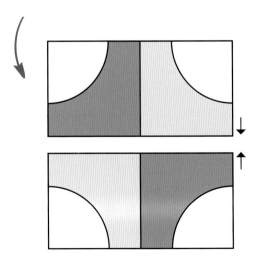

Sew the paired units together into the final block

BLOCK 56: This and That

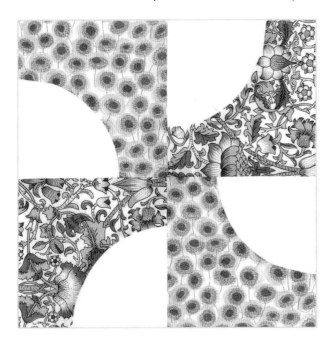

INFO

- Block Size: 6½in (16.5cm) unfinished, 6in (15.2cm) finished
- Seams: scant ¼in (0.4–0.5cm) and ¼in (0.6cm)
- Press Seams: To one side and open. Press after each sewing step.

CUTTING

- White Fabric: four of template B
- Fabric F4: two of template A
- Fabric F7: two of template A

Refer to the start of the Piecing with Templates chapter for the templates.

CONSTRUCTION

1. Following the **Sewing Curves Method**, use a scant ¼in (0.4–0.5cm) seam to sew one of template A fabric pieces (fabric F4) to a template B fabric piece (white fabric) to make the unit shown. Then repeat to make an identical unit.

2. Following step 1, sew two more units using the remaining template A (fabric F7) and template B (white fabric) pieces.

3. Sew the units together as shown following the **Standard Piecing Method**. Use a ¼in (0.6cm) seam and press seams open, first sewing them together in pairs, then joining the paired units together.

4. Evenly trim down the whole block to 6½in (16.5cm) square if it is not this size already. Block is complete. Press and store safely.

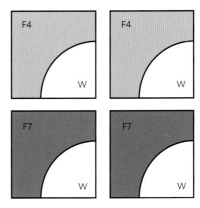

Use the patchwork templates to make the four units shown

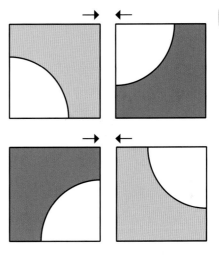

Sew the units together in pairs

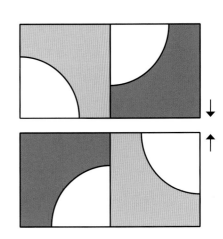

Sew the paired units together into the final block

BLOCK 57: Polka Dot

INFO

- Block Size: 6½in (16.5cm) unfinished, 6in (15.2cm) finished
- Seams: scant ¼in (0.4–0.5cm) and ¼in (0.6cm)
- Press Seams: To one side and open. Press after each sewing step.

CUTTING

- White Fabric: four of template A
- Fabric F1: two of template B
- Fabric F3: two of template B

Refer to the start of the Piecing with Templates chapter for the templates.

CONSTRUCTION

I. Following the **Sewing Curves Method**, use a scant ¼in (0.4–0.5cm) seam to sew one of template A fabric pieces (white fabric) to a template B fabric piece (fabric F1) to make the unit shown. Then repeat to make an identical unit.

2. Following step 1, sew two more units using the remaining template A (white fabric) and template B (fabric F3) pieces.

3. Sew the units together as shown following the **Standard Piecing Method**. Use a ¼in (0.6cm) seam and press seams open, first sewing them together in pairs, then joining the paired units together.

4. Evenly trim down the whole block to 6½in (16.5cm) square if it is not this size already. Block is complete. Press and store safely.

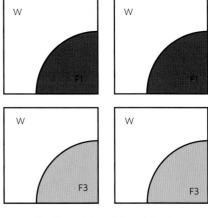

Use the patchwork templates to make four of the units shown

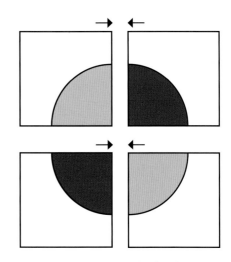

Sew the units together in pairs

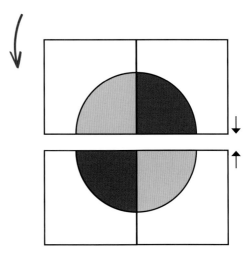

Sew the paired units together into the final block

BLOCK 58: Rob Peter to Pay Paul

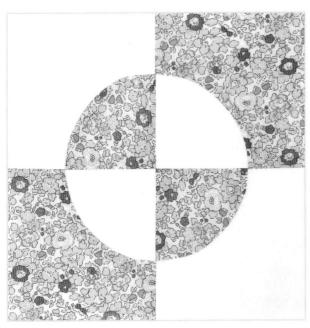

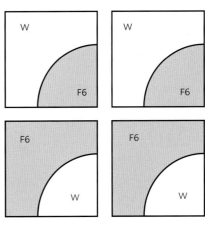

Use the patchwork templates to make four of the units shown

INFO

- Block Size: 6½in (16.5cm) unfinished, 6in (15.2cm) finished
- Seams: scant ¼in (0.4–0.5cm) and ¼in (0.6cm)
- Press Seams: To one side and open. Press after each sewing step.

CUTTING

- White Fabric: two of template A and two of template B
- Fabric F6: two of template A and two of template B

Refer to the start of the Piecing with Templates chapter for the templates.

CONSTRUCTION

1. Following the **Sewing Curves Method**, use a scant ¼in (0.4–0.5cm) seam to sew one of template A fabric pieces (white fabric) to a template B fabric piece (fabric F6) to make the unit shown. Then repeat to make an identical unit.

2. Following step 1, sew two more units using the remaining template A (fabric F6) and template B (white fabric) pieces.

3. Sew the units together as shown following the **Standard Piecing Method**. Use a ¼in (0.6cm) seam and press seams open, first sewing them together in pairs, then joining the paired units together.

4. Evenly trim down the whole block to 6½in (16.5cm) square if it is not this size already. Block is complete. Press and store safely.

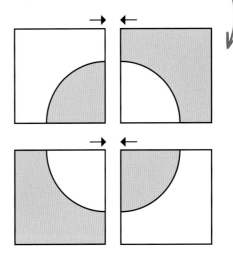

Sew the units together in pairs

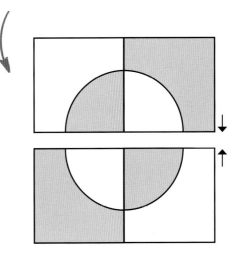

Sew the paired units together into the final block

BLOCK 59: *Melon Patch*

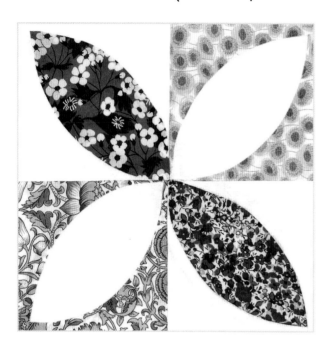

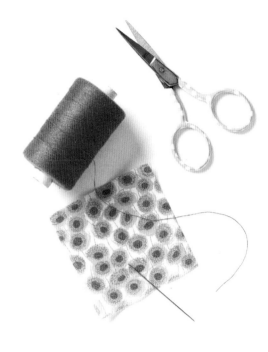

INFO

- Block Size: 6½in (16.5cm) unfinished, 6in (15.2cm) finished
- Seams: scant ¼in (0.4–0.5cm)
- Press Seams: To one side and open. Press after each sewing step.

CUTTING

- White Fabric: two of template C and four of template D
- Fabric F1: one of template D
- Fabric F2: two of template C
- Fabric F7: two of template C
- Fabric F8: one of template D

Refer to the start of the Piecing with Templates chapter for the templates.

CONSTRUCTION

1. Following the **Sewing Curves Method**, sew two template C fabric pieces (white fabric) to a template D fabric piece (fabric F1) to make the unit shown. Evenly trim down to 3½ x 3½in (8.9 x 8.9cm) square.

2. Sew together two template C fabric pieces (white fabric) to a template D fabric piece (fabric F8) in the same way and trim evenly.

3. Sew together two template C fabric pieces (fabric F2) to a template D fabric piece (white fabric) in the same way and trim evenly.

4. Sew together two template C fabric pieces (fabric F7) to a template D fabric piece (white fabric) in the same way and trim evenly.

5. Sew the units together as shown following the **Standard Piecing Method** and pressing seams open, first sewing the units together in pairs, then joining the paired units together.

6. Evenly trim down the whole block to 6½in (16.5cm) square if it is not this size already. Block is complete. Press and store safely.

Fabric Focus

Emma & Georgina is inspired by Liberty Fabrics' large collection of Victorian pattern books. It is based on two different tiny, dense, floral prints: Emma, which was first produced on Tana Lawn® in the 1970s, and Georgina, which was launched in 2000.

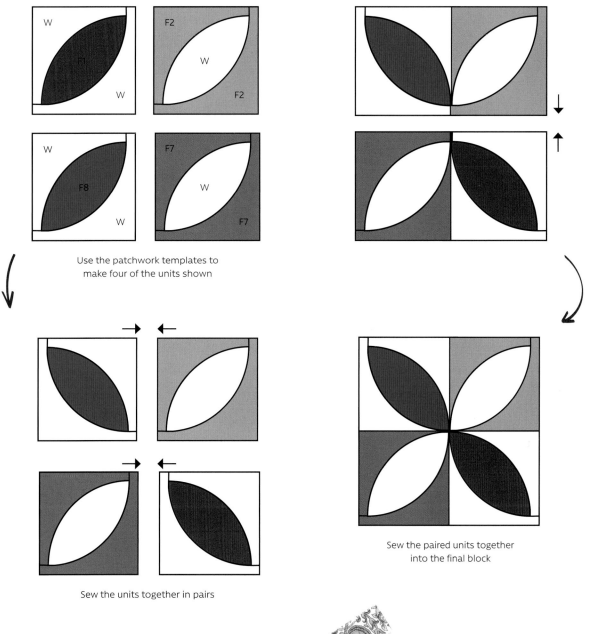

Use the patchwork templates to
make four of the units shown

Sew the units together in pairs

Sew the paired units together
into the final block

BLOCK 60: *Kathy's Star*

CONSTRUCTION

1. Following the **Sewing Curves Method**, sew two template J fabric pieces (white fabric) to a template K fabric piece (fabric F8) to make the unit shown. Evenly trim down to 2½ x 2½in (6.4 x 6.4cm) square.

2. Repeat step 1 three more times to make a total of four identical units.

3. Following the **Standard Piecing Method**, sew one of templates E and G fabric pieces (white fabric) to one of template F fabric pieces (fabric F5) to make the unit shown. Press seams to one side.

4. Repeat step 3 three more times to make a total of four identical units. Evenly trim down all units to 2½ x 2½in (6.4 x 6.4cm) square.

5. Sew the units together as shown following the **Standard Piecing Method** and pressing seams open, first sewing the units together in sections with the 2½ x 2½in (6.4 x 6.4cm) F2 fabric square, then joining the sections together.

6. Evenly trim down the whole block to 6½in (16.5cm) square if not this size already. Block is complete. Press and store safely.

INFO

- Block Size: 6½in (16.5cm) unfinished, 6in (15.2cm) finished
- Seams: scant ¼in (0.4–0.5cm)
- Press Seams: To one side and open. Press after each sewing step.

CUTTING

- White Fabric: eight of template J, four of template E and four of template G
- Fabric F2: one 2½ x 2½in (6.4 x 6.4cm)
- Fabric F5: four of template F
- Fabric F8: four of template K

Refer to the start of the Piecing with Templates chapter for the templates.

Fabric Focus

Xanthe Sunbeam showcases beautiful fields of sunbeam sunflowers. Originally from the Spring/Summer 2013 'Flower Show' collection, this print features a collage of delicately drawn sunflowers inspired by the Abbey Garden on the island of Tresco.

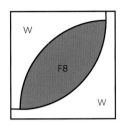

Use the patchwork templates to
make four of the units shown

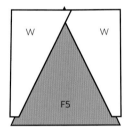

Use the patchwork templates to
make four of the units shown

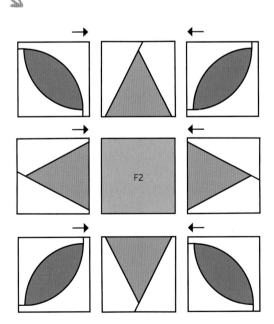

Sew the units together with the
remaining fabric square into sections

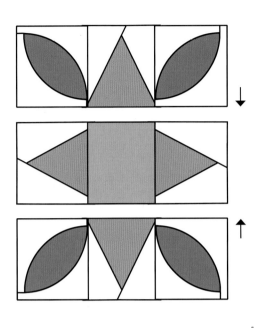

Sew the sections together into the final block

English Paper Piecing

ABOUT ENGLISH PAPER PIECING (EPP)

EPP is an easy hand sewing technique which involves small pieces of fabric being wrapped around paper before being sewn together. The paper provides stability when sewing and helps ensure the shape of the piece is accurate. Common shapes are hexagons, diamonds, triangles and squares. EPP typically involves straight lines, but gentle curves are also possible to achieve. It is a very cost effective method of sewing as it involves minimal equipment.

Quilt blocks commonly using this construction method include Granny Flowers, Clamshell and Dresden Plate.

Recommended Tools: thread conditioner, soluble fabric glue pen, hand sewing needle

EPP TEMPLATE AND FABRIC CUTTING METHOD

1. Trace the EPP template onto at least 120gsm paper, transferring all identifying text, and ensuring to reverse the template to make a mirrored shape when instructed to do so. Repeat as many times as required. Cut out the paper templates using paper scissors.

2. Press all fabric flat. Lay out the exact quantity and orientation (reversed or not) of each paper template required onto the indicated fabrics, wrong side of fabric facing up. Secure each paper shape in place using either a dab of soluble glue (our preferred method) or a small-headed pin. Be sure to leave a ¼in (0.6cm) gap around the outside of *each* of the paper shapes as this will be your seam allowance.

3. Cut around each shape, being sure to include the ¼in (0.6cm) seam allowance on each. I recommend using a rotary cutter and mat to cut out your shapes, however it may also be completed using scissors.

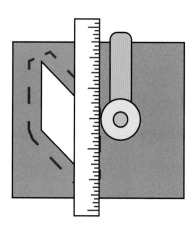

Add a ¼in (0.6cm) seam allowance as you cut

HANDY TIP

On sharp points, cut a beveled edge no less than ⅛in (0.3cm) away from the corners to help reduce bulk in the seams and save on fabric. On shallower corners, grade the corner down by only a small amount or not at all, as you desire.

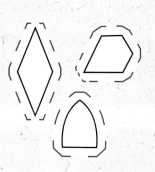

EPP PREPARATION METHOD

STRAIGHT EDGE SHAPES

Use one of the following methods to wrap the fabric around the straight edged papers:

Glue tacking (basting)

This is my preferred method. Place the paper shape on the wrong side of the cut fabric shape, leaving the ¼in (0.6cm) seam allowance of fabric around all the edges of the paper shape. Glue along one edge of the paper and carefully fold the fabric over the edge, lightly pressing it in place. Repeat for all sides of the shape working in a single direction until the paper is wrapped by the fabric on all sides.

Thread tacking (basting)

Place the paper shape on the wrong side of the cut fabric shape. Fold the fabric around the edge of the paper. Tack (baste) in place through the fabric and paper, starting and ending each tacked (basted) shape with a knot and using stitches approx. ⅜in (1cm) long. There is no need to be neat as these stitches will be removed later.

Repeat for all sides of the shape working in a single direction until the paper is wrapped by the fabric on all sides. You will need to make sure there is a stitch at each corner to hold the folded fabric in place.

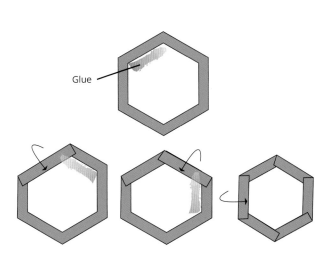

Glue

Tacking (basting) with glue

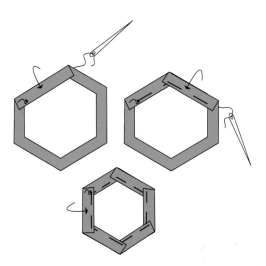

Tacking (basting) with thread

HANDY TIPS

Store all the templates required to make each block in an envelope (one for each block), writing the block number and name on the front of the envelope.

When required to cut the same number of same shaped pieces out of several fabrics, you can layer the fabrics on top of each other and multi cut. You can cut approximately four layers of Tana Lawn® fabric at the same time, so stack up what you can and pin one set of paper shapes through all layers of fabric. Once cut, simply attach paper shapes to the cut pieces that do not yet have paper shapes attached. If multi cutting in this way, you must use a rotary cutter and mat to cut out the shapes as cutting multiple layers accurately with scissors is far more difficult.

Completing all the gluing or tacking (basting) for a block or project in one go is handy as you can then take the fully prepared shapes 'out and about' and sew wherever you go.

EPP is really mobile. It's ideal to take on holiday, to waiting rooms or your local sewing group. Store everything in a clean cosmetics bag large enough to hold your prepared shapes, needle, small scissors, thimble and thread.

Look up from your EPP for 30 seconds or so at least once every half hour. Focus on things in the distance – a sign, a dog walker, a cloud – and let your eyes adjust to seeing faraway objects to give them a break from close work.

CONVEX SHAPES

Use one of the following methods to wrap the fabric around convex curved papers:

Thread tacking (basting)

My preferred method for curved sections, this technique may be used in combination with glued straight or concave sections. If the shape has any concave or straight sections, glue tack (baste) the concave sections first, then glue or thread tack (baste) the straight sections before thread tacking (basting) the convex curves (alternatively, you can use glue).

Place the paper shape on the wrong side of the fabric, leaving the ¼in (0.6cm) seam allowance of fabric around all the edges of the paper shape. Take a hand sewing needle and thread, and knot the end of the thread. Sew a running stitch with even stitch length along the fabric of the curved section. Gently pull on the loose length of thread to gather the fabric around the curve. Once happy with how the fabric is gathered, knot the loose thread end close to the fabric to secure.

Glue tacking (basting)

You can use glue as an alternative to thread tacking (basting) curved sections. Glue along the convex edge and press the fabric to the glue so the fabric gathers around the curve. It is helpful to start pressing at even points along the curve, gradually closing the remaining gaps one section at a time to ensure even gathers. For example, start pressing down at the halfway point, then the quarter points, eighth points, sixteenth points, and so on, until the whole curved length is pressed to the glue.

Single curved edge example   Circle example

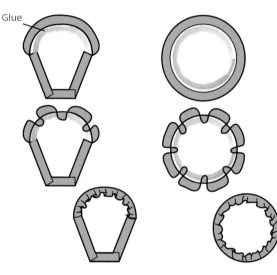

Glue

Single curved edge example   Circle example

CONCAVE SHAPES

My preferred method for concave curved sections is using glue. I do not recommend thread tacking (basting) concave edges.

Glue tacking (basting)

Place the paper shape on the wrong side of the fabric leaving the ¼in (0.6cm) seam allowance of fabric around all the edges of the paper shape. Use scissors to make small cuts into the concave fabric edge at regular invervals, stopping about ⅛in (0.3cm) away from the edge of the paper. Glue along the concave edge and press the fabric to the glue so it hugs the curve. If the fabric is not sitting flat easily you may need to clip into the seam allowance a little bit more to encourage the fabric to stretch and form the curve. Be careful not to clip too close to the edge of the shape. Glue tack (baste) the concave edges first before either glue or thread tacking (basting) any straight or convex edges.

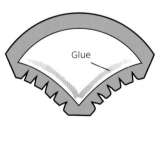

Glue

Concave edge example

EPP ASSEMBLY METHOD

STRAIGHT EDGE SHAPES

1. Referring to the individual block instructions, lay the fabric shapes out flat to make sure all the pieces are oriented correctly.

2. Place a pair of neighbouring fabric shapes right sides together. Stitch together along one edge only, using whipstitch: needle in on one side, out the other and back around to the side you started on to push it in again. Make about 12–16 stitches per inch and stitch as close to the edge of the shapes as you can so as not to pierce through the paper, picking up just a few threads of each fabric piece with the needle as you stitch. This makes the seams strong and the stitches almost invisible. Be precise – if stitches are made further down from the edge of the shapes and pierce through the paper, they will be seen from the right side! Knot the thread at the start of the first shape only; use the same length of thread to sew as many shapes together as possible before it runs out, then knot the thread). Open out.

Tip: If the block is radial, it is a good idea to start with the central shapes and work out from there, adding each 'ring' of shapes in turn.

3. Keep adding shapes, joining them using whipstitch. Follow the block instruction pages as a guide for where to place particular shapes and continue until the EPP unit is complete. Don't be scared to fold the work-in-progress EPP unit different ways in order to make it easier to sew the edges together; simply iron it flat afterwards to remove any creases.

4. Remove all papers from the completed EPP unit. If glue tacked (basted), dab the folded down seam allowances with a little water to help release the fabric from the paper. If thread tacked (basted), carefully snip away the tacking (basting) stitches, then pull the papers out.

Tip: If undamaged, removed papers may be used again for another project; simply iron them without steam to make them crisp and flat again.

5. Press the completed EPP unit flat, being careful to keep all seam allowances still folded back underneath the shapes at the edges. Spray starch can help to achieve a lovely crisp finish. If the seam allowances on thin, pointy sections overhang the front of the completed EPP unit at any point, do not worry; they will be dealt with later.

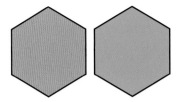

Place the shapes down flat

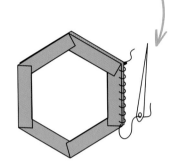

Whip stitch along their joining edge

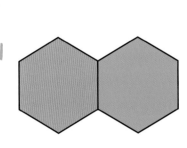

Open out

CURVED SHAPES

1. Place the two curved pieces right sides up on a hard, flat surface. Their curved joining edges should be flush together. Use a piece of low tack tape to stick together.

2. Flip the pieces over and place back down. Use a hand sewing needle and thread to stitch a flat whipstitch onto their wrong sides, knotting the thread at the start: needle in on one side, out the other and back around to the side you started on to push it in again. Make stitches as close together as you can, picking up ⅛in (0.3cm) or less of each fabric piece with the needle as you stitch.

3. Once the pieces are secured, you can remove the tape, and continue to add shapes as required to complete the EPP unit, and finish as steps 4 and 5 of **Straight Edge Shapes**.

Place the shapes together and tape

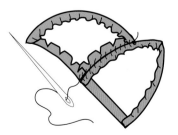

Whipstitch while flat

EPP APPLIQUÉ METHOD

BLIND STITCH BY HAND

Sometimes called hidden ladder stitch or invisible stitch, this hand sewing method is a great way to achieve a super clean look to your quilt top. It will take longer, but the neat results are worth the effort.

Using either a thread colour to match the block or a neutral colour, use blind stitches around the outside edge of the completed EPP unit to secure it to the backing fabric. To do this, tie a knot in one end of the thread and insert the needle from the reverse of the background fabric very close to the edge of the block.

Insert the tip of the needle sideways into the edge of the EPP unit; the needle should run along inside the creased edge and not pierce through to the top side of the EPP unit. Pierce the needle back through the underside of the EPP unit, catching a small section of the turned in seam allowance with the needle, no more than ¼in (0.6cm), for a secure stitch.

Then pass the needle directly back through the backing fabric, move the needle tip along on the underside no more than ¼in (0.6cm), push the needle back up through the backing fabric to the front and insert the tip of the needle sideways into the edge of the EPP unit again. Repeat around all outside edges of the EPP unit.

Once all edges of the EPP unit are blind stitched down, pass the needle back onto the wrong side of the backing fabric and knot to secure.

Tip: If you find the seam allowances on thin, pointy sections overhang the front of the block at any point, simply trim them down to ⅛in (0.3cm) from the folded tip, then tuck them back under the unit to hide them before stitching to secure. This can be done when using both hand or machine appliqué methods.

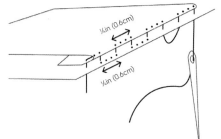

Evenly pass the needle inside the seam allowance and out from the underside

APPLIQUÉ BY SEWING MACHINE

This is a satisfyingly fast way to attach the EPP units to the background fabric, especially if using machine straight stitch. Alternatively use a zig zag stitch or other decorative stitch to create more of a feature of the thread.

Positioning the EPP unit on the background fabric as advised, sew all around just inside the outer edge of the block (about 0.1–0.2cm from the edge).

At the points, with the needle down, lift the foot and pivot the fabric to follow the edges of the shapes. Stitch right into the corners and the very tips of shapes.

Secure the stitching by reverse stitching (back-tacking) a little at the beginning and end of sewing.

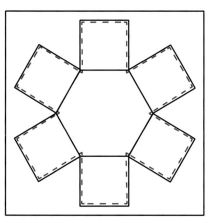

Straight stitch example

APPLIQUÉ BY HAND

This can provide an opportunity to make more of a feature of your appliqué and emphasise the handmade quality of your work.

Positioning the EPP unit on the background fabric as advised, thread a hand sewing needle with your chosen thread. Tie a knot in one end of the thread and insert the needle from the back very close to the edge of the EPP unit.

Sew all around the outside of the EPP unit using a backstitch or running stitch close to the very edge of the block (about 0.1–0.2cm from the edge) for a more subtle finish. Alternatively, use a blanket stitch for a more rustic, handmade look.

Tip: For a subtle finish, choose a neutral thread colour or one that matches the EPP unit being appliquéd. Or, for a bolder look, choose a contrasting thread colour. An embroidery hoop will help keep the area you are appliquéing taut.

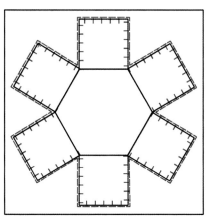

Blanket stitch example

HANDY TIPS

A sharp, longer needle makes sewing together the prepared fabric shapes easier. Use a size 9-11 (9 being longer than 11). Make sure that the eye of the needle is not so small that it punctures your finger. This is especially important if you are sewing lots of blocks in one sitting, although using a thimble can help. A gold tipped needle is also a good choice.

It is a good idea to anchor the thread to the needle to stop the thread from pulling through. Firstly, tie a knot at the bottom of the thread as usual. Then simply tie a knot with the other end of the thread around the eye of the needle (see diagram). This keeps the thread more securely attached to the needle and stops the need for endless re-threading.

Once you have threaded your needle, run the thread through your fingers two or three times to reduce twisting. If you wish, you can use a wax or a thread conditioner.

Posture is really important when you are sitting and hand sewing for hours. Placing your work on a cushion that elevates it to your natural arm level can really help with this. Try to sit comfortably and with your back in its natural shape, and stand up for a little bit once every hour to keep from becoming too immobile. Sewing with a good light source is essential, too, to prevent eye strain.

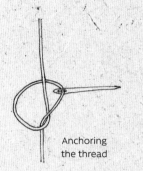

Anchoring the thread

RUNNING STITCH METHOD

Lines of decorative running stitches can enhance your finished EPP blocks.

1. Use a heat erasable pen to mark the desired line of stitching onto the front of the fabric. This may be skipped if you wish, however it is a good idea to prevent you from unintentionally stitching off course.

2. Take a hand sewing needle and thread it. You may use a double strand to achieve a thicker thread if desired; if using embroidery thread, split the strands to achieve the thread thickness you prefer. Knot the end of the thread.

3. Insert the needle into the block from the reverse side, pulling it through fully until the knot is securely at the back. Pass the needle back through the front of the block to the reverse, pulling it fully through. Pass the needle back up through the block to the front again. Continue in this way following the desired line of stitching.

4. Finish the line of stitching with the needle on the reverse of the block and tie a knot, snipping off the thread tails for a neater finish.

Tip: The distance between stitches and the stitch length can be even or uneven to achieve different effects.

Pass the needle up and down through the fabric

BLOCK 61: *Simple Heart*

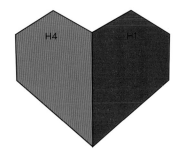

Join the two halves of the heart as shown

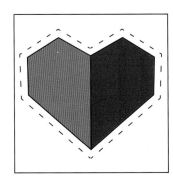

Sew the EPP unit to the white square and outline with running stitch

INFO

- Block Size: 6½in (16.5cm) unfinished, 6in (15.2cm) finished

CUTTING

- White Fabric: one 6½ x 6½in (16.5 x 16.5cm)
- Fabrics H1 and H4

CONSTRUCTION

1. Following the **EPP Template and Fabric Cutting Method** and the **EPP Preparation Method**, cut out and prepare the fabric shapes required using the template provided, and reversing the template as instructed to do so.

2. Following the **EPP Assembly Method**, sew the prepared fabric shapes together along their joined edges as shown.

3. Following the **EPP Appliqué Method**, sew the completed EPP unit centrally onto the white fabric square as shown.

4. Following the **Running Stitch Method**, stitch the decorative lines in colours of your choice. Block is complete. Press and store safely.

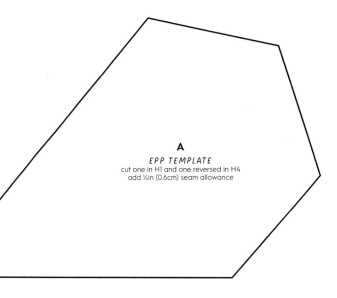

A
EPP TEMPLATE
cut one in H1 and one reversed in H4
add ¼in (0.6cm) seam allowance

BLOCK 62: Hexi Flower

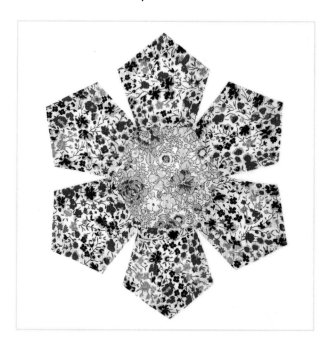

Join the parts of the
flower as shown

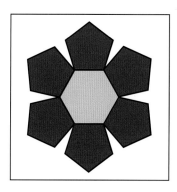

Sew the EPP unit to the white square

INFO

- Block Size: 6½in
  (16.5cm) unfinished, 6in
  (15.2cm) finished

CUTTING

- White Fabric: one 6½ x
  6½in (16.5 x 16.5cm)
- Fabrics G7 and G10

CONSTRUCTION

1. Following the **EPP Template and
Fabric Cutting Method** and the **EPP
Preparation Method**, cut out and
prepare the fabric shapes required
using the templates provided.

2. Following the **EPP Assembly
Method**, sew the prepared fabric
shapes together along their joined
edges as shown.

3. Following the **EPP Appliqué
Method**, sew the completed EPP
unit centrally onto the white fabric
square as shown. Block is complete.
Press and store safely.

A
EPP TEMPLATE
cut six in G10
add ¼in (0.6cm) seam allowance

B
EPP TEMPLATE
cut one in G7
add ¼in (0.6cm) seam allowance

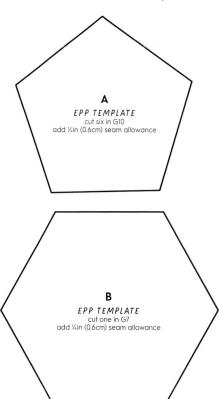

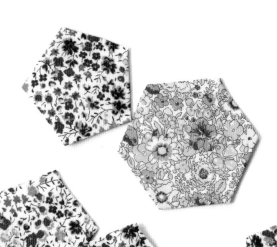

BLOCK 63: Grandmother's Fan

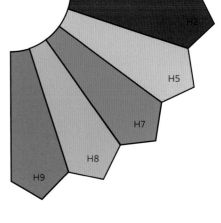

Join the shapes as shown

INFO

- Block Size: 6½in (16.5cm) unfinished, 6in (15.2cm) finished

CUTTING

- White Fabric: one 6½ x 6½in (16.5 x 16.5cm)
- Fabrics H2, H5, H7, H8 and H9

CONSTRUCTION

1. Following the **EPP Template and Fabric Cutting Method** and the **EPP Preparation Method**, cut out and prepare the fabric shapes required using the template provided.

2. Following the **EPP Assembly Method**, sew the prepared fabric shapes together along their joined edges as shown.

3. Following the **EPP Appliqué Method**, sew the completed EPP unit in the corner of the white fabric square as shown, leaving a ¼in (0.6cm) gap between the edge of the background fabric and the edges of the EPP unit. Block is complete. Press and store safely.

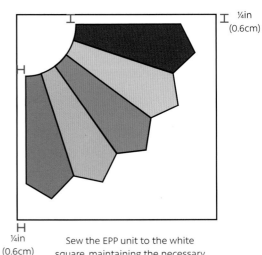

¼in (0.6cm)

¼in (0.6cm)

Sew the EPP unit to the white square, maintaining the necessary gap for the seam allowance

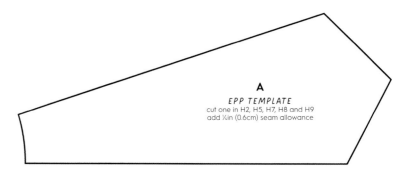

A
EPP TEMPLATE
cut one in H2, H5, H7, H8 and H9
add ¼in (0.6cm) seam allowance

BLOCK 64: Six-Pointed Star

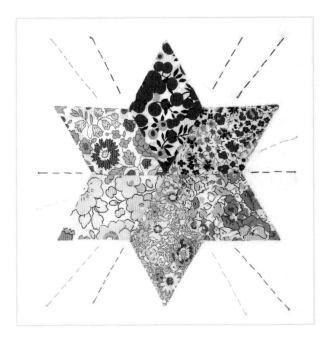

INFO

- Block Size: 6½in (16.5cm) unfinished, 6in (15.2cm) finished

CUTTING

- White Fabric: one 6½ x 6½in (16.5 x 16.5cm)
- Fabrics G1, G4, G6, G7, G8 and G10

CONSTRUCTION

1. Following the **EPP Template and Fabric Cutting Method** and the **EPP Preparation Method**, cut out and prepare the fabric shapes required using the template provided.

2. Following the **EPP Assembly Method**, sew the prepared fabric shapes together along their joined edges as shown.

3. Following the **EPP Appliqué Method**, sew the completed EPP unit centrally onto the white fabric square as shown.

4. Following the **Running Stitch Method**, stitch the decorative lines in colours of your choice. Block is complete. Press and store safely.

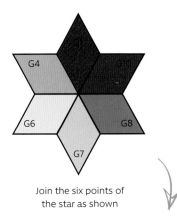

Join the six points of the star as shown

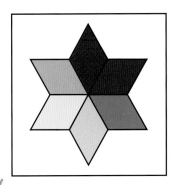

Sew the EPP unit to the white square

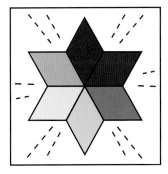

Add running stitch lines

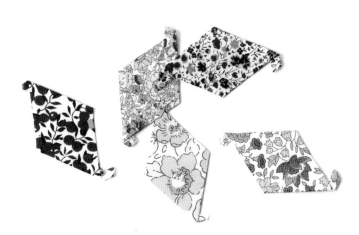

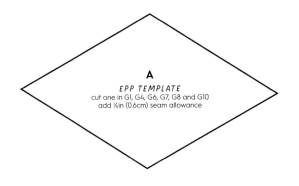

A
EPP TEMPLATE
cut one in G1, G4, G6, G7, G8 and G10
add ¼in (0.6cm) seam allowance

BLOCK 65: *Hexagon Star Variation*

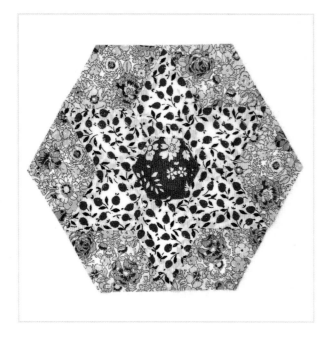

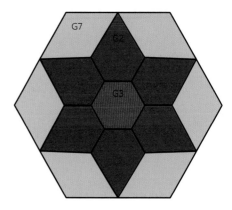

Join the shapes as shown

INFO

- Block Size: 6½in (16.5cm) unfinished, 6in (15.2cm) finished

CUTTING

- White Fabric: one 6½ x 6½in (16.5 x 16.5cm)
- Fabrics G2, G3 and G7

CONSTRUCTION

1. Following the **EPP Template and Fabric Cutting Method** and the **EPP Preparation Method**, cut out and prepare the fabric shapes required using the templates provided.

2. Following the **EPP Assembly Method**, sew the prepared fabric shapes together along their joined edges as shown.

3. Following the **EPP Appliqué Method**, sew the completed EPP unit centrally onto the white fabric square as shown. Be sure to leave a ¼in (0.6cm) gap around the outside for the seam allowance. Block is complete. Press and store safely.

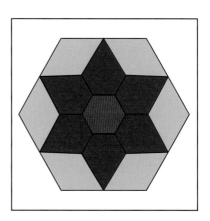

Sew the EPP unit to the white square

A
EPP TEMPLATE
cut six in G2
add ¼in (0.6cm) seam allowance

B
EPP TEMPLATE
cut one in G3
add ¼in (0.6cm) seam allowance

C
EPP TEMPLATE
cut six in G7
add ¼in (0.6cm) seam allowance

BLOCK 66: *Granny Flower*

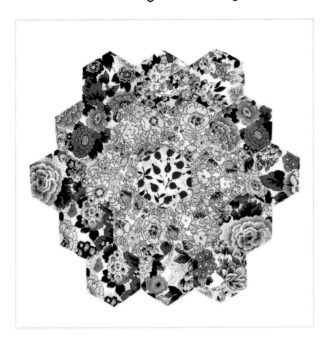

Join the hexagons as shown

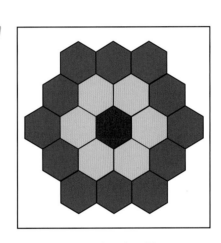

Sew the EPP unit to the white square

INFO

- Block Size: 6½in (16.5cm) unfinished, 6in (15.2cm) finished

CUTTING

- White Fabric: one 6½ x 6½in (16.5 x 16.5cm)
- Fabrics G2, G7 and G9

CONSTRUCTION

1. Following the **EPP Template and Fabric Cutting Method** and the **EPP Preparation Method**, cut out and prepare the fabric shapes required using the template provided.

2. Following the **EPP Assembly Method**, sew the prepared fabric shapes together along their joined edges as shown.

3. Following the **EPP Appliqué Method**, sew the completed EPP unit centrally onto the white fabric square as shown. Be sure to leave a ¼in (0.6cm) gap around the outside for the seam allowance. Block is complete. Press and store safely.

A
EPP TEMPLATE
cut one in G2, six in G7 and twelve in G9
add ¼in (0.6cm) seam allowance

Fabric Focus

Amelie is a classic Liberty floral dating from the 1930s and was originally printed at Liberty's Merton printworks. It features a fresh layout of roses, carnations and daisies.

BLOCK 67: *Hexagon Star*

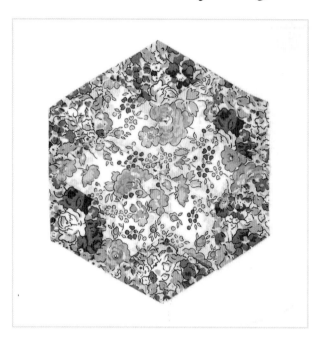

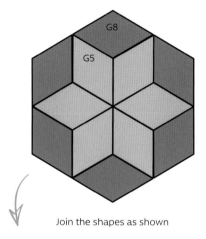

Join the shapes as shown

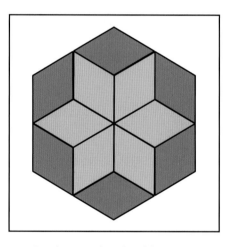

Sew the EPP unit to the white square

INFO

- Block Size: 6½in (16.5cm) unfinished, 6in (15.2cm) finished

CUTTING

- White Fabric: one 6½ x 6½in (16.5 x 16.5cm)
- Fabrics G5 and G8

CONSTRUCTION

1. Following the **EPP Template and Fabric Cutting Method** and the **EPP Preparation Method**, cut out and prepare the fabric shapes required using the template provided.

2. Following the **EPP Assembly Method**, sew the prepared fabric shapes together along their joined edges as shown.

3. Following the **EPP Appliqué Method**, sew the completed EPP unit centrally onto the white fabric square as shown. Be sure to leave a ¼in (0.6cm) gap around the outside for the seam allowance. Block is complete. Press and store safely.

A
EPP TEMPLATE
cut six in G5 and G8
add ¼in (0.6cm) seam allowance

BLOCK 68: Mosaic Star

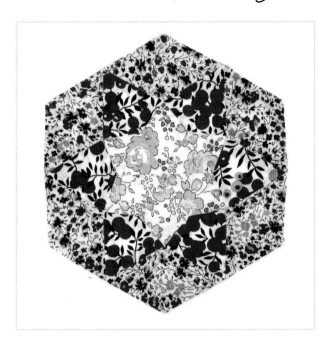

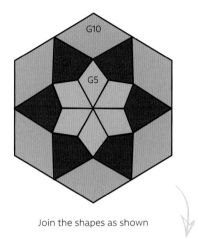

Join the shapes as shown

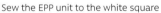

Sew the EPP unit to the white square

INFO

- Block Size: 6½in (16.5cm) unfinished, 6in (15.2cm) finished

CUTTING

- White Fabric: one 6½ x 6½in (16.5 x 16.5cm)
- Fabrics G1, G5 and G10

CONSTRUCTION

1. Following the **EPP Template and Fabric Cutting Method** and the **EPP Preparation Method**, cut out and prepare the fabric shapes required using the templates provided.

2. Following the **EPP Assembly Method**, sew the prepared fabric shapes together along their joined edges as shown.

3. Following the **EPP Appliqué Method**, sew the completed EPP unit centrally onto the white fabric square as shown. Be sure to leave a ¼in (0.6cm) gap around the outside for the seam allowance. Block is complete. Press and store safely.

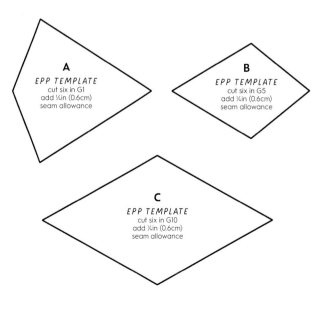

A
EPP TEMPLATE
cut six in G1
add ¼in (0.6cm)
seam allowance

B
EPP TEMPLATE
cut six in G5
add ¼in (0.6cm)
seam allowance

C
EPP TEMPLATE
cut six in G10
add ¼in (0.6cm)
seam allowance

BLOCK 69: Kaleidoscope

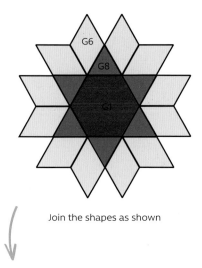

Join the shapes as shown

Sew the EPP unit to the white square

INFO

- Block Size: 6½in (16.5cm) unfinished, 6in (15.2cm) finished

CUTTING

- White Fabric: one 6½ x 6½in (16.5 x 16.5cm)
- Fabrics G1, G6 and G8

CONSTRUCTION

1. Following the **EPP Template and Fabric Cutting Method** and the **EPP Preparation Method**, cut out and prepare the fabric shapes required using the templates provided.

2. Following the **EPP Assembly Method**, sew the prepared fabric shapes together along their joined edges as shown.

3. Following the **EPP Appliqué Method**, sew the completed EPP unit centrally onto the white fabric square as shown. Be sure to leave a ¼in (0.6cm) gap between the edge of the background fabric and the edges of the EPP unit for the seam allowance. Block is complete. Press and store safely.

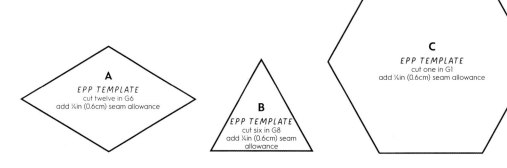

A
EPP TEMPLATE
cut twelve in G6
add ¼in (0.6cm) seam allowance

B
EPP TEMPLATE
cut six in G8
add ¼in (0.6cm) seam allowance

C
EPP TEMPLATE
cut one in G1
add ¼in (0.6cm) seam allowance

BLOCK 10: *Geometric Flower*

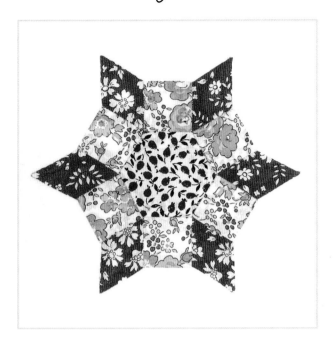

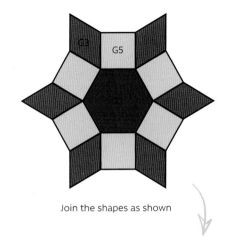

Join the shapes as shown

INFO

- Block Size: 6½in (16.5cm) unfinished, 6in (15.2cm) finished

CUTTING

- White Fabric: one 6½ x 6½in (16.5 x 16.5cm)
- Fabrics G2, G3 and G5

CONSTRUCTION

1. Following the **EPP Template and Fabric Cutting Method** and the **EPP Preparation Method**, cut out and prepare the fabric shapes required using the templates provided.

2. Following the **EPP Assembly Method**, scw the prepared fabric shapes together along their joined edges as shown.

3. Following the **EPP Appliqué Method**, sew the completed EPP unit centrally onto the white fabric square as shown. Be sure to leave a ¼in (0.6cm) gap between the edge of the background fabric and the edges of the EPP unit for the seam allowance. Block is complete. Press and store safely.

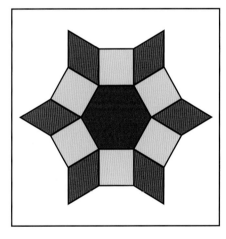

Sew the EPP unit to the white square

A
EPP TEMPLATE
cut six in G5
add ¼in (0.6cm)
seam allowance

B
EPP TEMPLATE
cut six in G3
add ¼in (0.6cm)
seam allowance

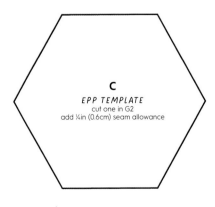

C
EPP TEMPLATE
cut one in G2
add ¼in (0.6cm) seam allowance

BLOCK 71: *Eight-Pointed Star*

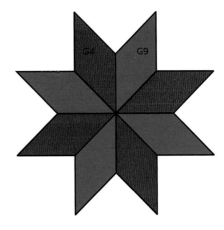

Join the eight points of the star as shown

INFO

- Block Size: 6½in (16.5cm) unfinished, 6in (15.2cm) finished

CUTTING

- White Fabric: one 6½ x 6½in (16.5 x 16.5cm)
- Fabrics G4 and G9

CONSTRUCTION

1. Following the **EPP Template and Fabric Cutting Method** and the **EPP Preparation Method**, cut out and prepare the fabric shapes required using the template provided.

2. Following the **EPP Assembly Method**, sew the prepared fabric shapes together along their joined edges as shown.

3. Following the **EPP Appliqué Method**, sew the completed EPP unit centrally onto the white fabric square as shown. Be sure to leave a ¼in (0.6cm) gap between the edge of the background fabric and the edges of the EPP unit for the seam allowance. Block is complete. Press and store safely.

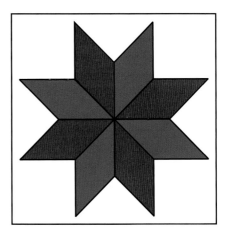

Sew the EPP unit to the white square

A
EPP TEMPLATE
cut four in G4 and G9
add ¼in (0.6cm) seam allowance

BLOCK 72: *Six-Petalled Flower*

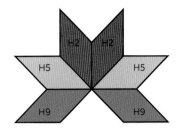

Join the petal shapes as shown

INFO

- Block Size: 6½in (16.5cm) unfinished, 6in (15.2cm) finished

CUTTING

- White Fabric: one 6½ x 6½in (16.5 x 16.5cm)
- Fabrics H2, H5, H7 and H9

CONSTRUCTION

1. Following the **EPP Template and Fabric Cutting Method**, cut out the fabric shapes required using template A. Following the **Raw Edge Appliqué Preparation Method**, prepare required fabric pieces using templates B and C.

2. Following the **EPP Preparation Method**, prepare the template A 'petal' pieces. Following the **EPP Assembly Method**, sew them together along their joined edges as shown.

3. Following the **Raw Edge Appliqué Method**, sew template B and C fabric pieces onto the white fabric square as shown.

4. Following the **EPP Appliqué Method**, sew the completed EPP unit onto the white fabric square on top of the stem as shown. Block is complete. Press and store safely.

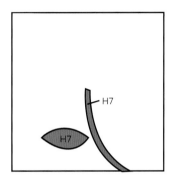

Appliqué the stem and leaf to the white square

Sew the EPP unit in place

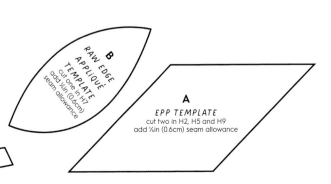

C
RAW EDGE APPLIQUÉ TEMPLATE
cut one in H7
add ¼in (0.6cm) seam allowance

B
RAW EDGE APPLIQUÉ TEMPLATE
cut one in H7
add ¼in (0.6cm) seam allowance

A
EPP TEMPLATE
cut two in H2, H5 and H9
add ¼in (0.6cm) seam allowance

BLOCK 13: Shamrock

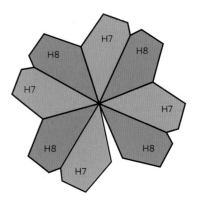

Join the leaf shapes as shown

Appliqué the stem to the white square

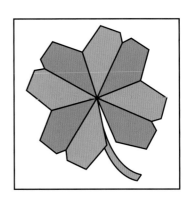

Sew the EPP unit in place

INFO

- Block Size: 6½in (16.5cm) unfinished, 6in (15.2cm) finished

CUTTING

- White Fabric: one 6½ x 6½in (16.5 x 16.5cm)
- Fabrics H7 and H8

CONSTRUCTION

1. Following the **EPP Template and Fabric Cutting Method**, cut out the fabric shapes required using template A, and reversing the template as instructed to do so. Following the **Raw Edge Appliqué Preparation Method**, prepare required fabric piece using template B.

2. Following the **EPP Preparation Method**, prepare the template A 'leaf' pieces. Following the **EPP Assembly Method**, sew them together along their joined edges as shown.

3. Following the **Raw Edge Appliqué Method**, sew Template B 'stem' piece onto the white fabric square as shown.

4. Following the **EPP Appliqué Method**, sew the completed EPP unit onto the white fabric square on top of the stem as shown. Block is complete. Press and store safely.

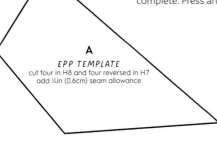

A
EPP TEMPLATE
cut four in H8 and four reversed in H7
add ¼in (0.6cm) seam allowance

B
RAW EDGE APPLIQUÉ TEMPLATE
cut one in H7
add ¼in (0.6cm) seam allowance

BLOCK 74: Simple Butterfly

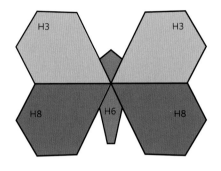

Join the shapes as shown

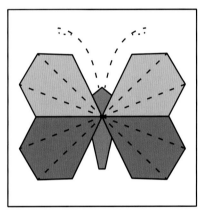

Sew the EPP unit to the white square and add running stitch lines

INFO

- Block Size: 6½in (16.5cm) unfinished, 6in (15.2cm) finished

CUTTING

- White Fabric: one 6½ x 6½in (16.5 x 16.5cm)
- Fabrics H3, H6 and H8

CONSTRUCTION

1. Following the **EPP Template and Fabric Cutting Method** and the **EPP Preparation Method**, cut out and prepare the fabric shapes required using the templates provided.

2. Following the **EPP Assembly Method**, sew the prepared fabric shapes together along their joined edges as shown.

3. Following the **EPP Appliqué Method**, sew the completed EPP unit centrally onto the white fabric square as shown.

4. Following the **Running Stitch Method**, stitch the decorative lines in colours of your choice. Block is complete. Press and store safely.

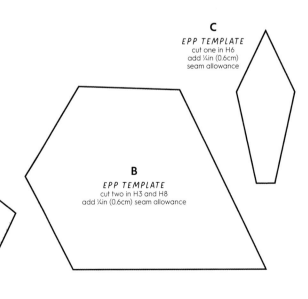

C
EPP TEMPLATE
cut one in H6
add ¼in (0.6cm)
seam allowance

B
EPP TEMPLATE
cut two in H3 and H8
add ¼in (0.6cm) seam allowance

A
EPP TEMPLATE
cut one in H6
add ¼in (0.6cm)
seam allowance

BLOCK 75: Diamond

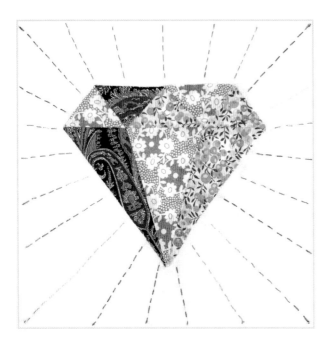

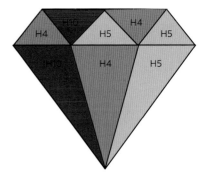

Join the shapes as shown

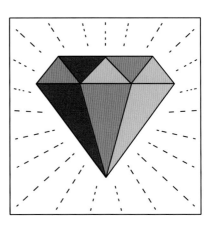

Sew the EPP unit to the white square
and add running stitch lines

INFO

- Block Size: 6½in (16.5cm) unfinished, 6in (15.2cm) finished

CUTTING

- White Fabric: one 6½ x 6½in (16.5 x 16.5cm)
- Fabrics H4, H5 and H10

CONSTRUCTION

1. Following the **EPP Template and Fabric Cutting Method** and the **EPP Preparation Method**, cut out and prepare the fabric shapes required using the templates provided, and reversing templates A and B as instructed to do so.

2. Following the **EPP Assembly Method**, sew the prepared fabric shapes together along their joined edges as shown.

3. Following the **EPP Appliqué Method**, sew the completed EPP unit centrally onto the white fabric square as shown.

3. Following the **Running Stitch Method**, stitch the decorative lines in colours of your choice. Block is complete. Press and store safely.

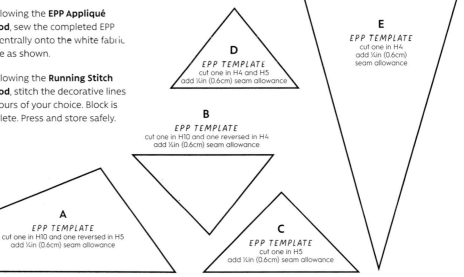

D
EPP TEMPLATE
cut one in H4 and H5
add ¼in (0.6cm) seam allowance

E
EPP TEMPLATE
cut one in H4
add ¼in (0.6cm)
seam allowance

B
EPP TEMPLATE
cut one in H10 and one reversed in H4
add ¼in (0.6cm) seam allowance

A
EPP TEMPLATE
cut one in H10 and one reversed in H5
add ¼in (0.6cm) seam allowance

C
EPP TEMPLATE
cut one in H5
add ¼in (0.6cm) seam allowance

BLOCK 76: Five-Pointed Star

INFO

- Block Size: 6½in (16.5cm) unfinished, 6in (15.2cm) finished

CUTTING

- White Fabric: one 6½ x 6½in (16.5 x 16.5cm)
- Fabrics G3 and G4

CONSTRUCTION

1. Following the **EPP Template and Fabric Cutting Method** and the **EPP Preparation Method**, cut out and prepare the fabric shapes required using the template provided, and reversing the template as instructed to do so.

2. Following the **EPP Assembly Method**, sew the prepared fabric shapes together along their joined edges as shown.

Tip: Remember, before sewing the star together, lay it out flat to make sure all the pieces are oriented correctly.

3. Following the **EPP Appliqué Method**, sew the completed EPP unit centrally onto the white fabric square as shown.

4. Following the **Running Stitch Method**, stitch the decorative lines in colours of your choice. Block is complete. Press and store safely.

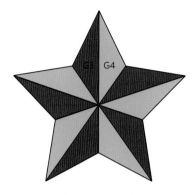

Join the shapes as shown

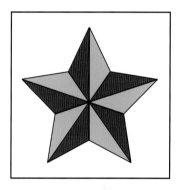

Sew the EPP unit to the white square

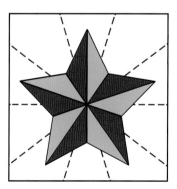

Add running stitch lines

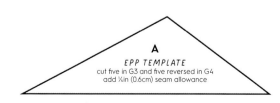

A

EPP TEMPLATE
cut five in G3 and five reversed in G4
add ¼in (0.6cm) seam allowance

BLOCK 77: Mixed Dresden

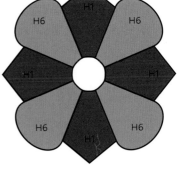

Join the shapes as shown

INFO

- Block Size: 6½in (16.5cm) unfinished, 6in (15.2cm) finished

CUTTING

- White Fabric: one 6½ x 6½in (16.5 x 16.5cm) and template A
- Fabrics H1 and H6

CONSTRUCTION

1. Following the **EPP Template and Fabric Cutting Method**, cut out the fabric shapes required using the templates provided.

2. Following the **EPP Preparation Method**, prepare the template B and C fabric pieces. Following the **EPP Assembly Method**, sew them together along their joined edges.

3. Following the **EPP Appliqué Method**, sew the EPP unit centrally onto the white fabric square.

4. Following the **EPP Preparation Method** for convex shapes, prepare template A fabric piece; sew it onto the centre of the block, following the **EPP Appliqué Method**. Block is complete. Press and store safely.

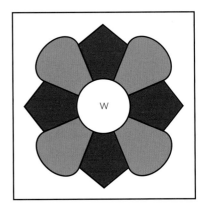

Sew the EPP unit to the white square and appliqué the circle over the centre

A
EPP TEMPLATE
cut one in white fabric
add ¼in (0.6cm) seam allowance

B
EPP TEMPLATE
cut four in H1
add ¼in (0.6cm) seam allowance

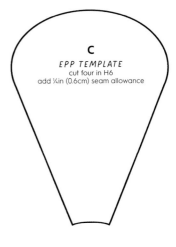

C
EPP TEMPLATE
cut four in H6
add ¼in (0.6cm) seam allowance

BLOCK 78: Dresden Plate

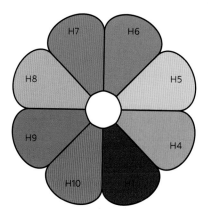

Join the shapes as shown

INFO

- Block Size: 6½in (16.5cm) unfinished, 6in (15.2cm) finished

CUTTING

- White Fabric: one 6½ x 6½in (16.5 x 16.5cm) and template A
- Fabrics H1, H4, H5, H6, H7, H8, H9 and H10

CONSTRUCTION

1. Following the **EPP Template Preparation and Cutting Method**, cut out the fabric shapes required using the templates provided.

2. Following the **EPP Preparation Method**, prepare the template B fabric pieces. Following the **EPP Assembly Method**, sew them together along their joined edges as shown.

3. Following the **EPP Appliqué Method**, sew the EPP unit centrally onto the white fabric square

4. Following the **EPP Preparation Method** for convex shapes, prepare the template A fabric piece; sew it onto the centre of the block, following the **EPP Appliqué Method**. Block is complete. Press and store safely.

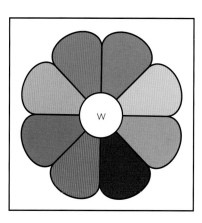

Sew the EPP unit to the white square and appliqué the fabric circle onto the centre

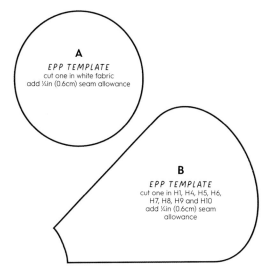

A
EPP TEMPLATE
cut one in white fabric
add ¼in (0.6cm) seam allowance

B
EPP TEMPLATE
cut one in H1, H4, H5, H6,
H7, H8, H9 and H10
add ¼in (0.6cm) seam
allowance

BLOCK 79: English Rose

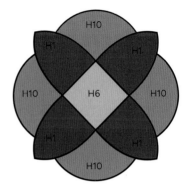

Join the shapes as shown

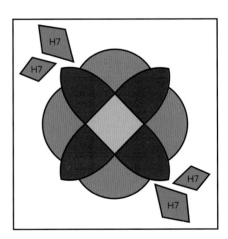

Sew the EPP unit to the white square,
then sew the leaves in place

INFO

- Block Size: 6½in (16.5cm) unfinished, 6in (15.2cm) finished

CUTTING

- White Fabric: one 6½ x 6½in (16.5 x 16.5cm)
- Fabrics H1, H6, H7 and H10

CONSTRUCTION

1. Following the **EPP Template Preparation and Cutting Method**, cut out the fabric shapes required using the templates provided.

2. Following the **EPP Preparation Method**, prepare all pieces.

3. Following the **EPP Assembly Method**, sew template A, D and E fabric pieces together along their joined edges as shown. Then, following the **EPP Appliqué Method**, sew the completed EPP unit centrally onto the white fabric square.

4. Following the **EPP Appliqué Method**, sew template B and C fabric pieces onto the block, leaving a ¼in (0.6cm) gap around the outside for the seam allowance. Block is complete. Press and store safely.

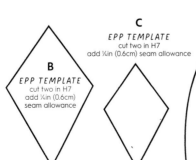

A
EPP TEMPLATE
cut one in H6
add ¼in (0.6cm)
seam allowance

B
EPP TEMPLATE
cut two in H7
add ¼in (0.6cm)
seam allowance

C
EPP TEMPLATE
cut two in H7
add ¼in (0.6cm) seam allowance

D
EPP TEMPLATE
cut four in H1
add ¼in (0.6cm)
seam allowance

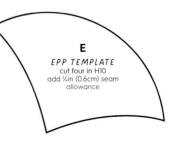

E
EPP TEMPLATE
cut four in H10
add ¼in (0.6cm) seam
allowance

BLOCK 80: *Shell*

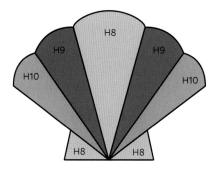

Join the shapes as shown

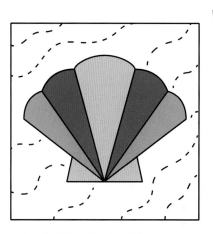

Sew the EPP unit to the white square and add running stitch lines

INFO

- Block Size: 6½in (16.5cm) unfinished, 6in (15.2cm) finished

CUTTING

- White Fabric: one 6½ x 6½in (16.5 x 16.5cm)
- Fabrics H8, H9 and H10

CONSTRUCTION

1. Following the **EPP Template and Fabric Cutting Method** and the **EPP Preparation Method**, cut out and prepare the fabric shapes required using the templates provided, and reversing templates A, B and C as instructed to do so.

2. Following the **EPP Assembly Method**, sew the prepared fabric shapes together along their joined edges as shown.

3. Following the **EPP Appliqué Method**, sew the EPP unit centrally onto the white fabric square.

4. Following the **Running Stitch Method**, stitch the decorative lines. Block is complete. Press and store safely.

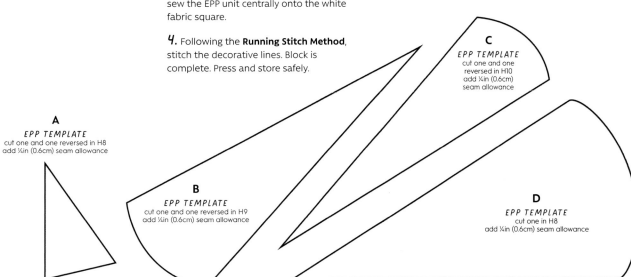

A
EPP TEMPLATE
cut one and one reversed in H8
add ¼in (0.6cm) seam allowance

B
EPP TEMPLATE
cut one and one reversed in H9
add ¼in (0.6cm) seam allowance

C
EPP TEMPLATE
cut one and one reversed in H10
add ¼in (0.6cm) seam allowance

D
EPP TEMPLATE
cut one in H8
add ¼in (0.6cm) seam allowance

Raw Edge Appliqué

ABOUT RAW EDGE APPLIQUÉ

Raw edge appliqué involves cut pieces of fabric being placed onto a background and sewn down to secure. It is a simple and fast method of appliqué. It may be likened to collaging with fabric and intricate, often organic, pictorial designs can be easily achieved. The edges of each cut fabric piece are left raw and unbound, with stitches close to the edge helping to prevent fraying. Stitches may be completed using the sewing machine or by hand, and may be a simple running/straight stitch or more decorative.

Types of quilts commonly using this construction method include Pictoral, Autograph/Album and Broderie Perse.

Recommended Tools: double-sided fabric adhesive, craft glue stick, scrap cotton fabric, heat erasable pen; fray stop may also prove useful

RAW EDGE APPLIQUÉ PREPARATION METHOD

Use the following method to prepare your raw edge appliqué pieces. All raw edge appliqué templates have been provided in the orientation required for this preparation method. However, some will also need to be reversed to make a mirrored pair of shapes, so be sure to do this when instructed.

1. Roughly cut a piece of double-sided fabric adhesive, using paper scissors, to be slightly larger than the template or group of templates you intend to cut out. Iron the fabric adhesive onto the wrong side of the fabric.

2. Trace the templates required onto standard printer paper (80gsm) using a pen or pencil. As well as the template letter and any cutting information, it's a good idea to add the block number and name to each template. Roughly cut around the traced template using paper scissors.

3. Use a standard craft glue stick to glue the paper template traced side up onto the adhesive backing side of the fabric. Ensure the area of the traced shape is within the area of the adhesive backing. Cut out the traced shape using fabric scissors. Leave the paper template attached to the cut shape for easy identification.

HANDY TIPS

The glue side of the double-sided fabric adhesive feels slightly rough to touch and looks shiny. The paper side feels smooth. Never place your iron onto the glue side as this dirties the iron and is very difficult to remove. Similarly, try not to iron any of the glue onto your ironing board.

To be safe when working with double-sided fabric adhesive, always iron it between scrap cotton fabric pieces. Have one scrap piece covering the ironing board and another covering the fabric to protect your iron.

If fitting lots of shapes onto a smaller piece of fabric it would be best to simply iron adhesive to the entire fabric piece. This is called 'block fusing'.

If tracing multiple shapes to be cut out of the same fabric, do leave appropriate space between the shapes for ease of cutting. However, do keep in mind the dimensions of the fabric and if you think it will be a tight fit, it's safest to cut out a piece of adhesive to match.

RAW EDGE APPLIQUÉ METHOD

1. Peel away the paper backing from the adhesive-backed fabric shape and place it right side up on top of the background fabric. Iron in place. If the shapes need to be ironed down in a certain order, be sure to follow that as directed.

2. Sew around the edge of the shape, about ⅟₁₆in (0.1–0.2cm) from the edge, sewing right up into any points. Stitches may be made by hand or with a sewing machine. On the sewing machine you could use straight stitch, zig zag stitch or any other decorative stitch to sew along the shape's edge. With a hand sewing needle and thread you could use a running stitch, backstitch or blanket stitch. A straight stitch/running stitch would be simplest and fastest; a zig zag/blanket stitch creates more of a feature of the thread. Match thread colour to the fabric for a seamless finish or choose a contrasting colour for emphasis.

3. Repeat steps 1 and 2 with each layer of shapes as needed, sewing each layer down before the next is added.

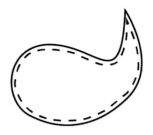

Straight/running stitch
by machine or hand

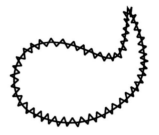

Zig zag stitch by machine

Blanket stitch by hand

Be sure to stitch into points/tips of shapes

HANDY TIPS

When peeling away the adhesive's paper backing, take a needle and lightly score the paper backing, just enough to cause a thin tear. This will make it easy to remove.

The nature of raw edge appliqué means the cut fabric shapes may fray a little around their edges, but fray stop can be helpful in preventing this. Apply it before ironing the cut shapes to the background fabric.

Drop the feed dog, if your sewing machine can do so. This allows total control over the stitch length and direction. It may take some practice to gain confidence sewing this way, but once mastered it will make sewing curves much easier.

If you cannot drop the feed dogs, simply pause sewing and pivot the fabric with the needle down as often as necessary to achieve smoothly curved stitching.

A free-motion quilting foot allows for more visibility in the area being sewn and therefore helps greatly with raw edge appliqué. If using a regular foot, however, simply pause sewing, leave the needle down and lift the foot to check your positioning.

TEMPLATES

You will need these templates for Blocks 83, 85, 87, 89, 94, 95 and 99. For all other blocks, the required templates are shown on the block instruction pages. All templates are shown at full size and printable versions can be downloaded from www.bookmarkedhub.com. Be sure to also reverse the template when instructed to do so.

C
RAW EDGE APPLIQUÉ TEMPLATE
cut three in J6

D
RAW EDGE APPLIQUÉ TEMPLATE
cut one in J6

BLOCK 89
STRAWBERRIES

A
RAW EDGE APPLIQUÉ TEMPLATE
cut one in J7

E
RAW EDGE APPLIQUÉ TEMPLATE
cut one in J6

B
RAW EDGE APPLIQUÉ TEMPLATE
cut one in J7

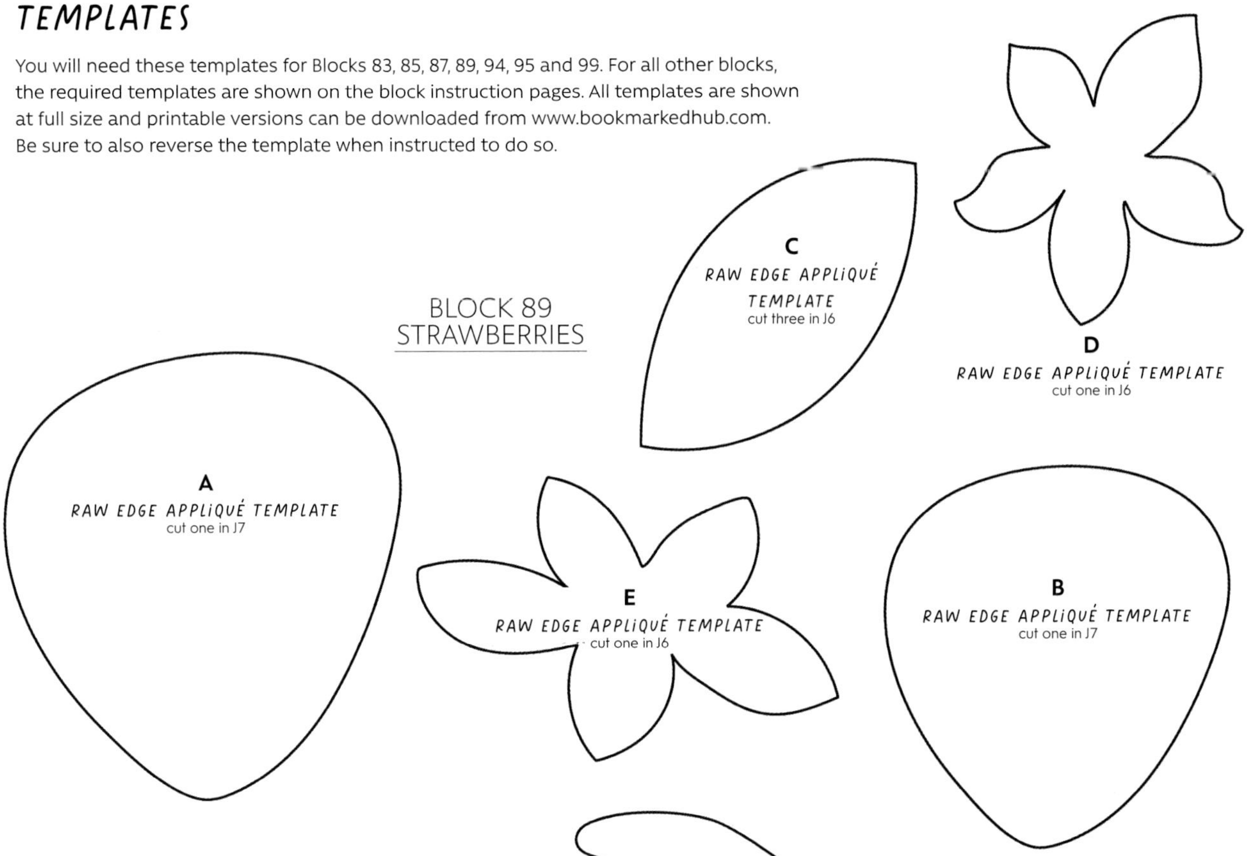

BLOCK 83
MONSTERA LEAF

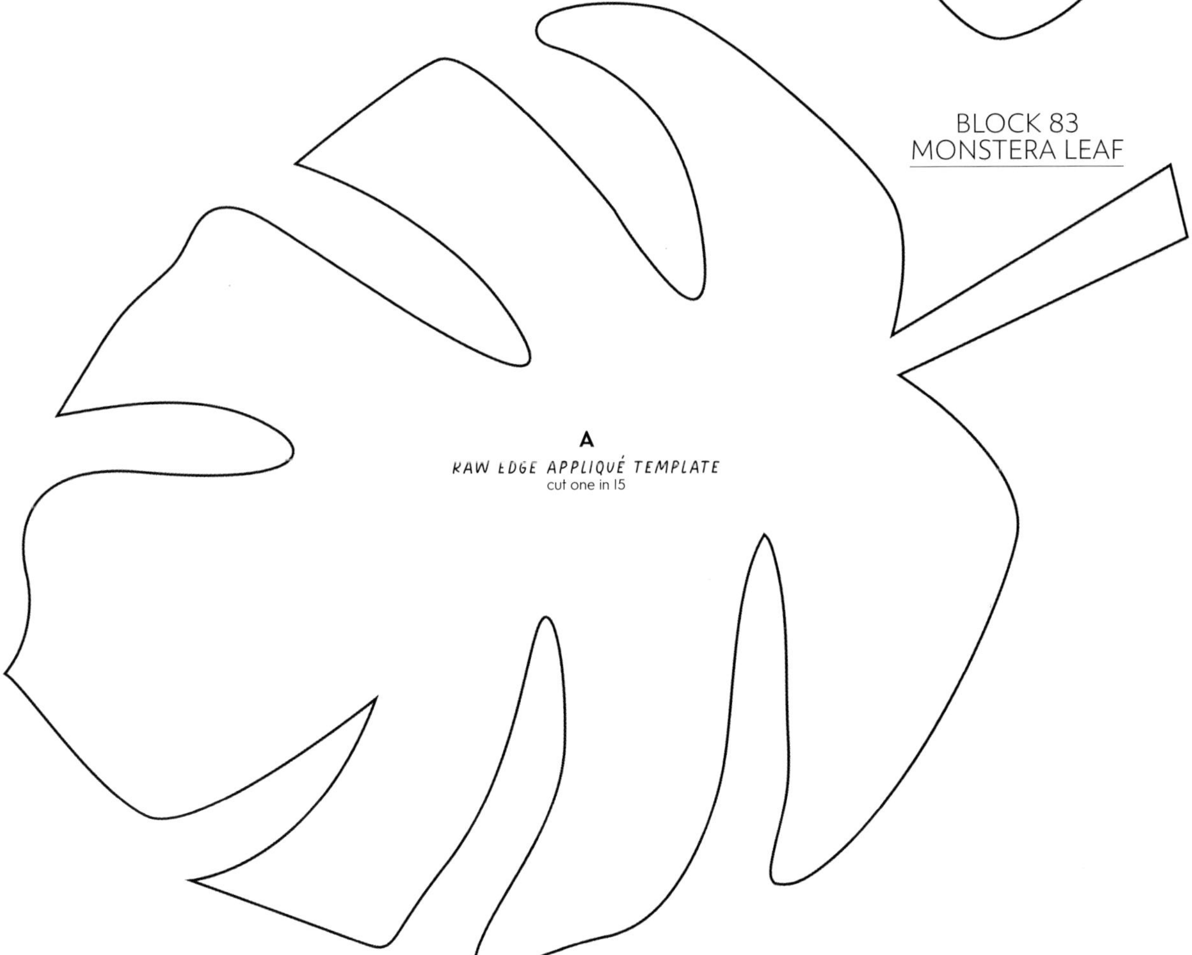

A
RAW EDGE APPLIQUÉ TEMPLATE
cut one in I5

RAW EDGE APPLIQUÉ

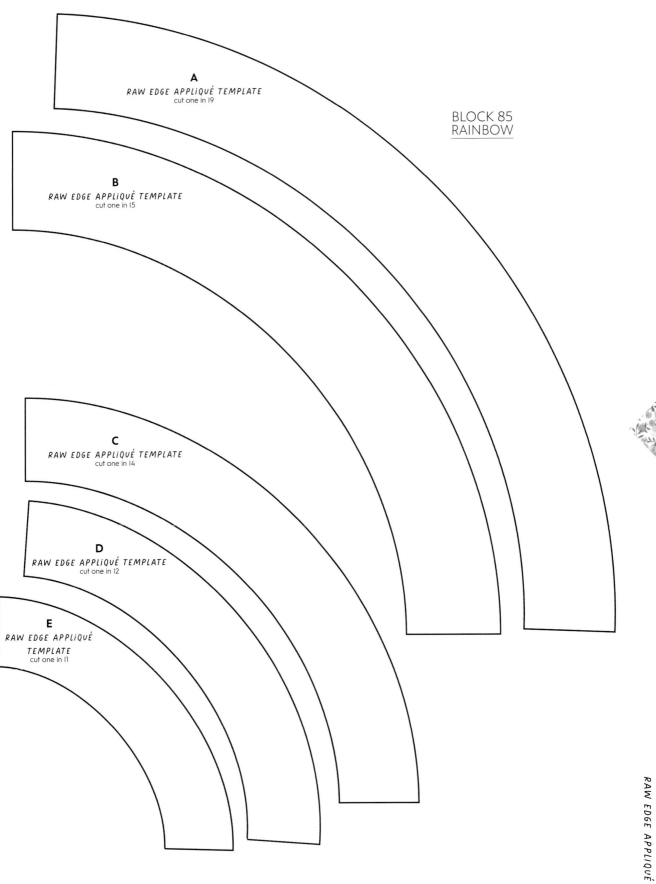

A
RAW EDGE APPLIQUÉ TEMPLATE
cut one in 19

B
RAW EDGE APPLIQUÉ TEMPLATE
cut one in 15

C
RAW EDGE APPLIQUÉ TEMPLATE
cut one in 14

D
RAW EDGE APPLIQUÉ TEMPLATE
cut one in 12

E
RAW EDGE APPLIQUÉ TEMPLATE
cut one in 11

BLOCK 85
RAINBOW

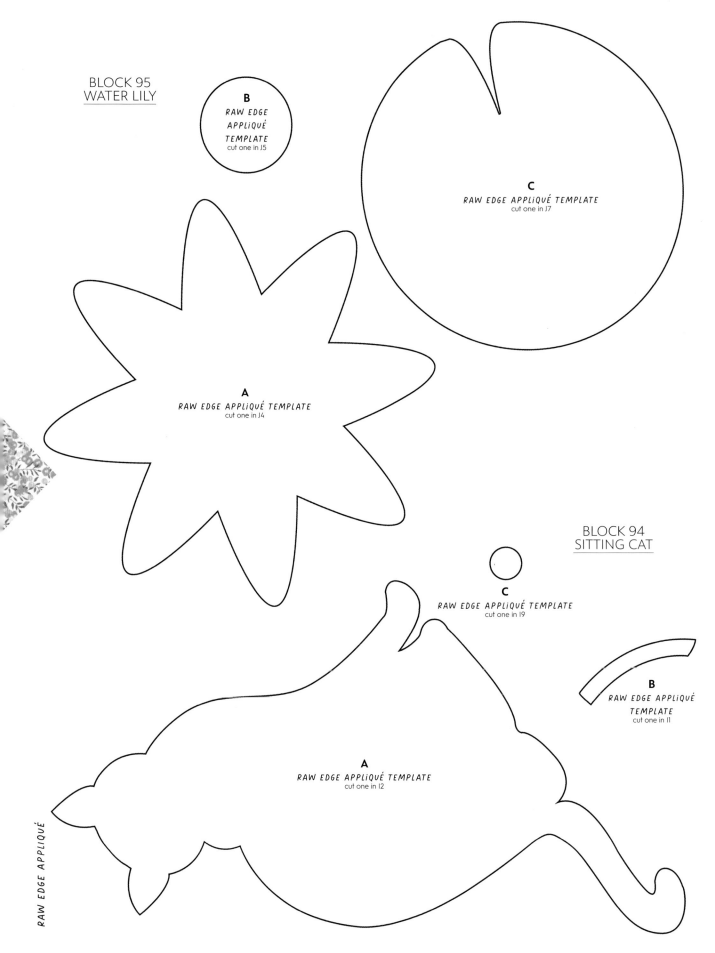

BLOCK 95
WATER LILY

B

RAW EDGE APPLIQUÉ TEMPLATE
cut one in J5

C

RAW EDGE APPLIQUÉ TEMPLATE
cut one in J7

A

RAW EDGE APPLIQUÉ TEMPLATE
cut one in J4

BLOCK 94
SITTING CAT

C

RAW EDGE APPLIQUÉ TEMPLATE
cut one in I9

B

RAW EDGE APPLIQUÉ TEMPLATE
cut one in I1

A

RAW EDGE APPLIQUÉ TEMPLATE
cut one in I2

RAW EDGE APPLIQUÉ

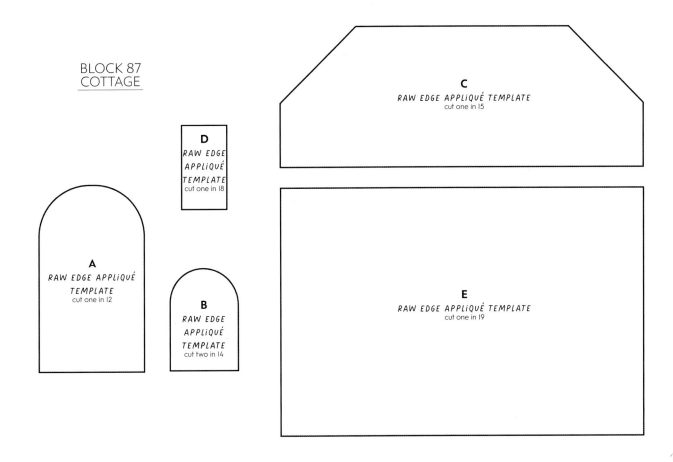

BLOCK 87
COTTAGE

D
RAW EDGE APPLIQUÉ TEMPLATE
cut one in 18

C
RAW EDGE APPLIQUÉ TEMPLATE
cut one in 15

A
RAW EDGE APPLIQUÉ TEMPLATE
cut one in 12

B
RAW EDGE APPLIQUÉ TEMPLATE
cut two in 14

E
RAW EDGE APPLIQUÉ TEMPLATE
cut one in 19

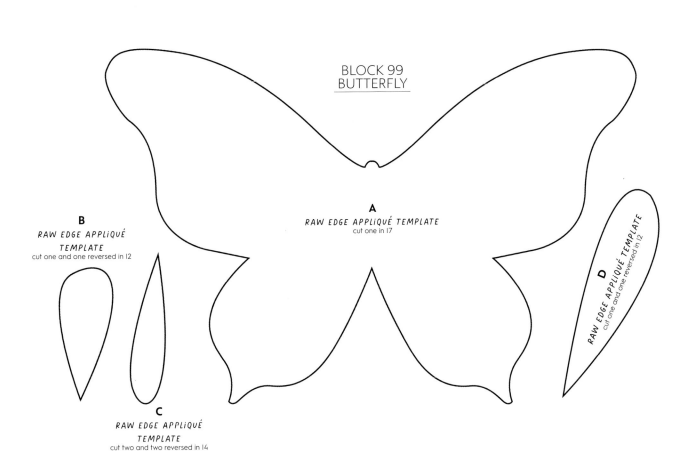

BLOCK 99
BUTTERFLY

B
RAW EDGE APPLIQUÉ TEMPLATE
cut one and one reversed in 12

A
RAW EDGE APPLIQUÉ TEMPLATE
cut one in 17

C
RAW EDGE APPLIQUÉ TEMPLATE
cut two and two reversed in 14

D
RAW EDGE APPLIQUÉ TEMPLATE
cut one and one reversed in 12

BLOCK 81: Double Heart

Sew the shapes to the white square
in the layer order specified

INFO

- Block Size: 6½in (16.5cm) unfinished, 6in (15.2cm) finished

CUTTING

- White Fabric: one 6½ x 6½in (16.5 x 16.5cm)
- Fabrics I1 and I2

CONSTRUCTION

1. Following the **Raw Edge Appliqué Preparation Method**, prepare the fabric pieces.

2. Following the **Raw Edge Appliqué Method**, iron and sew the shapes centrally onto the white fabric square in the layer order shown. Block is complete. Press and store safely.

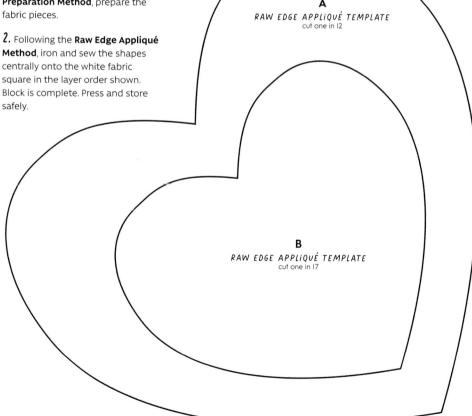

A
RAW EDGE APPLIQUÉ TEMPLATE
cut one in I2

B
RAW EDGE APPLIQUÉ TEMPLATE
cut one in I7

BLOCK 82: *Shooting Stars*

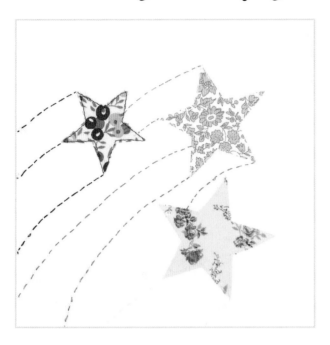

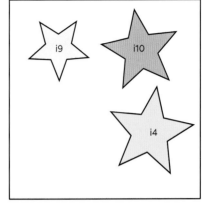

Sew the shapes to the white square

INFO

- Block Size: 6½in (16.5cm) unfinished, 6in (15.2cm) finished

CUTTING

- White Fabric: one 6½ x 6½in (16.5 x 16.5cm)
- Fabrics I4, I9 and I10

CONSTRUCTION

1. Following the **Raw Edge Appliqué Preparation Method**, prepare all the fabric pieces.

2. Following the **Raw Edge Appliqué Method**, iron and sew the shapes onto the white fabric square as shown. Be sure to leave a ¼in (0.6cm) gap around the outside for the seam allowance.

3. Following the **Running Stitch Method**, stitch the decorative lines in colours of your choice. Block is complete. Press and store safely.

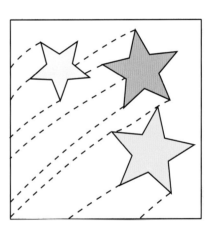

Add running stitch lines

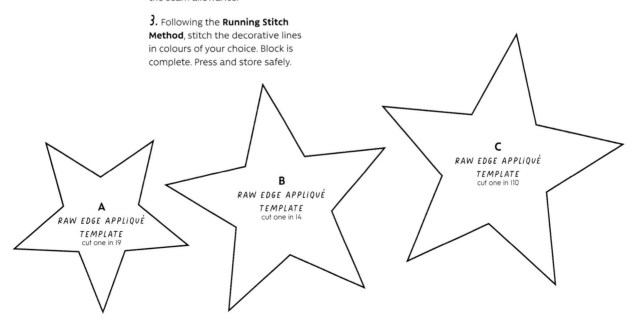

A
RAW EDGE APPLIQUÉ TEMPLATE
cut one in I9

B
RAW EDGE APPLIQUÉ TEMPLATE
cut one in I4

C
RAW EDGE APPLIQUÉ TEMPLATE
cut one in I10

BLOCK 83: Monstera Leaf

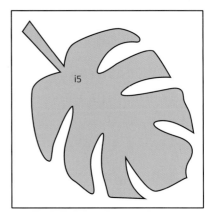

Sew the shape to the white square

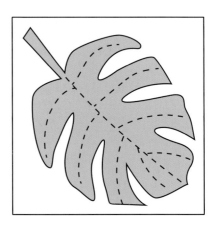

Add running stitch lines

INFO

- Block Size: 6½in (16.5cm) unfinished, 6in (15.2cm) finished

CUTTING

- White Fabric: one 6½ x 6½in (16.5 x 16.5cm)
- Fabric I5

Refer to the start of the Raw Edge Appliqué chapter for the template.

CONSTRUCTION

I. Following the **Raw Edge Appliqué Preparation Method**, prepare the fabric piece.

2. Following the **Raw Edge Appliqué Method**, iron and sew the shape centrally onto the white fabric square as shown. Be sure to leave a ¼in (0.6cm) gap between the edge of the background fabric and the edges of the appliqué for the seam allowance.

3. Following the **Running Stitch Method**, stitch the decorative lines in colours of your choice. Block Is complete. Press and store safely.

BLOCK 84: Butterfly Trio

Sew the shapes to the white square

Add running stitch lines

INFO

- Block Size: 6½in (16.5cm) unfinished, 6in (15.2cm) finished

CUTTING

- White Fabric: one 6½ x 6½in (16.5 x 16.5cm)
- Fabrics J2, J5 and J10

CONSTRUCTION

1. Following the **Raw Edge Appliqué Preparation Method**, prepare the fabric pieces.

2. Following the **Raw Edge Appliqué Method**, iron and sew the shapes onto the white fabric square as shown. Be sure to leave a ¼in (0.6cm) gap around the outside for the seam allowance.

3. Following the **Running Stitch Method**, stitch the decorative lines in colours of your choice. Block is complete. Press and store safely.

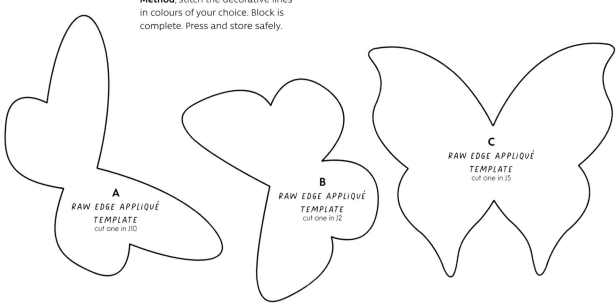

A
RAW EDGE APPLIQUÉ TEMPLATE
cut one in J10

B
RAW EDGE APPLIQUÉ TEMPLATE
cut one in J2

C
RAW EDGE APPLIQUÉ TEMPLATE
cut one in J5

BLOCK 85: Rainbow

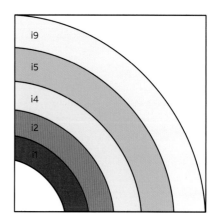

Sew the shapes to the white square

INFO

- Block Size: 6½in (16.5cm) unfinished, 6in (15.2cm) finished

CUTTING

- White Fabric: one 6½ x 6½in (16.5 x 16.5cm)
- Fabrics I1, I2, I4, I5 and I9

Refer to the start of the Raw Edge Appliqué chapter for the templates.

CONSTRUCTION

1. Following the **Raw Edge Appliqué Preparation Method**, prepare all the fabric pieces.

2. Following the **Raw Edge Appliqué Method**, iron and sew the shapes onto the white fabric square as shown. Be sure to leave a ¼in (0.6cm) gap between the edge of the background fabric and the edges of the appliqué for the seam allowance. Block is complete. Press and store safely.

Fabric Focus

Alice W was created for Spring/Summer 2015, to celebrate 150 years since the first publication of Lewis Carroll's Alice's Adventures in Wonderland. It is loosely inspired by an archival 1936 print by D.S., the enigmatic Liberty designer. Small playing-card symbols form a unique sub pattern between the daisies.

BLOCK 86: Flying Bird

Sew the shapes to the white square,
then add running stitch lines

INFO

- Block Size: 6½in (16.5cm) unfinished, 6in (15.2cm) finished

CUTTING

- White Fabric: one 6½ x 6½in (16.5 x 16.5cm)
- Fabrics 12 and 16

CONSTRUCTION

1. Following the **Raw Edge Appliqué Preparation Method**, prepare the fabric pieces.

2. Following the **Raw Edge Appliqué Method**, iron and sew the shapes onto the white fabric square as shown. Be sure to leave a ¼in (0.6cm) gap around the outside for the seam allowance.

3. Following the **Running Stitch Method**, stitch the decorative lines in colours of your choice. Block is complete. Press and store safely.

B
RAW EDGE APPLIQUÉ
TEMPLATE
cut one in 12

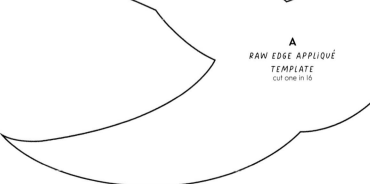

A
RAW EDGE APPLIQUÉ
TEMPLATE
cut one in 16

BLOCK 87: *Cottage*

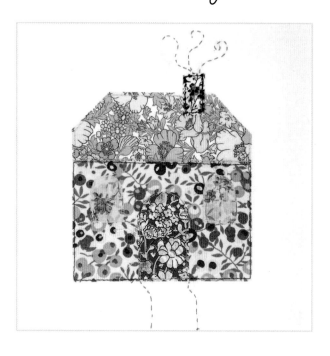

INFO

- Block Size: 6½in (16.5cm) unfinished, 6in (15.2cm) finished

CUTTING

- White Fabric: one 6½ x 6½in (16.5 x 16.5cm)
- Fabrics I2, I4, I5, I8 and I9

Refer to the start of the Raw Edge Appliqué chapter for the templates.

CONSTRUCTION

1. Following the **Raw Edge Appliqué Preparation Method**, prepare all the fabric pieces.

2. Following the **Raw Edge Appliqué Method**, iron and sew the shapes centrally onto the white fabric square in the layer order shown.

3. Following the **Running Stitch Method**, stitch the decorative lines in colours of your choice. Block is complete. Press and store safely.

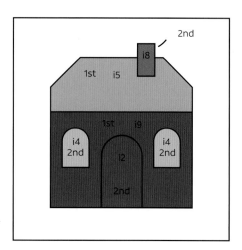

Sew the shapes to the white square in the layer order specified

Add running stitch lines

BLOCK 88: *Bloom*

Sew the shapes to the white square

INFO

- Block Size: 6½in (16.5cm) unfinished, 6in (15.2cm) finished

CUTTING

- White Fabric: one 6½ x 6½in (16.5 x 16.5cm)
- Fabrics J3 and J5

CONSTRUCTION

1. Following the **Raw Edge Appliqué Preparation Method**, prepare the fabric pieces.

2. Following the **Raw Edge Appliqué Method**, iron and sew the shapes centrally onto the white fabric square as shown. Be sure to leave a ¼in (0.6cm) gap between the edge of the background fabric and the edges of the appliqué for the seam allowance. Block is complete. Press and store safely.

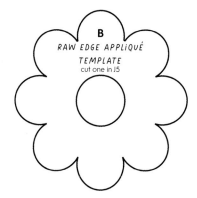

B
RAW EDGE APPLIQUÉ TEMPLATE
cut one in J5

A
RAW EDGE APPLIQUÉ TEMPLATE
cut five in J3

BLOCK 89: Strawberries

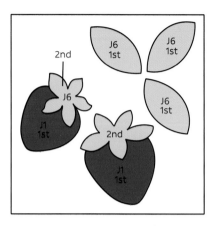

Sew the shapes to the white square
in the layer order specified

Add running stitch lines

INFO

- Block Size: 6½in (16.5cm) unfinished, 6in (15.2cm) finished

CUTTING

- White Fabric: one 6½ x 6½in (16.5 x 16.5cm)
- Fabrics J1 and J6

Refer to the start of the Raw Edge Appliqué chapter for the templates.

CONSTRUCTION

1. Following the **Raw Edge Appliqué Preparation Method**, prepare all the fabric pieces.

2. Following the **Raw Edge Appliqué Method**, iron and sew the shapes onto the white fabric square in the layer order shown. Be sure to leave a ¼in (0.6cm) gap between the edge of the background fabric and the edges of the appliqué for the seam allowance.

3. Following the **Running Stitch Method**, stitch the decorative lines in colours of your choice. Block is complete. Press and store safely.

Fabric Focus

Elysian Day is an archival classic, characterised by its exuberant retro-infused blooms. The design first appeared in a pattern book dating from the late 1910s or early 1920s and was originally used for both dress and furnishing fabrics.

BLOCK 90: *Tulips*

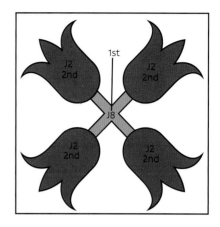

Sew the shapes to the white square
in the layer order specified

INFO

- Block Size: 6½in (16.5cm) unfinished, 6in (15.2cm) finished

CUTTING

- White Fabric: one 6½ x 6½in (16.5 x 16.5cm)
- Fabrics J2 and J8

CONSTRUCTION

1. Following the **Raw Edge Appliqué Preparation Method**, prepare the fabric pieces.

2. Following the **Raw Edge Appliqué Method**, iron and sew the shapes centrally onto the white fabric square in the layer order shown. Be sure to leave a ¼in (0.6cm) gap between the edge of the background fabric and the edges of the appliqué for the seam allowance. Block is complete. Press and store safely.

A
RAW EDGE APPLIQUÉ TEMPLATE
cut one in J8

B
RAW EDGE APPLIQUÉ TEMPLATE
cut four in J2

BLOCK 91: Petal Power

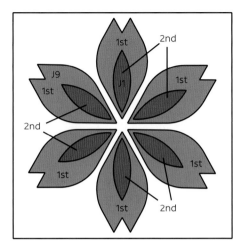

Sew the shapes to the white square
in the layer order specified

INFO

- Block Size: 6½in (16.5cm) unfinished, 6in (15.2cm) finished

CUTTING

- White Fabric: one 6½ x 6½in (16.5 x 16.5cm)
- Fabrics J1 and J9

CONSTRUCTION

1. Following the **Raw Edge Appliqué Preparation Method**, prepare the fabric pieces.

2. Following the **Raw Edge Appliqué Method**, iron and sew the shapes centrally onto the white fabric square in the layer order shown. Be sure to leave a ¼in (0.6cm) gap between the edge of the background fabric and the edges of the appliqué for the seam allowance. Block is complete. Press and store safely.

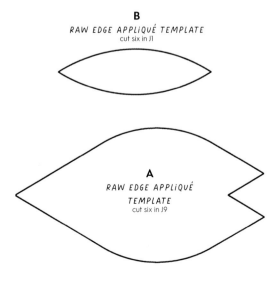

B
RAW EDGE APPLIQUÉ TEMPLATE
cut six in J1

A
RAW EDGE APPLIQUÉ TEMPLATE
cut six in J9

BLOCK 92: Dragonfly

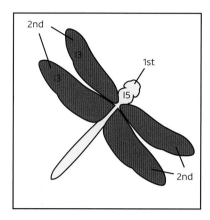

Sew the shapes to the white square
in the layer order specified

INFO

- Block Size: 6½in (16.5cm) unfinished, 6in (15.2cm) finished

CUTTING

- White Fabric: one 6½ x 6½in (16.5 x 16.5cm)
- Fabrics I3 and I5

CONSTRUCTION

1. Following the **Raw Edge Appliqué Preparation Method**, prepare all the fabric pieces.

2. Following the **Raw Edge Appliqué Method**, iron and sew the shapes onto the white fabric square in the layer order shown.

3. Following the **Running Stitch Method**, stitch the decorative lines in colours of your choice. Block is complete. Press and store safely.

Add running stitch lines

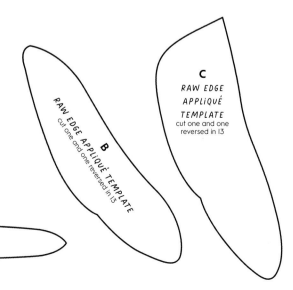

A
RAW EDGE APPLIQUÉ TEMPLATE
cut one in I5

B
RAW EDGE APPLIQUÉ TEMPLATE
cut one and one reversed in I3

C
RAW EDGE APPLIQUÉ TEMPLATE
cut one and one reversed in I3

BLOCK 93: Plum Blossom

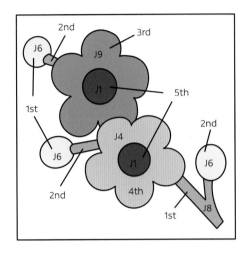

Sew the shapes to the white square
in the layer order specified

INFO

- Block Size: 6½in (16.5cm) unfinished, 6in (15.2cm) finished

CUTTING

- White Fabric: one 6½ x 6½in (16.5 x 16.5cm)
- Fabrics J1, J4, J6, J8 and J9

CONSTRUCTION

1. Following the **Raw Edge Appliqué Preparation Method**, prepare all the fabric pieces.

2. Following the **Raw Edge Appliqué Method**, iron and sew the shapes onto the white fabric square in the layer order shown. Be sure to leave a ¼in (0.6cm) gap between the edge of the background fabric and the edges of the appliqué for the seam allowance. Block is complete. Press and store safely.

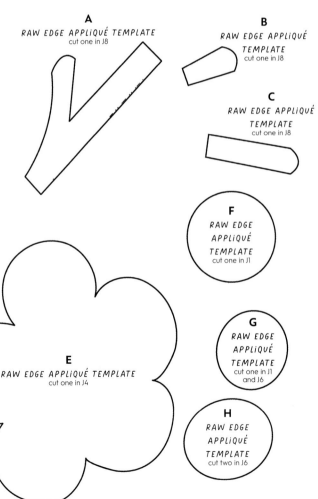

A
RAW EDGE APPLIQUÉ TEMPLATE
cut one in J8

B
RAW EDGE APPLIQUÉ TEMPLATE
cut one in J8

C
RAW EDGE APPLIQUÉ TEMPLATE
cut one in J8

F
RAW EDGE APPLIQUÉ TEMPLATE
cut one in J1

G
RAW EDGE APPLIQUÉ TEMPLATE
cut one in J1 and J6

H
RAW EDGE APPLIQUÉ TEMPLATE
cut two in J6

D
RAW EDGE APPLIQUÉ TEMPLATE
cut one in J9

E
RAW EDGE APPLIQUÉ TEMPLATE
cut one in J4

BLOCK 94: *Sitting Cat*

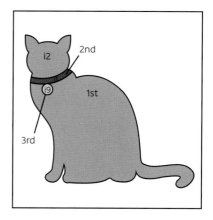

Sew the shapes to the white square
in the layer order specified

Add running stitch lines

INFO

- Block Size: 6½in
  (16.5cm) unfinished, 6in
  (15.2cm) finished

CUTTING

- White Fabric: one 6½ x
  6½in (16.5 x 16.5cm)
- Fabrics I1, I2 and I9

Refer to the start of
the Raw Edge Appliqué
chapter for the templates.

CONSTRUCTION

1. Following the **Raw Edge Appliqué
Preparation Method**, prepare the
fabric pieces.

2. Following the **Raw Edge Appliqué
Method**, iron and sew the shapes
onto the white fabric square in the
layer order shown.

3. Following the **Running Stitch
Method**, stitch the decorative lines
in colours of your choice. Block is
complete. Press and store safely.

BLOCK 95: Water Lily

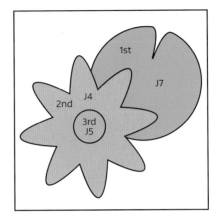

Sew the shapes to the white square
in the layer order specified

Add running stitch lines

INFO

- Block Size: 6½in (16.5cm) unfinished, 6in (15.2cm) finished

CUTTING

- White Fabric: one 6½ x 6½in (16.5 x 16.5cm)
- Fabrics J4, J5 and J7

Refer to the start of the Raw Edge Appliqué chapter for the templates.

CONSTRUCTION

1. Following the **Raw Edge Appliqué Preparation Method**, prepare the fabric pieces.

2. Following the **Raw Edge Appliqué Method**, iron and sew the shapes onto the white fabric square in the layer order shown. Be sure to leave a ¼in (0.6cm) gap between the edge of the background fabric and the edges of the appliqué for the seam allowance.

3. Following the **Running Stitch Method**, stitch the decorative lines in colours of your choice. Block is complete. Press and store safely.

BLOCK 96: Autumn Berries

Sew the shapes to the white square
in the layer order specified

INFO

- Block Size: 6½in (16.5cm) unfinished, 6in (15.2cm) finished

CUTTING

- White Fabric: one 6½ x 6½in (16.5 x 16.5cm)
- Fabrics J7 and J8

CONSTRUCTION

1. Following the **Raw Edge Appliqué Preparation Method**, prepare the fabric pieces.

2. Following the **Raw Edge Appliqué Method**, iron and sew the shapes onto the white fabric square in the layer order shown. Be sure to leave a ¼in (0.6cm) gap between the edge of the background fabric and the edges of the appliqué for the seam allowance. Block is complete. Press and store safely.

A
RAW EDGE APPLIQUÉ TEMPLATE
cut one in J7

B
RAW EDGE APPLIQUÉ TEMPLATE
cut two in J8

C
RAW EDGE APPLIQUÉ TEMPLATE
cut one in J8

BLOCK 97: Sprig

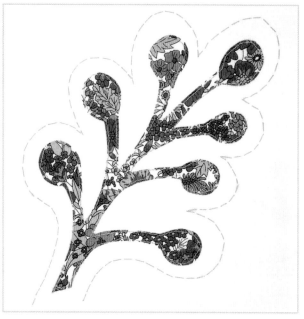

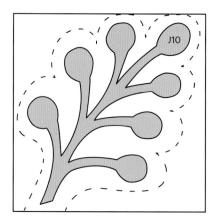

Sew the shape to the white square
then add running stitch outline

INFO

- Block Size: 6½in
  (16.5cm) unfinished, 6in
  (15.2cm) finished

CUTTING

- White Fabric: one 6½ x
  6½in (16.5 x 16.5cm)
- Fabric J10

CONSTRUCTION

1. Following the **Raw Edge Appliqué Preparation Method**, prepare the fabric piece.

2. Following the **Raw Edge Appliqué Method**, iron and sew the shape onto the white fabric square as shown. Be sure to leave a ¼in (0.6cm) gap between the edge of the background fabric and the edges of the appliqué for the seam allowance.

3. Following the **Running Stitch Method**, stitch the decorative lines in colours of your choice. Block is complete. Press and store safely.

A
RAW EDGE APPLIQUÉ TEMPLATE
cut one in J10

BLOCK 98: Bumblebee

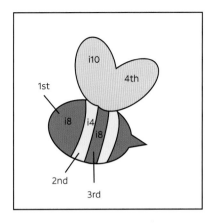

Sew the shapes to the white square
in the layer order specified

Add running stitch lines

INFO

- Block Size: 6½in
  (16.5cm) unfinished, 6in
  (15.2cm) finished

CUTTING

- White Fabric: one 6½ x
  6½in (16.5 x 16.5cm)
- Fabrics I4, I8 and I10

CONSTRUCTION

1. Following the **Raw Edge Appliqué Preparation Method**, prepare all the fabric pieces.

2. Following the **Raw Edge Appliqué Method**, iron and sew the shapes onto the white fabric square in the layer order shown.

3. Following the **Running Stitch Method**, stitch the decorative lines in colours of your choice. Block is complete. Press and store safely.

A
RAW EDGE APPLIQUÉ TEMPLATE
cut one in I8

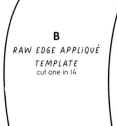

B
RAW EDGE APPLIQUÉ
TEMPLATE
cut one in I4

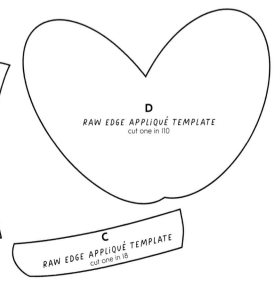

D
RAW EDGE APPLIQUÉ TEMPLATE
cut one in I10

C
RAW EDGE APPLIQUÉ TEMPLATE
cut one in I8

BLOCK 99: *Butterfly*

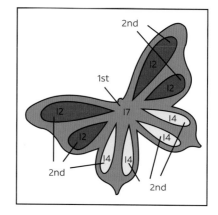

Sew the shapes to the white square
in the layer order specified

Add running stitch lines

INFO

- Block Size: 6½in
  (16.5cm) unfinished, 6in
  (15.2cm) finished

CUTTING

- White Fabric: one 6½ x
  6½in (16.5 x 16.5cm)

- Fabrics I2, I4 and I7

Refer to the start of
the Raw Edge Appliqué
chapter for the template.

CONSTRUCTION

1. Following the **Raw Edge Appliqué Preparation Method**, prepare all the fabric pieces.

2. Following the **Raw Edge Appliqué Method**, iron and sew the shapes onto the white fabric square in the layer order shown. Be sure to leave a ¼in (0.6cm) gap between the edge of the background fabric and the edges of the appliqué for the seam allowance.

3. Following the **Running Stitch Method**, stitch the decorative lines in colours of your choice. Block is complete. Press and store safely.

BLOCK 100: Art Nouveau Flower

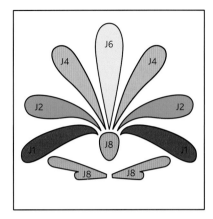

Sew the shapes to the white square

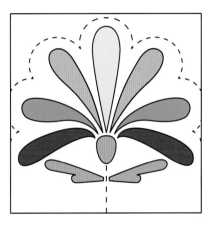

Add running stitch lines

INFO

- Block Size: 6½in (16.5cm) unfinished, 6in (15.2cm) finished

CUTTING

- White Fabric: one 6½ x 6½in (16.5 x 16.5cm)
- Fabrics J1, J2, J4, J6 and J8

CONSTRUCTION

1. Following the **Raw Edge Appliqué Preparation Method**, prepare all the fabric pieces.

2. Following the **Raw Edge Appliqué Method**, iron and sew the shapes onto the white fabric square as shown. Be sure to leave a ¼in (0.6cm) gap between the edge of the background fabric and the edges of the appliqué for the seam allowance.

3. Following the **Running Stitch Method**, stitch the decorative lines in colours of your choice. Block is complete. Press and store safely.

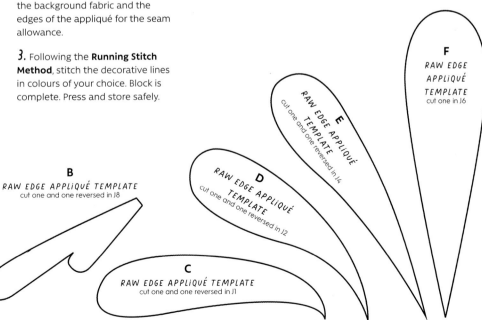

A
RAW EDGE APPLIQUÉ TEMPLATE
cut one in J8

B
RAW EDGE APPLIQUÉ TEMPLATE
cut one and one reversed in J8

C
RAW EDGE APPLIQUÉ TEMPLATE
cut one and one reversed in J1

D
RAW EDGE APPLIQUÉ TEMPLATE
cut one and one reversed in J2

E
RAW EDGE APPLIQUÉ TEMPLATE
cut one and one reversed in J4

F
RAW EDGE APPLIQUÉ TEMPLATE
cut one in J6

Layout, Sashing & Borders

QUILT BLOCK LAYOUT

Now for the super exciting part: deciding on the final quilt block layout! The blocks must be arranged as a 10 x 10 grid, but where you place each block within that grid is entirely your choice. Mix and match, switch, adjust, rotate and compose to your heart's content. Have fun and listen to your creative instincts! If you are unsure, however, I suggest following the same layout that I used on my quilt as shown.

Once you are happy with how the blocks are looking in the grid, take a good quality photo and print it. You should be able to clearly identify each block in the photo. Note the top and bottom edges of the grid and label the rows from 1–10 for your reference. Keep this handy to refer to.

Recommended Tools: camera

Top

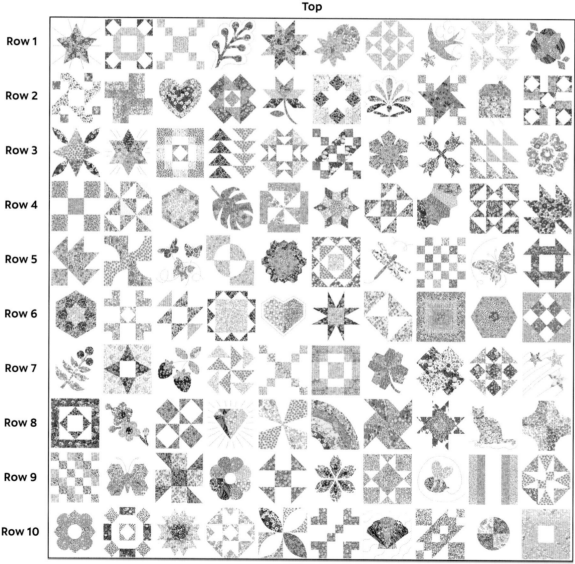

Row 1
Row 2
Row 3
Row 4
Row 5
Row 6
Row 7
Row 8
Row 9
Row 10

Bottom

HANDY TIPS

Good light is your friend. Never decide on your quilt layout in poor lighting!

A balanced layout is preferable. Try spreading any 'heavy' blocks (ones with darker fabrics or more solidly coloured block edges) and 'light' blocks (ones with lots of white space) as evenly as possible throughout the grid.

Try to avoid grouping blocks of similar colour in the same area (unless , of course, you are going for a colourwash look!).

Make sure the orientation of each block is as it should be. Some blocks may be rotated in any direction while others have a definite top and bottom edge.

Once you have your block arrangement in place, stand back and look at it from a distance. Sometimes what looks good close up isn't so further away.

Our preferences can change so it is worth sitting on your arrangement for a little while. Will you still like it tomorrow? I confess it took me days to decide on my own block layout.

SASHING, BORDERS AND BINDING

Sashing

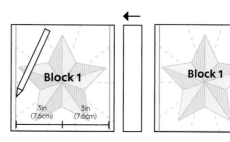

Mark stitch lines onto the block, attach the
sashing strip, then mark a stitch line on the strip

INFO

- Seams: According to the marked stitching lines*
- Press Seams: In towards the sashing unless stated otherwise. Press after each sewing step.

CUTTING

- White Fabric: ninety 1 x 6½in (2.6 x 16.5cm), thirty-nine 1 x 22in (2.6 x 55.9cm) and four 1 x 1in (2.6 x 2.6cm)

Note: *To ensure that the grid lines up perfectly once sewn together, I have given you more steps than is usual for sashing. I do recommend taking the extra time to mark all the stitching lines as instructed, as this will ensure that your sashing aligns perfectly.*

Tip: Trim any overhanging sashing strip down so it is square and in line with the block.

CONSTRUCTION

1. Take nine 1 x 6½in (2.6 x 16.5cm) white fabric sashing strips and Blocks 1–10 from a single row. Find the middle of a block at its top and bottom edge with a 6in (15.2cm) square grid ruler or a regular grid ruler. Draw a line with a heat erasable pen 3in (7.6cm) from the centre at either side. These will be your stitching lines (marked as blue in the diagrams). Repeat for all blocks.

2. Using one 1 x 6½in (2.6 x 16.5cm) white fabric sashing strip and Block 1, sew the strip onto the right-hand side of the block following the **Standard Piecing Method**, using the marked stitching line on the block in place of the usual ¼in (0.6cm) seam line on this occasion. Press seams towards sashing.

3. Measure ½in (1.3cm) along the sashing strip from the seam and draw a stitching line to ensure even spacing.

4. Take the next block and sew the units shown, aligning the stitching lines. Continue sewing and drawing the stitching lines, alternating sashing strips and blocks in this way until the whole row has formed, ending with Block 10.

5. Take the completed row and find the centre point of each block at its side edges using a 6in (15.2cm) square grid ruler or a regular grid ruler. Draw a stitching line in heat erasable pen 3in (7.6cm) either side of the centre point at the top and bottom of each block. These stitching lines will ensure that each block will be 6in (15.2cm) square once the rows are sashed together. Set completed row aside.

6. Repeat steps 1–5 until all ten rows have been sewn together.

7. Now to join the rows together. Start by sewing the long sashing strips by sewing three of the 1 x 22in (2.6 x 55.9cm) strips together as shown. Repeat twelve times more. You will have a total of thirteen long sashing strips. Set four aside.

8. Take one long sashing strip and sew it onto the bottom of Row 1 as shown, stitching along the drawn line from step 5. Press seams in towards sashing. Measure ½in (1.3cm) in from the seam and draw a stitching line along the whole length of the sashing strip to ensure even spacing. Set completed row aside.

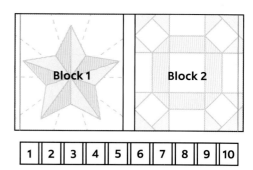

Sew the next block on, aligning the marked
stitching lines, then repeat to piece the row

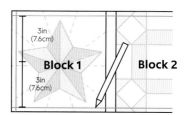

Mark the stitching lines on the top
and bottom of each pieced row

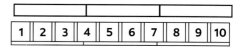

Sew three strips together to make a long sashing
strip, and sew to the bottom of each row

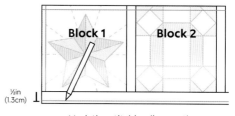

Mark the stitching line on the
joined sashing strips

9. Repeat step 8 to join long sashing strips to Rows 2–9.

10. Sew completed Row 2 onto Row 1 as shown, sewing directly on the stitching line and ensuring sashing is aligned with the row above, so your grid lines up.

11. Continue to sew Rows 3–9 on in the same way as shown. Then sew Row 10 onto the bottom as shown.

Tip: During the process of stitching and pressing, the erasable pen marks may have disappeared. If so, redraw the stitching lines around all four outside edges of the joined rows before sewing the next step.

12. Now to add sashing strips to the edges of the joined rows. Take two of the set aside long sashing strips from step 7 and sew them to either side of the joined rows as shown, sewing along the marked stitching lines. Press seams towards outer edge.

13. Sew the 1 x 1in (2.6 x 2.6cm) squares of white fabric onto each end of the remaining two long sashing strips. Then sew these longer strips onto the top and bottom as shown, sewing along the marked stitching lines. Press seams towards outer edge.

The sashing is now complete.

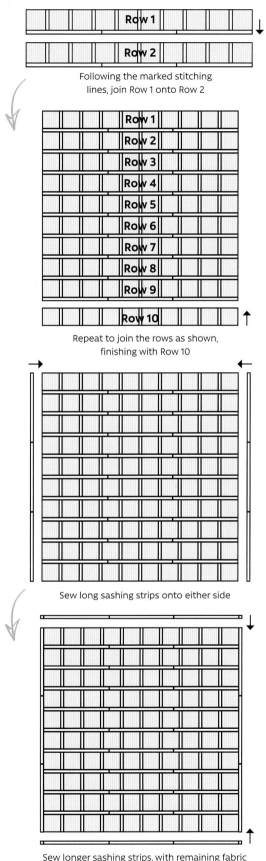

Following the marked stitching lines, join Row 1 onto Row 2

Repeat to join the rows as shown, finishing with Row 10

Sew long sashing strips onto either side

Sew longer sashing strips, with remaining fabric squares attached, onto the top and bottom

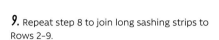

Border 1

INFO

- Seams: ¼in (0.6cm)
- Press Seams: Open. Press after each sewing step.

CUTTING

- Fabrics A3, A4, A6, E4, E6, E9, G1, G7, G10, I6: one 3½ x 13in (8.9 x 33cm)

CONSTRUCTION

1. Following the **Strip Piecing Method**, sew the 3½ x 13in (8.9 x 33cm) strips of each fabric together to make the strip set as shown.

2. Cut the strip set at 1¼in (3.2cm) intervals to make ten 1¼ x 30½in (3.2 x 77.5cm) smaller units. Discard any leftover fabric.

3. Sew all of the strips together end to end to make one very long border strip, following the **Standard Piecing Method**. You can gently wrap the long length of the border strip around a piece of thick cardboard or tubing to help keep it neat and more manageable.

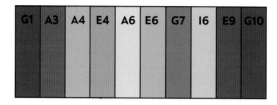

G1	A3	A4	E4	A6	E6	G7	I6	E9	G10

Sew the strips into one large strip set

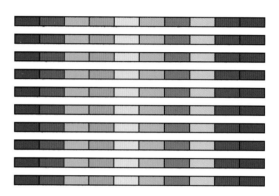

Subcut into ten smaller units

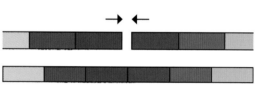

Sew the strips end to end to make one very long strip

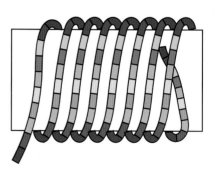

Arrange the very long strip neatly for easy handling

4. Align one end of the long border strip at one side of the quilt. Sew along this side to attach. Trim the border strip so it is square and in line with the edge of the quilt top.

5. Align the end of the long border strip at the next side of the quilt top. Sew along this side to attach. Trim the border strip so it is square and in line with the edge of the quilt top.

6. Repeat steps 4 and 5 along the remaining two sides of the quilt top, working sequentially so the rainbow continues around. Press.

Border 1 is now complete.

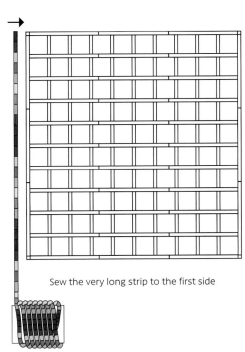

Sew the very long strip to the first side

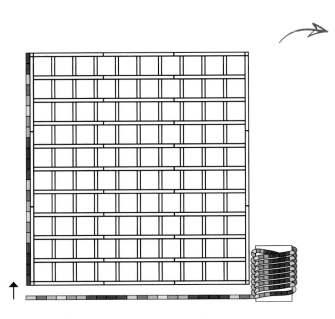

Sew the very long strip to the next side

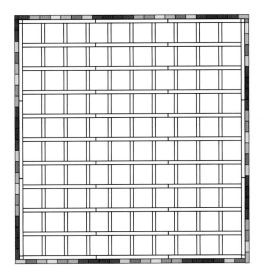

Continue to sew the very long strip around the remaining sides

Border 2

INFO

- Seams: ¼in (0.6cm)
- Press Seams: Open. Press after each sewing step.

CUTTING

- Fabrics A3, A4, A6, E4, E6, E9, G1, G7, G10, I6: one 3½ x 13in (8.9 x 33cm) and two 1½ x 3½in (3.8 x 8.9cm)

CONSTRUCTION

1. Following the **Strip Piecing Method**, sew the 3½ x 13in (8.9 x 33cm) strips of each fabric together to make the strip set as shown.

2. Cut the strip set at 1¼in (3.2cm) intervals to make eight 1¼ x 30½in (3.2 x 77.5cm) smaller units. Discard any leftover fabric.

3 Following the **Standard Piecing Method**, sew the 1½ x 3½in (3.8 x 8.9cm) strips of each fabric end to end, to make two more strips with the fabric order running as shown. You will now have a total of ten strips.

4. Sew all of the strips together end to end to make one very long border strip, following the **Standard Piecing Method**. You can gently wrap the long length of the border strip around a piece of thick cardboard or tubing to help keep it neat and more manageable.

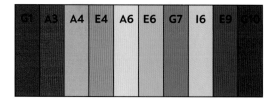

Sew the long strips into one large strip set

Subcut into eight smaller units

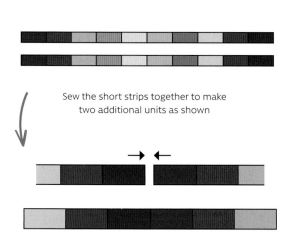

Sew the short strips together to make two additional units as shown

Sew all of the strips end to end to make one very long strip

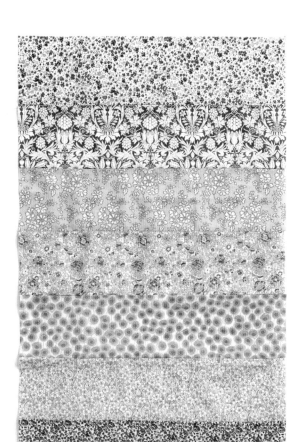

5. Align one end of the long border strip at one side of the quilt. Stagger the border strip so that the seams sit directly in the middle of the strips on Border 1. Ensure the same fabrics do not appear in the same position where they sit adjacent to Border 1. Sew along this side to attach. Trim the border strip at top and bottom so it is square and in line with the edge of the quilt.

6. Repeat step 5 along the remaining three sides of the quilt, working sequentially so the rainbow continues around. Press.

Border 2 is now complete.

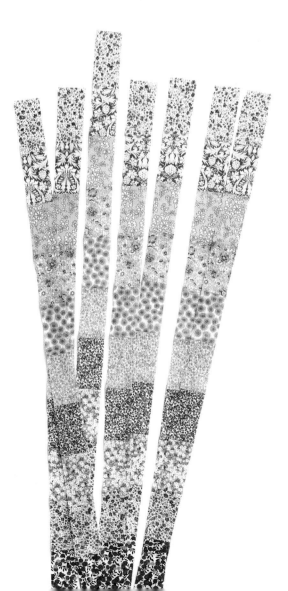

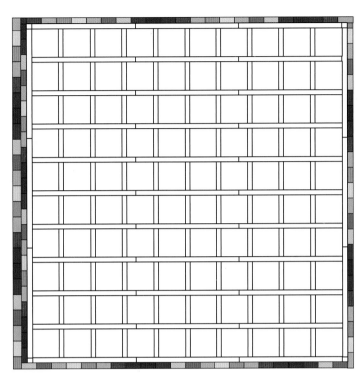

Sew the very long strip onto one side, staggering seams with Border 1

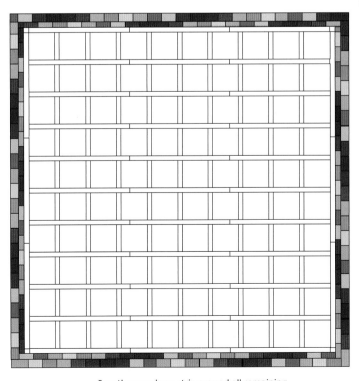

Sew the very long strip around all remaining sides, staggering the seams as shown

Border 3

INFO

- Seams: ¼in (0.6cm)
- Press Seams: Open. Press after each sewing step.

CUTTING

- White Fabric: four 2 x 43½in (5.1 x 110.5cm), four 2 x 15in (5.1 x 38.1cm) and four 2 x 13½in (5.1 x 34.3cm)

CONSTRUCTION

1. Following the **Standard Piecing Method**, sew two of the 2 x 13½in (5.1 x 34.3cm) strips onto either end of one 2 x 43½in (5.1 x 110.5cm) strip to make one 70½in (179.1cm) long strip. Repeat once more. You will have two identical long strips.

2. Sew two of the 2 x 15in (5.1 x 38.1cm) strips onto either end of one 2 x 43½in (5.1 x 110.5cm) strip to make one 73½in (186.7cm) long strip. Repeat once more. You will have two identical long strips.

3. Sew the 70½in (179.1cm) long strips onto each side of the quilt top as shown.

4. Sew the 73½in (186.7cm) long strips onto the top and bottom of the quilt top as shown. Press. The quilt top will now measure 73½in (186.7cm) square.

Border 3 is now complete.

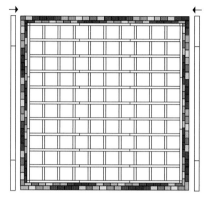

Sew the shorter of the pieced white fabric strips onto either side

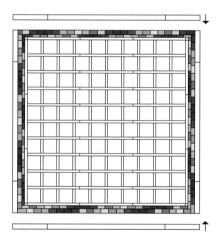

Sew the longer of the pieced white fabric strips onto the top and bottom

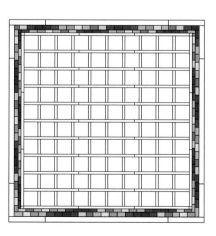

Border 3 is complete

Border 4

INFO

- Seams: ¼in (0.6cm) and scant ¼in (0.4–0.5cm)
- Press Seams: To one side. Press after each sewing step.

CUTTING

- White Fabric: 100 3½ x 3½in (8.9 x 8.9cm)
- Fabrics A8, A10, B1, B6, B7, C6, C7, D3, D4, E2, F2, F3, F4, F10, G3, G9, I1, I4, J7, J8: twenty 2⅛ x 2⅛in (5.4 x 5.4cm)

CONSTRUCTION

1. Following the **Diamond in a Square Method**, use a scant ¼in (0.4–0.5cm) seam to sew four of the 2⅛ x 2⅛in (5.4 x 5.4cm) I1 fabric squares onto a 3½ x 3½in (8.9 x 8.9cm) white fabric square to make the unit shown. Evenly trim down to 3½ x 3½in (8.9 x 8.9cm) square. Repeat to make four more identical units, to give you a total of five units.

2. Repeat step 1 using G3 fabric squares and a white fabric square; then F2 fabric squares and a white fabric square; then F3 fabric squares and a white fabric square; and so on until you have used all of the squares. You will now have five identical units in each of the twenty coloured fabrics. This makes a total of 100 Diamond in a Square units.

3. Following the **Standard Piecing Method**, sew the units together using a ¼in (0.6cm) seam into four long strips as shown. Ensure the fabric order matches the diagrams exactly. Each coloured fabric's number is shown next to the strip. One strip will be for the left-hand side, one strip for the right-hand side, one strip for the top and one strip for the bottom.

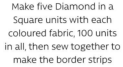

Make five Diamond in a Square units with each coloured fabric, 100 units in all, then sew together to make the border strips

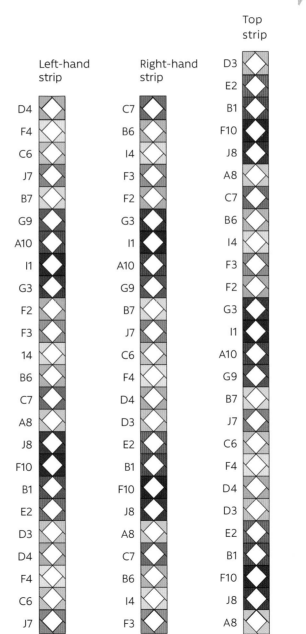

Left-hand strip	Right-hand strip	Top strip	Bottom strip
D4	C7	D3	B7
F4	B6	E2	G9
C6	I4	B1	A10
J7	F3	F10	I1
B7	F2	J8	G3
G9	G3	A8	F2
A10	I1	C7	F3
I1	A10	B6	I4
G3	G9	I4	B6
F2	B7	F3	C7
F3	J7	F2	A8
I4	C6	G3	J8
B6	F4	I1	F10
C7	D4	A10	B1
A8	D3	G9	E2
J8	E2	B7	D3
F10	B1	J7	D4
B1	F10	C6	F4
E2	J8	F4	C6
D3	A8	D4	J7
D4	C7	D3	B7
F4	B6	E2	G9
C6	I4	B1	A10
J7	F3	F10	I1
		J8	G3
		A8	F2

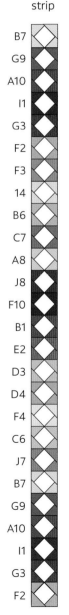

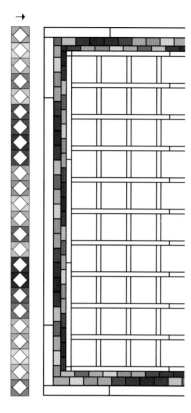

4. Sew the left-hand strip onto the left side of the quilt as shown. Ensure fabric D4 is at the top of the strip and fabric J7 is at the bottom of the strip.

5. Sew the right-hand strip onto the right side of the quilt as shown. Ensure fabric C7 is at the top of the strip and fabric F3 is at the bottom of the strip.

6. Sew the top strip onto the top edge of the quilt as shown. Ensure fabric D3 is on the left of the strip and fabric A8 is on the right of the strip.

7. Sew the bottom strip onto the bottom edge of the quilt as shown. Ensure fabric B7 is on the left of the strip and fabric F2 is on the right of the strip. Press.

Border 4 is now complete.

Sew the left-hand strip onto the quilt top

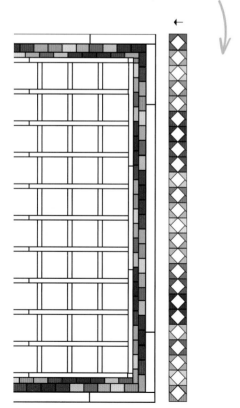

Sew the right-hand strip onto the quilt top

Fabric D3   **Fabric A8**

Sew the top strip onto the quilt top

Fabric B7   **Fabric F2**

Sew the bottom strip onto the quilt top

Border 5

INFO

- Seams: ¼in (0.6cm)
- Press Seams: Open. Press after each sewing step.

CUTTING

- White Fabric: four 2 x 43½in (5.1 x 110.5cm), four 2 x 19in (5.1 x 48.3cm) and four 2 x 18in (5.1 x 45.7cm)

CONSTRUCTION

1. Following the **Standard Piecing Method**, sew two of the 2 x 19in (5.1 x 48.3cm) strips onto either end of one 2 x 43½in (5.1 x 110.5cm) strip to make one strip 80½in (204.5cm) long. Repeat once more. You will have two identical long strips.

2. Sew two of the 2 x 18in (5.1 x 45.7cm) strips onto either end of one 2 x 43½in (5.1 x 110.5cm) strip to make one 78½in (199.4cm) long strip. Repeat once more. You will have two identical long strips.

3. Sew two of the 78½in (199.4cm) long strips onto each side of the quilt top as shown.

4. Sew the 80½in (204.5cm) long strips onto the top and bottom of the quilt top as shown. Press. The quilt top will now measure 78½in (199.4cm) square. Border 5 is now complete.

The quilt top is now complete.

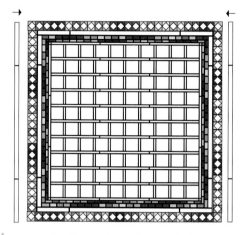

Sew the shorter of the pieced white fabric strips onto either side

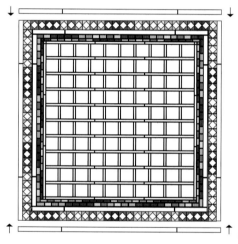

Sew the longer of the pieced white fabric strips onto the top and bottom

The quilt top is complete

Quilting & Binding

FINISHING YOUR QUILT

There are three main steps to finishing a quilt: making the quilt sandwich, quilting and binding.

The quilt sandwich process involves putting all the layers of the quilt together (backing, wadding/batting and quilt top). This usually only happens once the whole quilt top has been sewn together. This is followed by quilting, which involves stitches being sewn through the layers of the quilt (called 'quilting'), either by hand or machine. The quilting process is both practical and decorative. The main purpose of the stitches is to hold all the layers of the quilt together securely – therefore there is a minimum level of quilting that should be completed. However, any further quilting detail or decoration is entirely up to you. Quilting may also be passed to a professional with a long-arm quilting machine if desired. Finally, the quilt is bound around all of its sides, encasing the raw fabric and wadding (batting) edges to finish the quilt neatly.

Recommended Tools: spray tacking (basting) glue, free-motion quilting foot, walking quilting foot, large quilting/embroidery hoop

CUTTING

To finish your quilt you will need the following:

- Backing Fabric: 90 x 90in (228 x 228cm)
- Wadding (Batting): 90 x 108in (228 x 274cm)
- Binding Fabric: four 2½ x 84in (6.4 x 213cm) strips

QUILT SANDWICH METHOD

1. Press the backing fabric and quilt top flat. Lay your backing fabric right side down on a large flat surface. Ensure there are no wrinkles or creases. Lay the wadding (batting) centrally on top. Be careful that the backing fabric does not wrinkle or crease as the wadding (batting) is laid down.

2. Lay the completed quilt top centrally on top of the wadding (batting), right side facing up. You should have at least 4–5in (10.2–12.7cm) excess of wadding (batting) and backing fabric around all outside edges. This is a safety allowance for any edge that hasn't turned out completely straight and ensures there will be no area on the front of the quilt that won't be backed by the wadding (batting) and backing fabric.

3. Tack (baste) the three layers of the quilt sandwich together with rows of stitches 8–10in (20–25cm) apart. There is no need to be neat as these stitches will be removed later.

Tip: Make your tacking (basting) stitches using a brightly coloured thread. This will ensure the stitches are easier to find and remove later. Alternatively, use wash-out fabric adhesive to or quilting safety pins to hold the layers together.

HANDY TIPS

I recommend a backing fabric that complements your quilt top and goes well with the binding. Larger-scale prints are well suited. You could even piece your backing fabric from smaller bits of fabric for a stunning quilt both front and back.

The binding should match the colours of the quilt top well, or provide a bold frame to 'finish' the quilt. Sometimes fabrics look very different when you can only see a small section of them, so it is a good idea to cover all but a strip of the prospective binding fabric and hold your quilt top up to it to give you the best idea of what it will look like.

I recommend using a white or off-white wadding so its colour does not impact the look of the quilt front. An 80% cotton/20% polyester blend or 100% cotton wadding (batting) are good lightweight choices, while a bamboo blend or wool blend wadding (batting) are super soft and warm, but heavier. The thicker (but not necessarily heavier) the wadding (batting) the more challenging it will be to quilt, so keep that in mind when making your choice.

Backing

Wadding (batting)

Quilt top

The quilt sandwich

QUILTING METHODS

The minimum distance between rows of quilting is 4in (10.2cm), or according to the instructions for your wadding (batting). Choose one of the following four methods to quilt your quilt sandwich:

FREE-MOTION QUILTING

1. Switch the foot on your sewing machine to the free-motion quilting foot if you have one (or you can use the standard foot – it will just require being more careful). Also use a slightly longer stitch length than normal (I recommend 3.5–4).

2. With the right side of the quilt facing up, sew any pattern you like onto the surface of the quilt. If you wish to stitch a detailed design, fitting a large embroidery hoop around the area will help keep it taut. You can draw a design on your quilt using an erasable fabric pen – this method quilting is particularly good for organic, curved lines.; either design freely or buy templates to follow.

STRAIGHT LINE MACHINE QUILTING

Use the standard sewing foot on your machine and a slightly longer stitch length than normal (I recommend 3.5–4). With the quilt facing right side up, sew any straight pattern you like onto its surface, perhaps outlining blocks or shapes.

Tip: A walking foot is a great investment when it comes to straight line machine quilting. Although they can be on the expensive side, they will make sewing through the quilt layers much easier.

HAND QUILTING

1. Place the area you wish to quilt inside a quilting/embroidery hoop to keep it from creasing and stop the layers moving out of place. However, do not pull your quilt completely taut within the hoop as you will need to be able to manipulate the fabric as you stitch.

2. Thread your needle and tie a knot at the end of the thread. Start working from the back side of the quilt, sew through the quilt, bringing the needle and thread to the front and then pass it back through to the back of the quilt. It is very important to keep your stitches even and consistent when hand quilting. Stitches may be as short or long as you wish but I recommend five stitches per inch (2.5cm) to start as standard. You can sew several stitches at a time before pulling the needle through.

3. When you run out of thread, pull your needle to the back of the quilt and knot against the backing fabric, or make three small stitches on top of each other to secure. Rethread the needle and start again.

PROFESSIONAL QUILTING

If you do not wish to complete the quilting yourself, you could have it quilted by a professional long-arm quilting company – you may find one local to you. Long-arm quilting is especially good for detailed allover patterns. Typically there will be a library of quilting patterns to choose from, including florals or geometrics, and celebratory themes from wedding motifs to 'baby' patterns, including building blocks and teddy bears. They can even quilt bespoke designs, which is what I have done on the Alice's Wonderland Sampler Quilt.

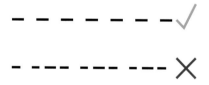

Keep your hand quilting stitches consistently spaced

Work several stitches at a time

BE CREATIVE!

Ultimately, it is up to your own personal taste how bold you decide to make the quilting, whether you use coloured thread or not, and how much quilting you do. Feel free to quilt whatever pattern you like – the final design choice is yours. However, if you are unsure about where to quilt, I recommend at least a minimum of straight line quilting by machine to 'stitch in the ditch' (sewing directly into the ditch of the seam) along the outside seams on each block and some of the borders, as shown.

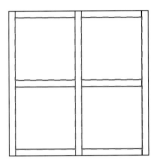

'Stitch in the ditch' around the outside
of all 100 square blocks

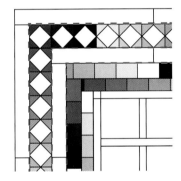

'Stitch in the ditch' around the outside edges
of Border 2 and Border 4 as shown

For more detailed quilting, use a combination of quilting methods using a neutral thread colour into every white fabric shape in patchwork blocks and patchwork Border 4, or around coloured EPP or appliquéd shapes, as demonstrated in the following diagrams.

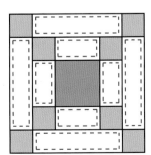 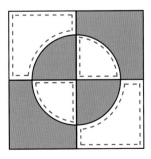

Stitching a little short of ¼in (0.6cm) inside the edge of all
individual white fabric shapes on all patchwork blocks

 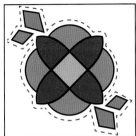

Stitching a little short of ¼in (0.6cm) outside the
edge of the appliqué and EPP shapes

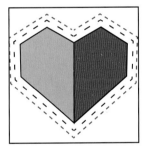

Stitching a little short of ¼in (0.6cm) outside the stitches
on any shapes outlined in hand stitching detail

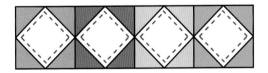

Stitching a little short of ¼in (0.6cm) inside the edge
of all white fabric shapes on Border 4 as shown

If you used safety pins to tack (baste), remove these as you come to them while quilting. Once quilting is complete, carefully remove any tacking (basting) stitches if you made any. Lastly, trim the wadding (batting) and backing down so that it is in line with the square quilt top, with no overhanging edges.

Tip: Hand quilting will be a long-term project, but one that is just as mindful as the slower stitching experience of EPP. Pick it up whenever you feel the desire, I hope you enjoy every stitch.

STRIP BINDING METHOD

Choose one of the following two methods to bind your quilt with your binding strips:

MACHINE FINISHING

1. Along one edge of each binding strip, fold over ¼in (0.6cm) onto the wrong side. Press.

2. Align the unfolded side of one binding strip against one edge of the quilt back, right sides of fabric together. Pin in place and sew the binding to the reverse of the quilt, ¼in (0.6cm) from the edge.

3. Press the binding out to the side and then fold it around the raw edge of the quilt to the front. Turn the quilt over and, ensuring that the binding covers up the stitches from step 2, topstitch the folded edge of the binding to the front of the quilt. On the back, your stitches should lie next to the binding. Trim the ends of the binding level with the top and bottom edges.

4. Repeat steps 2 and 3 on the opposite side of the quilt with another binding strip.

5. Take another binding strip and repeat step 2 along the top edge on the back of the quilt, this time leaving at least ⅜in (1cm) of the binding strip overhanging the quilt at both ends.

6. Press the binding up to the top and then fold both overhanging ends of the binding around the edge of the quilt to the front. Fold the rest of the binding strip down over the top edge, towards the front of the quilt and covering the raw edge. Topstitch, ensuring the stitches made in step 5 are covered.

7. Repeat steps 5 and 6 at the bottom edge of the quilt with the remaining binding strip.

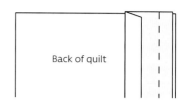

Sew binding strip along unfolded edge to one side of the back, right sides together

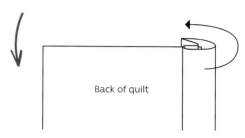

Press out and bring around to the front

Sew the strip down on the front; add binding strip to opposite side in the same way

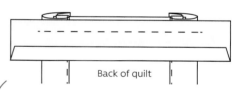

Sew binding strip to the top edge of the back

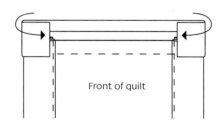

Press up and bring the edges around to the front

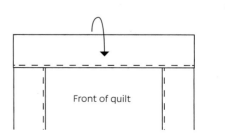

Fold the strip down over the top edge

HAND FINISHING

Follow the **Machine Finishing** instructions as written but with the following alterations:

In step 2: Align the unfolded side of one binding strip against one edge of the quilt *front*, right sides of fabric together.

In step 3: Press the binding out to the side and then fold it around the raw edge of the quilt to the *back*. Then, use blind stitch by hand with a needle and thread to hand sew the folded edge of the binding to the quilt on the *back*. This results in a very neat and clean finish, with no stitching visible on the binding at the front or back.

In step 5: Sew the binding strip to the *front* of the quilt.

In step 6: Fold both overhanging ends of the binding around the edge of the quilt to the *back*. Then, fold the rest of the binding strip down over the top edge, towards the *back* of the quilt. Use blind stitch by hand to sew the binding strip down, leaving no visible stitching.

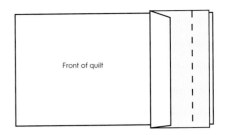

In step 2, sew the binding strip to one side of the *front*

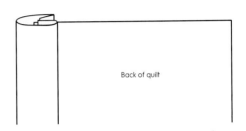

In step 3, press the binding out and bring around to the *back*

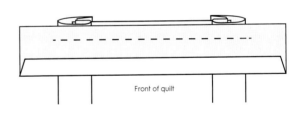

In step 5, sew the binding strip to the top edge of the quilt *front*

HANDY TIPS

If you need to complete a quilt fast, machine finishing the binding is a good choice but stitching will be visible on the front of the quilt.

For a neat, clean look, hand finishing the binding is the way to go. It will take longer to complete but the results are well worth the effort as it leaves no visible stitching.

When choosing binding fabric, make sure the print looks good as only a long, thin strip. You may be surprised with what does and doesn't work so it is worth experimenting. Avoid fabrics with large-scale prints.

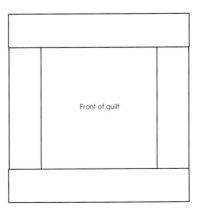

In step 6, blind stitch by hand to finish the binding on the *back* so there is no visible stitching on the front (or back!) of the quilt

ABOUT THE AUTHOR

Alice has always loved playing with fabrics, finding particular joy in combining colours. Finding a snippet of Liberty amongst her grandmother's quilting stash of worn out dresses and vintage fabrics was always a highlight, and from there her passion for Liberty fabrics grew.

Trained in scientific research, Alice kept her passion for sewing alive throughout her Ph.D in genetics, selling handmade bags at student fairs. It was from here that she started her business, Alice Caroline. Alice now enjoys running her business and designing sewing patterns and kits, which are stocked in the iconic Liberty of London store. Alice Caroline specialises in Liberty fabrics, sending Liberty fabrics, patterns and kits all over the world.

Alice lives and works in Gloucestershire, UK.

LIBERTY FABRIC STOCKISTS

UK

Alice Caroline
www.alicecaroline.com
Liberty Fabric specialist with a huge range of classic, seasonal and exclusive Liberty prints. Free worldwide shipping options. Alice's Wonderland Quilt kits available.

Instagram: @alicecarolinefabrics
Pinterest: @alicecaroline
Facebook: Alice Caroline Liberty Fabrics
YouTube: @alicecarolinefabrics
TikTok: @alicecarolinefabrics

Liberty London
www.libertylondon.com

Sew & Quilt
www.sewandquilt.co.uk

AUSTRALIA & NEW ZEALAND

Tessuti
www.tessuti-shop.com

The Fabric Store
www.thefabricstoreonline.com

Annie's Country Quilt Store
www.anniesquilts.co.nz

The Strawberry Thief
www.thestrawberrythief.com.au

EUROPE

Stragier
www.stragier.com

Telerie Spadari Milano
www.teleriespadari.it

Gårda Textil
www.gardatextil.se

USA

Jones & Vandermeer
www.jonesandvandermeer.com

Morris Textiles
www.morristextiles.com

The Intrepid Thread
www.intrepidthread.com

DuckaDilly
www.duckadilly.com

JAPAN

Liberty Japan
www.liberty-japan.co.jp

Lilymeru
www.lilymeru.etsy.com

ChokiChoki22
www.chokichoki22.etsy.com

GENERAL FABRICS & HABERDASHERY

Please support your local fabric shop in the first instance where possible. They may not have Liberty in particular, but they will undoubtedly have your necessary haberdashery, as well as cotton quilting fabrics for you to coo over!

THANKS

This book would not exist without the creative brilliance and dedication of Laura Enriquez - your tireless efforts have shaped this work. Special thanks to Kathy Knight and Lara Pearce for their determination, meticulous sewing and pattern testing. Also to Jo at LouLouRioux who spent many hours beautifully bespoke quilting the Wonderland Quilt. Thank you to our loyal customers who gave valuable feedback whilst they enjoyed making this quilt as a year-long block of the month project. My heartfelt gratitude to the whole Alice Caroline team for their unwavering support - I am truly grateful for all of your invaluable contribution and commitment to excellence, which has undoubtedly enriched the essence of this book.

Index

A DAVID AND CHARLES BOOK
© David and Charles, Ltd 2024

David and Charles is an imprint of David and Charles, Ltd
Suite A, Tourism House, Pynes Hill, Exeter, EX2 5WS

Text and Designs © Alice Caroline 2024
Layout and Photography © David and Charles, Ltd 2024

First published in the UK and USA in 2024

A catalogue record for this book is available from the British Library.

ISBN-13: 9781446312773 paperback
ISBN-13: 9781446312797 EPUB
ISBN-13: 9781446312780 PDF

This book has been printed on paper from approved suppliers and made from pulp from sustainable sources.

Printed in China through Asia Pacific Offset for:
David and Charles, Ltd
Suite A, Tourism House, Pynes Hill, Exeter, EX2 5WS

10 9 8 7 6 5 4 3 2 1

Publishing Director: Ame Verso
Managing Editor: Jeni Chown
Project Editor: Cheryl Brown
Head of Design: Anna Wade
Designers: Sam Staddon and Jo Webb
Pre-press Designer: Susan Reansbury
Illustrations: Laura Enriquez
Art Direction: Prudence Rogers
Photography: Jason Jenkins
Production Manager: Beverley Richardson

Full-size printable versions of the templates are available to download free from www.bookmarkedhub.com. Search for this book by the title or ISBN: the files can be found under 'Book Extras'. Membership of the Bookmarked online community is free.

David and Charles publishes high-quality books on a wide range of subjects. For more information visit www.davidandcharles.com.

Share your makes with us on social media using #dandcbooks and follow us on Facebook and Instagram by searching for @dandcbooks.

Layout of the digital edition of this book may vary depending on reader hardware and display settings.